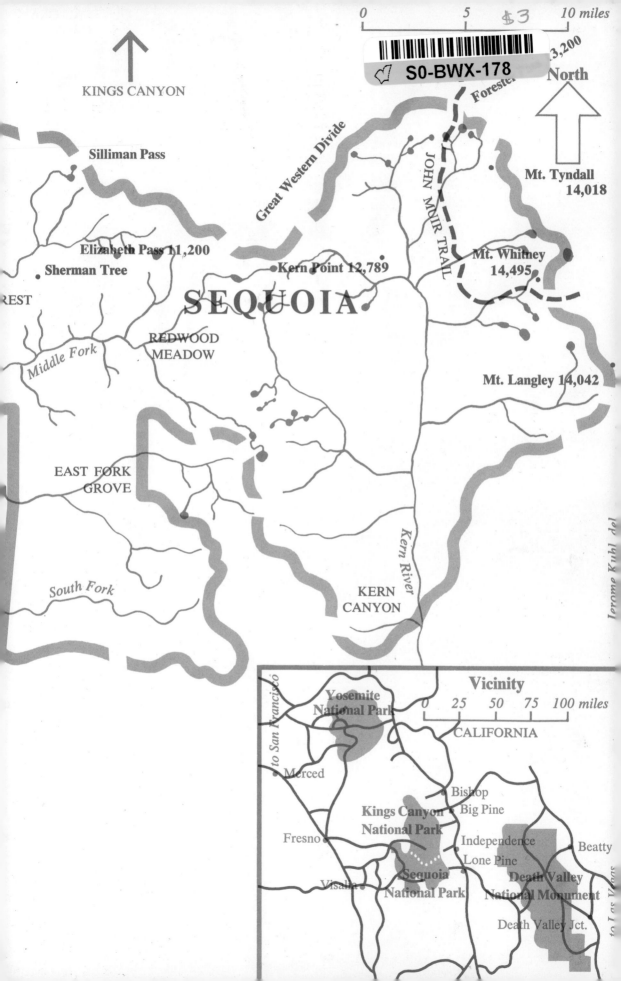

SOUTH OF YOSEMITE

JOHN MUIR, explorer, naturalist, amateur geologist, and leader of the conservation movement in the United States, was born in Scotland in 1838 and spent his boyhood in Wisconsin. He attended the University of Wisconsin, wandered in Canada, the South, and Cuba, then found his way to his promised land in California. His abiding concern throughout most of his adult life was the preservation of the country's parks and forests. Although his writing belongs to geology and glaciology as much as it does to conservation literature, the work which consumed most of his energies was the campaign he waged for Federal action to establish a system of National Parks and Forest Reserves. He died on Christmas Eve in 1914.

FREDERIC R. GUNSKY is a native San Franciscan with a lifelong enthusiasm for the mountains of the West, especially the Sierra Nevada. As a columnist for and former editor of the *Sierra Club Bulletin,* and a trip leader and scout for Sierra Club outings, he has hiked many of the routes pioneered by John Muir. In 1962 he edited Muir's *The Yosemite* for the Natural History Library. During the preparation of *South of Yosemite* he camped with the photographer, Philip Hyde, in the high country of Kings Canyon National Park and joined him in the search for landscapes to illustrate Muir's text.

PHILIP HYDE's photographs have appeared in a number of magazines and books, including *The Last Redwoods, Time and the River Flowing,* and *The Wild Cascades,* published by the Sierra Club.

Just before the alpenglow began to fade, two crimson clouds came streaming across the summit like wings of flame, rendering the sublime scene yet more intensely impressive; then came darkness and the stars.

OVERLEAF: *Ritter Range and the Minarets, from Minaret Summit, Minarets Wilderness Area*

Selected writings by John Muir

SOUTH OF YOSEMITE

Edited and with a foreword by

FREDERIC R. GUNSKY

With photographs by PHILIP HYDE

Sketches by JOHN MUIR

Published for the

American Museum of Natural History

The Natural History Press

Garden City, New York

The Natural History Press, publisher for The American Museum of Natural History, is a division of Doubleday and Company, Inc. Directed by a joint editorial board made up of members of the staff of both the Museum and Doubleday, the Natural History Press publishes books and periodicals in all branches of the life and earth sciences, including anthropology and astronomy. The Natural History Press has its editorial offices at The American Museum of Natural History, Central Park West at 79th Street, New York, New York 10024, and its business offices at 501 Franklin Avenue, Garden City, New York 11530.

FOREWORD

"There is no gorge gulch or gouge 'finer than Yosemite' that I know of, but many well worth seeing & telling each with its own wonders," John Muir wrote to his friend and editor, Robert Underwood Johnson, in 1902 when they were debating the scope of the book which was published ten years later as *The Yosemite*. At one time Muir proposed the title, "The Yosemite and Other Yosemites." The other gorges, gulches, and gouges he meant to include were the great valleys of the Sierra Nevada south of the Merced and Tuolumne which he had studied in the 1870s and which had supplied evidence for his then controversial theory of the glacial origin of those majestic land forms.

Despite more ambitious plans, *The Yosemite* was a Muir-style guidebook to one national park. It also served as a climactic campaign document in the fight to prevent the damming of the Tuolumne at Hetch Hetchy. The impending loss of that yosemite overshadowed Muir's first intention. It was forty years since he had promised, "I will go over all this Yosemite region this fall and write it up in some form or other." That was in 1872, his fourth year of residence in the valley which others were to call incomparable. He himself wanted to compare it with other regions, to test his scientific insights, to widen his experience and to confirm his transcendental joy in the blazing mountain light.

Before the year was out he had climbed alone to the peak of Mount Ritter. The next summer and fall saw him in the Minarets and then all the way south among the peaks, canyons, and groves of the San Joaquin, Kings, Kern, and Kaweah watersheds. "The Kings River yosemite," he discovered, had "two Washington Columns and nearly two North Domes, but no lakes and few meadows." He climbed Mount Whitney two months after its first ascent and bragged, "Give me a summer and a bunch of matches and a sack of meal and I will climb every mountain in the region."

Muir was enjoying himself but he had a serious purpose. In 1872 and

1873, and again in 1875 and 1877, when he spent many months south of Yosemite, he was extending his knowledge of the Sierra in order to make good his claim to be its foremost interpreter. The legend of the bearded mountaineer in seven-league boots is a by-product. More important, the mountaineer had completed his Yosemite studies, verified them in other parts of the range, and gone forth to report what he had found.

Although Muir never produced a book about the "other yosemites," he wrote journal entries, letters, and newspaper and magazine articles in a fine fever of excitement during his decade of discovery. Readers of the daily press in San Francisco, and of *Overland, Scribner's* and *Harper's,* were treated to fresh-minted descriptions of high peaks, deep canyons, and big trees as seen by the West's most original naturalist. In later life, when Muir turned to making books, he tailored some of that writing to fit into chapters. W. F. Badé and Linnie Marsh Wolfe brought to light, after his death, letters and certain passages from the journals. This book, nevertheless, is the first to be focused on the region south of Yosemite, gathering together Muir's narratives of travel in the 1870s and the enthusiastic essays in natural history which resulted directly from those excursions.

II

At the age of seventy-six, John Muir was still repeating, "I have always said when urged to write that I would not spend precious time writing books until too old to climb mountains." Long before, from his hermit stronghold in Yosemite Valley, he had resisted the appeals of his friends in California and Wisconsin, and even such distinguished acquaintances as Emerson, Professor LeConte, and the president of the Massachusetts Institute of Technology, who wanted him to publish or lecture. He said he didn't know enough, that he wasn't ready. He remained in Yosemite almost continuously from 1868 to 1873, sometimes guiding visitors and impressing them with his knowledge and gift for expression, but holding back from committing himself to print.

By the summer of 1872, however, he knew that he was ripe for a change. He had had a taste of writing for money, when the New York *Tribune* published a piece of his on glaciers and others on Yosemite in winter and spring. He had proved to his own satisfaction not only that ice had carved the Yosemite landscape but that a living glacier was in motion on Mount Lyell. He knew the classic land forms, flowers, trees, birds, mammals, storms, and seasons of the Merced and Tuolumne as intimately as a man could. He had tried his skill, strength, and endurance on the rocks, in waterfalls, on avalanches, and in the upper branches of wind-tossed trees.

One thing was left to do before he came down from the mountains. He must see more of the Sierra Nevada to confirm his observations in the laboratory of Yosemite. There were bigger trees and forests to the south, grand canyons and great peaks, including the highest in the land, Mount Whitney. After the Sierra he was not quite sure where he would go. Perhaps he would tour the mountains of the world, as he had intended to do when he first came to California.

A letter to his mentor, Mrs. Jeanne C. Carr, in San Francisco, reveals what he was thinking in July 1872:

"I am approaching a kind of fruiting-time in this mountain work and I want very much to see you . . . All say *write,* but I don't know how or what, and besides I want to see North and South and the midland basins and the seacoast and all the lake-basins and the canyons, also the alps of every country and the continental glaciers of Greenland, before I write the book we have been speaking of; and all this will require a dozen years or twenty, and money. The question is what will I write now, etc. I have learned the alphabet of ice and mountain structure here, and I think I can read fast in other countries. I would let others write what I have read here, but that they make so damnable a hash of it and ruin so glorious a unit."

The decision he made, to travel south of Yosemite in these years, was a crucial one for Muir. He stayed to write for others what he read in California's mountains, and then in other parts of the West and in Alaska. The dream of farther travel was deferred, as his work and personal responsibilities came to govern his plans, and as his conscience told him that he must not only charm his readers but inspire and lead them to create new social mechanisms to conserve the forests and wild places he described.

III

When the act of Congress adding the Cedar Grove tract and Tehipite Valley to Kings Canyon National Park became law on August 6, 1965, a chapter of history in which John Muir played an important role was brought to a triumphant conclusion. The "one grand national park" he had urged became a reality, protecting the yosemites as well as the headwaters and sequoias of the Kings, Kern, and Kaweah drainages. There, where he had traced the paths of ancient glaciers and the distribution of Big Tree groves on the soil of their moraines, and where during the 1870s and 1880s he had enlarged his vision of a wilderness to be preserved, stands a memorial as tangible as Yosemite National Park, the John Muir Trail, the John Muir Wilderness Area of the Inyo and Sierra national forests, and the Sierra Club, all of which owe their beginnings to his creative energy.

History in this case moved slowly. There were proposals as early as 1879 to protect the sequoias which Muir's writings were helping to make known. The General Land Office suspended some of the forest lands from entry in the 1880s, and in 1890 a campaign parallel to Muir's and Johnson's for a Yosemite park resulted in establishment of Sequoia and General Grant national parks. But these were relatively small, limited to the sequoia forests of the Kings-Kaweah divide and tiny Grant Grove.

It was now that Muir and Johnson began their work of propaganda and persuasion to place all the high country and canyons of the Kings and Kern under Federal protection. Even before publication of Muir's article, "A Rival to the Yosemite," in the November 1891 issue of Johnson's *Century Magazine,* the editor carried the proof sheets to Washington to argue their case with members of Congress and the Secretary of Interior. Captain J. H. Dorst, in his first report as acting superintendent of Sequoia National Park, wrote that he was "in sympathy with any plan that will preserve the mountainous country in its natural state," and Muir called on the legislators "before it is too late to set apart this surpassingly glorious region for the recreation and well-being of humanity." He was simply bringing up to date his plea of 1876 in the Sacramento *Record-Union* to preserve the forests and ground cover from destruction by fire, ax, and overgrazing.

In 1893 the Sierra Forest Reserve was established by presidential proclamation. Although it did not have the more secure status of a national park, it withdrew from any new claim a large part of the Sierra Nevada. Yet, as Muir said in an *Atlantic Monthly* article in 1898, and continued to say, the Sierra Reserve was not adequate for the purposes of conservation. "Lumbermen are allowed to spoil it at their will, and sheep in uncountable ravenous hordes to trample it and devour every green leaf within reach; while the shepherds, like destroying angels, set innumerable fires, which burn not only the undergrowth of seedlings on which the permanence of the forest depends, but countless thousands of the venerable giants."

Repeated efforts were made to extend Sequoia National Park eastward and northward, to take in Mount Whitney, the Kern Canyon, and the South Fork and Middle Fork canyons of the Kings. None of these efforts succeeded during Muir's remaining years. It was not until 1926 that the "Greater Sequoia National Park" was a fact, while the Kings Canyon Wilderness National Park was a subject of controversy until 1940. One of the compromises, near the end of the legislative battle, was a change in the name. It was to have been "John Muir National Park," and then "John Muir-Kings Canyon National Park."

Francis Farquhar wrote in the *Sierra Club Bulletin* in 1941: "The main objective of creating a great national park to preserve as nearly as possible in its natural state the whole High Sierra of the Kings and the Kern, together with its forests, meadows, and canyons, has been substantially achieved. The question of Cedar Grove and Tehipite remains, but they are not immediately threatened and there are good grounds for believing that agitation for their conversion into reservoirs will subside. The time may come when there will be no opposition at all to their inclusion in the park."

The time did come, and there is now, in effect, "one grand national park." The mountains through which John Muir traveled in fall 1873 as the first modern Sierran, among the headwaters of the San Joaquin and the great wilderness rivers to the south, are protected in national forests and national parks. Thousands every year follow the John Muir Trail. In this selection of Muir's pioneering prose, they may read how it looked and felt, and what it meant to the mind and spirit, when the trails were few.

FREDERIC R. GUNSKY

6 January 1967
Sacramento, California

ACKNOWLEDGMENTS

Francis P. Farquhar long ago recommended turning to Muir's magazine articles for "a more contemporaneous feeling" than one gets by reading him in the final form of his books. Herbert F. Smith, in his discerning book *John Muir* (Twayne Publishers, 1965), observes that "his middle years—the years of most of his periodical contributions, 1870 to 1890—mark his high point as a writer. During these years his imagery is most vibrant; his concepts of nature are most shocking, yet still effective and believable; and his sense of the right word, the perfect metaphor, the exact example is most striking."

For those reasons, in selecting the text of *South of Yosemite,* every effort has been made to present Muir's original version, even when, as often occurred, he revised the material and used it again in his books. The manuscript journals are not available, but the excerpts edited by Linnie Marsh Wolfe in *John of the Mountains* have provided rich accounts of the trips south in the 1870s. Many manuscript letters have been read; those included are quoted from the originals or from W. F. Badé's *The Life and Letters of John Muir.* Newspaper and magazine articles have been transcribed directly. Paragraphs and sometimes longer passages have been omitted, but the structure of the writing is otherwise unchanged. Minor editing has been confined, in most cases, to spelling and punctuation (e.g., canyon for cañon, Kings for King's, Tehipite for Tehipitee, and the elimination of many of Muir's hyphens). Muir's adjective "yosemitic" has been avoided; the lower-case "yosemite" serves either as noun or adjective.

Thanks for many courtesies are extended to members of the staff of the California State Library, Sacramento; the Bancroft Library of the University of California, Berkeley; the Henry E. Huntington Library, San Marino; the Sierra Club, San Francisco; the National Park Service, Western

Region, San Francisco; and the U. S. Forest Service, California Region, San Francisco.

Also, to the publishers of Muir's writings now in the public domain, including Harper & Row and the present Sacramento *Union* and San Francisco *Examiner;* to James K. Page, Jr., and Sally N. Bates, of the Natural History Press; and to those individuals who encouraged the editor to complete this project, among them William F. Kimes, Newport Beach; Shirley Sargent, Yosemite; Muir's granddaughter, Jean H. Clark of Carson City; and a very patient wife, Gladys Gunsky.

A special word of gratitude is reserved for the photographer, Philip Hyde, of Taylorsville, good companion in the mountains, whose vision is akin to Muir's and keeps his spirit of a century ago alive in the Sierra today.

F. R. G.

Permission to reprint copyright or manuscript material has been received from the following:

Houghton Mifflin Company, for portions of *John of the Mountains,* edited by Linnie Marsh Wolfe (copyright 1938 by Wanda Muir Hanna); and *The Life and Letters of John Muir,* by W. F. Badé (copyright 1923 and 1924 by Houghton Mifflin Company);

Appleton-Century-Crofts for a portion of *The Yosemite,* by John Muir (copyright 1912, renewed 1940 by Wanda Muir Hanna);

The Huntington Library, San Marino, California, for a portion of a manuscript letter to Theodore P. Lukens dated January 10, 1899;

The Bancroft Library, University of California, Berkeley, for portions of manuscript letters to Mrs. John Bidwell, dated October 21, 1877, and to William Colby, dated January 15, 1907, and January 16, 1911.

CONTENTS

THE BIG TREES

ONE GRAND NATIONAL PARK

SOUTH OF YOSEMITE

FREE IN THE MOUNTAINS

Above this memorable spot, the face of the mountain is still more savagely hacked and torn. It is a maze of yawning chasms and gullies, in the angles of which rise beetling crags and piles of detached boulders that seem to have been gotten ready to be launched below.

OVERLEAF: *Minarets and Mt. Ritter from the upper basin of Dike Creek, Minarets Wilderness Area*

1. TO MOUNT RITTER

Since summer 1869, when John Muir at the age of thirty-one worked his way into the mountains above Yosemite Valley by herding a band of sheep, he had resisted every pull of the world outside. The journal he wrote that summer recorded his fascination and his intention to remain in the vicinity of "the famous valley, with its wonderful cliffs and groves, a grand page of mountain manuscript that I would gladly give my life to be able to read." He soon had glimpsed his Rosetta stone in the polished granite pavements and erratic boulders of the Tuolumne-Merced divide, and was reading the glacial history of the Sierra Nevada which no one else then understood so well.

Three years later he was still there, by now the legendary mountaineer, domiciled in the Valley, eloquent guide of visiting celebrities, protégé of Emerson, Tyndall, and Asa Gray, the firmly established advocate of a controversial theory of the glacial origin of Yosemite land forms. He had begun to be published, in The Overland Monthly *and the New York* Tribune. *Although reluctant to leave his sanctuary, Muir knew his "fruiting time" was near. To claim his due as the Sierra's most intimate naturalist-student he must see more of the range, beyond the watersheds of the Tuolumne and Merced.*

It was at this time, in October 1872, that he returned from a ten-day walk to Mount Lyell and found three artists waiting for him with a letter of introduction from Mrs. Jeanne Carr in San Francisco. They were William Keith (a fellow Scot who was to become his lifelong friend), Benoni Irwin, and Thomas Ross. They wanted Muir to take them to some point of vantage where they could paint one of those alpine grand views which were then in demand. His friend's letter, and perhaps Keith's congenial burr, won the day. "I'm going to take your painter boys with me into one of my best sanctums on your recommendation for holiness," Muir wrote to Mrs. Carr. He also took along Merrill Moores, sixteen, a family friend from the Middle West.

The grand view was of Mount Lyell from the Lyell Fork of the Tuolumne. Keith later entitled his romantic landscape, "Crown of the Sierra." As the painter boys were fully occupied sketching and making notes for a winter's work in their studios, Muir took advantage of the opportunity to follow the compass needle of his vocation. Alone, he crossed the pass leading south.

The three-day excursion, during which he made the first ascent of Mount Ritter (13,157 feet), is described in one of his best narratives. When it appeared in final form in The Mountains of California, *he called it "A Near View of the High Sierra."*

Early one bright morning in the middle of Indian summer, while the glacier meadows were still crisp with frost crystals, I set out from the foot of Mount Lyell, on my way down to Yosemite Valley. I had spent the past summer, and many preceding ones, exploring the glaciers that lie on the headwaters of the San Joaquin, Tuolumne, Merced, and Owens rivers; measuring and studying their movements, trends, crevasses, moraines, etc., and the part they had played during the period of their greater extension in the creation and development of the landscapes of this alpine wonderland. Having been cold and hungry so many times, and worked so hard, I was weary, and began to look forward with delight to the approaching winter, when I would be warmly snowbound in my Yosemite cabin, with plenty of bread and books; but a tinge of regret came on when I considered that possibly I was now looking on all this fresh wilderness for the last time.

Pursuing my lonely way down the valley, I turned again and again to gaze on the glorious picture, throwing up my arms to enclose it as in a frame. After long ages of growth in the darkness beneath the glaciers, through sunshine and storms, it seemed now to be ready and waiting for the elected artist, like yellow wheat for the reaper; and I could not help wishing that I were that artist. I had to be content, however, to take it into my soul. At length, after rounding a precipitous headland that puts out from the west wall of the valley, every peak vanished from sight, and I pushed rapidly along the frozen meadows, over the divide between the waters of the Merced and Tuolumne, and down through the lower forests that clothe the slopes of Clouds Rest, arriving in Yosemite in due time—which, with me, is *any* time. And, strange to say, among the first human beings I met here were two artists[1] who were awaiting my return.

---

[1] William Keith and Benoni Irwin had a letter of introduction from Mrs. Jeanne C. Carr of San Francisco. A third artist, Thomas Ross, and Muir's young friend Merrill Moores accompanied the party to the Lyell Fork.

Handing me letters of introduction, they inquired whether in the course of my explorations in the adjacent mountains I had ever come upon a landscape suitable for a large painting; whereupon I began a description of the one that had so lately excited my admiration. Then, as I went on further and further into details, their faces began to glow, and I offered to guide them to it, while they declared they would gladly follow, far or near, whithersoever I could spare the time to lead them.

Since storms might come breaking down through the fine weather at any time, burying the meadow colors in snow, and cutting off their retreat, I advised getting ready at once.

Our course lay out of the valley by the Vernal and Nevada falls, thence over the main dividing ridge to the Big Tuolumne Meadows, by the old Mono trail, and thence along the riverbank to its head. Toward the end of the second day, the Sierra Crown[2] began to come into view, and when we had fairly rounded the projecting headland mentioned above, the whole picture stood revealed in the full flush of the alpenglow. Now their enthusiasm was excited beyond bounds, and the more impulsive of the two dashed ahead, shouting and gesticulating and tossing his arms in the air like a madman. Here, at last, was a typical alpine landscape.

After feasting awhile, I proceeded to make camp in a sheltered grove a little way back from the meadow, where pine boughs could be obtained for beds, while the artists ran here and there, along the river bends and up the side of the canyon, choosing foregrounds for sketches. After dark, when our tea was made and a rousing fire kindled, we began to make our plans. They decided to remain here several days, at the least, while I concluded to make an excursion in the meantime to the untouched summit of Ritter.

It was now about the middle of October, the springtime of snow-flowers. The first winter clouds had bloomed, and the peaks were strewn with fresh crystals, without, however, affecting the climbing to any dangerous extent. And as the weather was still profoundly calm, and the distance to the foot of the mountain only a little more than a day, I felt that I was running no great risk of being stormbound.

Ritter is king of our Alps, and had never been climbed. I had explored the adjacent peaks summer after summer, and, but for the tendency to reserve a grand masterpiece like this for a special attempt, it seemed strange that in all these years I had made no effort to reach its commanding summit. Its height above sea level is about 13,300 feet,[3] and it is fenced

[2] Mount Lyell, 13,114 feet, on the boundary of the present Yosemite National Park.

[3] Actually 13,157 feet.

round by steeply inclined glaciers, and canyons of tremendous depth and ruggedness, rendering it comparatively inaccessible. But difficulties of this kind only exhilarate the mountaineer.

Next morning, the artists went heartily to their work and I to mine. My general plan was simply this: to scale the canyon wall, cross over to the eastern flank of the range, and then make my way southward to the northern spurs of Mount Ritter in compliance with the intervening topography; for to push on directly southward from camp through the innumerable peaks and pinnacles that adorn this portion of the axis of the range is simply impossible.[4]

Before I had gone a mile from camp, I came to the foot of a white cascade that beats its way down a rugged gorge in the canyon wall, from a height of about nine hundred feet, and pours its throbbing waters into the Tuolumne. Gladly I climbed along its dashing border, absorbing its divine music, and bathing from time to time in waftings of irised spray. Climbing higher, higher, new beauty came streaming on the sight: painted meadows, late-blooming gardens, peaks of rare architecture, lakes here and there, shining like silver, and glimpses of the forested lowlands seen far in the west. Over the summit, I saw the so-called Mono Desert lying dreamily silent in the thick, purple light—a desert of heavy sun glare beheld from a desert of ice-burnished granite. Here the mountain waters divide, flowing east to vanish in the volcanic sands and dry sky of the Great Basin; west, to flow through the Golden Gate to the sea.

Passing a little way down over the summit until I had reached an elevation of about 10,000 feet, I pushed on southward toward a group of savage peaks that stand guard about Ritter on the north and west, groping my way, and dealing instinctively with every obstacle as it presented itself. Here a huge gorge would be found cutting across my path, along the dizzy edge of which I scrambled until some less precipitous point was discovered where I might safely venture to the bottom and, selecting some feasible portion of the opposite wall, re-ascend with the same slow caution. Massive, flat-topped spurs alternate with the gorges, plunging abruptly from the shoulders of the snowy peaks, and planting their feet in the warm desert. These were everywhere marked and adorned with characteristic sculptures of the ancient glaciers that swept over this entire region like one vast ice-wind, and the polished surfaces produced by the ponderous flood are still so perfectly preserved that in many places the sunlight reflected from them is about as trying to the eyes as sheets of snow.

[4] In editing this sentence for *The Mountains of California,* Muir used for "impossible" the phrase "extremely difficult and dangerous at this time of year."

Now came the solemn, silent evening. Long, blue, spiky-edged shadows crept out across the snowfields, while a rosy glow, at first scarce discernible, gradually deepened and suffused every mountaintop, flushing the glaciers and the harsh crags above them. This was the alpenglow, to me one of the most impressive of all the terrestrial manifestations of God. At the touch of this divine light, the mountains seemed to kindle to a rapt, religious consciousness, and stood hushed like devout worshipers waiting to be blessed. Just before the alpenglow began to fade, two crimson clouds came streaming across the summit like wings of flame, rendering the sublime scene yet more intensely impressive; then came darkness and the stars.

Ritter was still miles away, but I could proceed no further that night. I found a good campground on the rim of a glacier basin about 11,000 feet above the sea. A small lake nestles in the bottom of it, from which I got water for my tea, and a storm-beaten thicket nearby furnished abundance of firewood. Somber peaks, hacked and shattered, circled halfway around the horizon, wearing a most savage aspect in the gloaming, and a waterfall chanted solemnly across the lake on its way down from the foot of a glacier.

I made my bed in a nook of the pine thicket, where the branches were pressed and crinkled overhead like a roof, and bent down around the sides. These are the best bedchambers our Alps afford—snug as squirrel nests, well ventilated, full of spicy odors, and with plenty of wind-played needles to sing one asleep. I little expected company, but, creeping in through a low side door, I found five or six birds nestling among the tassels. The night wind began to blow soon after dark; at first, only a gentle breathing, but increasing toward midnight to a violent gale that fell upon my leafy roof in ragged surges, like a cascade, and bearing strange sounds from the crags overhead. The waterfall sang in chorus, filling the old ice fountain with its solemn roar, and seeming to increase in power as the night advanced—fit voice for such a landscape. I had to creep out many times to the fire during the night; for it was biting cold and I had no blankets. Gladly I welcomed the morning star.

The dawn in the dry, wavering air of the desert was glorious. Everything encouraged my undertaking and betokened success. No cloud in the sky, no storm tone in the wind. Breakfast of bread and tea was soon made. I fastened a hard, durable crust to my belt by way of provision, in case I should be compelled to pass a night on the mountaintop; then, securing the remainder of my little stock from wolves and wood rats, I set forth free and hopeful.

On the southern shore of a frozen lake, I encountered an extensive field of hard, granular snow, up which I scampered in fine tone, intending to follow it to its head, and cross the rocky spur against which it leans, hoping thus to come direct upon the base of the main Ritter peak. The surface was pitted with oval hollows, made by stones and drifted pine needles that had melted themselves into the mass by the radiation of absorbed sun heat. These afforded good footholds, but the surface curved more and more steeply at the head, and the pits became shallower and less abundant, until I found myself in danger of being shed off like avalanching snow. I persisted, however, creeping on all fours, and shuffling up the smoothest places on my back, as I had often done on burnished granite, until, after slipping several times, I was compelled to retrace my course to the bottom, and make my way around the west end of the lake, and thence up to the summit of the divide between the headwaters of Rush Creek and the northernmost tributaries of the San Joaquin.

Arriving on the summit of this dividing crest, one of the most exciting pieces of pure wilderness was disclosed that the eye of man ever beheld. There, immediately in front, loomed the majestic mass of Mount Ritter, with a glacier swooping down its face nearly to my feet, then curving westward and pouring its frozen flood into a dark blue lake, whose shores were bound with precipices of crystalline snow; while a deep chasm drawn between the divide and the glacier separated the massive picture from everything else. Only the one sublime mountain in sight, the one glacier, and one lake; the whole veiled with one blue shadow—rock, ice, and water, without a single leaf.

Descending the divide in a hesitating mood, I picked my way across the yawning chasm at the foot, and climbed out upon the glacier.

I could not distinctly hope to reach the summit from this side, yet I moved on across the glacier as if driven by fate. Contending with myself, the season is too far spent, I said, and even should I be successful, I might be stormbound on the mountain; and in the cloud-darkness, with the cliffs and crevasses covered with snow, how could I escape? No; I must wait until next summer. I would only approach the mountain now, and inspect it, creep about its flanks, learn what I could of its history, holding myself ready to flee on the approach of the first storm cloud. But we little know until tried how much of the uncontrollable there is in us, urging across glaciers and torrents, and up dangerous heights, let the judgment forbid as it may.

I succeeded in gaining the foot of the cliff on the eastern extremity of the glacier, and discovered the mouth of a narrow avalanche gully, through which I began to climb, intending to follow it as far as possible, and at least obtain some fine wild views for my pains. Its general course is oblique to the plane of the mountain face, and the metamorphic slates of which it is built are cut by cleavage planes in such a way that they weather off in angular blocks, giving rise to irregular steps that greatly facilitate climbing on the sheer places. I thus made my way into a wilderness of crumbling spires and battlements, built together in bewildering combinations, and glazed in many places with a thin coating of ice, which I had to hammer off with a stone. The situation was becoming gradually more perilous; but, having passed several dangerous spots, I dared not think of descending; for, so steep was the entire ascent, one would inevitably fall to the glacier in case a single misstep were made.

At length, after attaining an elevation of about 12,800 feet, I found myself at the foot of a sheer drop in the bed of the avalanche channel I was tracing, which seemed absolutely to bar all further progress. It is only about forty-five or fifty feet high, and somewhat roughened by fissures and projections; but these seemed so slight and insecure, as footholds, that I tried hard to avoid the precipice altogether, by scaling the wall on either side. But, though less steep, the walls were smoother than the obstructing rock, and repeated efforts only showed that I must either go right ahead or turn back. The tried dangers beneath seemed even greater than that of the cliff in front; therefore, after scanning its face again and again, I began to scale it, picking my holds with intense caution. After gaining a point about halfway to the top, I was suddenly brought to a dead stop, with arms outspread, clinging close to the face of the rock, unable to move hand or foot either up or down. My doom appeared fixed. I *must* fall. There would be a moment of bewilderment, and then a lifeless rumble down the one general precipice to the glacier below.

When this final danger flashed upon me, I became nerve-shaken for the first time since setting foot on the mountain, and my mind seemed to fill with a stifling smoke. But this terrible eclipse lasted only a moment, when life blazed forth again with preternatural clearness. I seemed suddenly to become possessed of a new sense. The other self—the ghost of bygone experiences, Instinct, or Guardian Angel—call it what you will—came forward and assumed control. Then my trembling muscles became firm again, every rift and flaw in the rock was seen as through a microscope, and my limbs moved with a positiveness and precision with which I seemed to have nothing at all to do. Had I been borne aloft upon wings, my deliverance could not have been more complete.

Above this memorable spot, the face of the mountain is still more savagely hacked and torn. It is a maze of yawning chasms and gullies, in the angles of which rise beetling crags and piles of detached boulders that seem to have been gotten ready to be launched below. But the strange influx of strength I had received seemed inexhaustible. I found a way without effort, and soon stood upon the topmost crag in the blessed light.

Looking southward along the axis of the range, the eye is first caught by a row of exceedingly sharp and slender spires, which rise openly to a height of about a thousand feet, from a series of short, residual glaciers that lean back against their bases; their fantastic sculpture and the un-relieved sharpness with which they spring out of the ice rendering them peculiarly wild and striking. These are the Minarets, and beyond them you behold a most sublime wilderness of mountains, their snowy summits crowded together in lavish abundance, peak beyond peak, swelling higher, higher as they sweep on southward, until the culminating point of the range is reached on Mount Whitney, near the head of the Kern River, at an elevation of nearly 15,000 feet above the level of the sea.[5]

Westward, the general flank of the range is seen flowing sublimely away from the sharp summits, in smooth undulations; a sea of huge gray granite waves dotted with lakes and meadows, and fluted with stupendous canyons that grow steadily deeper as they recede in the distance. Below this gray region lies the dark forest zone, broken here and there by upswelling ridges and domes; and yet beyond is a yellow, hazy belt, marking the broad plain of the San Joaquin, bounded on its further side by the blue mountains of the coast.

Turning now to the northward, there in the immediate foreground is the glorious Sierra Crown, with Cathedral Peak a few miles to the left—a temple of marvelous architecture, hewn from the living rock; the gray, giant form of Mammoth Mountain, 13,000 feet high; Mounts Ord, Gibbs, Dana, Conness, Tower Peak, Castle Peak, and Silver Mountain, stretch-ing away in the distance, with a host of noble companions that are as yet nameless.[6]

Eastward, the whole region seems a land of pure desolation covered with beautiful light. The torrid volcanic basin of Mono, with its one bare lake fourteen miles long; Owens Valley and the broad lava tableland at its head, dotted with craters, and the massive Inyo Range, rivaling even the Sierra in height. These are spread, map-like, beneath you, with

[5] As later calculated by the U. S. Coast and Geodetic Survey, 14,495 feet.

[6] Several names used by Muir have not survived. These are not the present Mammoth, Castle, and Silver; Ord is not on any current map.

countless ranges beyond, passing and overlapping one another and fading on the glowing horizon.

But in the midst of these fine lessons and landscapes, I had to remember that the sun was wheeling far to the west, while a new way had to be discovered, at least to some point on the timberline where I could have a fire; for I had not even burdened myself with a coat. I first scanned the western spurs, hoping some way might appear through which I might reach the northern glacier, and cross its snout; or pass around the lake into which it flows, and thus strike my morning track. This route was soon sufficiently unfolded to show that, if practicable at all, it would require so much time that reaching camp that night would be out of the question. I therefore scrambled back eastward, descending the southern slopes obliquely at the same time. Here the crags seemed less formidable, and the head of a glacier that flows northeast came in sight, which I determined to follow as far as possible, hoping thus to make my way to the foot of the peak on the east side, and thence across the intervening canyons and ridges to camp.

The inclination of the glacier is quite moderate at the head, and, as the sun had softened the *névé*, I made safe and rapid progress, running and sliding, and keeping up a sharp outlook for crevasses. About half a mile from the head, there is an ice cascade, where the glacier pours over a sharp declivity, and is shattered into massive blocks separated by deep, blue fissures. Fortunately, the day had been warm enough to loosen the ice crystals so as to admit of hollows being dug in the rotten portions of the blocks, thus enabling me to pick my way with far less difficulty than I had anticipated.

Night drew near before I reached the eastern base of the mountain, and my camp lay many a rugged mile to the north; but ultimate success was assured. It was now only a matter of endurance and ordinary mountain-craft. The sunset was, if possible, yet more beautiful than that of the day previous. The Mono landscape seemed to be fairly saturated with warm, purple light. The peaks marshaled along the summit were in shadow, but through every notch and pass streamed vivid sun-fire, soothing and irradiating their rough, black angles, while companies of small, luminous clouds hovered above them like very angels of light.

Darkness came on, but I found my way by the trends of the canyons and the peaks projected against the sky. All excitement died with the light, and then I was weary. But the joyful sound of the waterfall across the lake was heard at last, and soon the stars were seen reflected in the lake itself. Taking my bearings from these, I discovered the little pine thicket in which my nest was, and then I had a rest such as only a mountaineer may enjoy. Afterward, I made a sunrise fire, went down to the lake, dashed water on my head, and dipped a cupful for tea. The revival brought about by bread and tea was as complete as the exhaustion from excessive enjoyment and toil had been. Then I crept beneath the pine tassels to bed. The wind was frosty and the fire burned low, but my sleep was none the less sound, and the evening constellations had swept far to the west before I awoke.

After warming and resting in the sunshine, I sauntered home—that is, back to the Tuolumne camp—bearing away toward a cluster of peaks that hold the fountain snows of one of the north tributaries of Rush Creek. Here I discovered a group of beautiful glacier lakes, nestled together in a grand amphitheater. Toward evening, I crossed the divide separating the Mono waters from those of the Tuolumne, and entered the glacier basin that now holds the fountain snows of the stream that forms the upper Tuolumne cascades. This stream I traced down through its many dells and gorges, meadows and bogs, reaching the brink of the main Tuolumne at dusk.

A loud whoop for the artists was answered again and again. Their campfire came in sight, and half an hour afterward I was with them. They seemed unreasonably glad to see me. I had been absent only three days; nevertheless, they had already been weighing chances as to whether I would ever return, and trying to decide whether they should wait longer or begin to seek their way back to the lowlands. Now their curious troubles were over. They packed their precious sketches, and next morning we set out homeward bound, and in two days entered the Yosemite Valley from the north by way of Indian Canyon.

"In the Heart of the California Alps,"
Scribner's Monthly, July 1880

The falls on the creek above
Lake Ediza, Mt. Ritter (left),
and Banner Peak,
Minarets Wilderness Area

2. THE MINARETS

Conscious of the attractions of the Ritter Range after his climbing adventure there the previous autumn, and pursuing further evidence of glacial action, Muir spent most of August 1873 among the head- waters of the North Fork of the Middle Fork of the San Joaquin River. Around Banner Peak and Mount Ritter, threading the passes of the Minarets, studying the icy architecture of that castellated ridge, he enjoyed "feast days" of lonely mountaineering.

He was no longer on familiar Yosemite granite. The glaciers of this range had cut and ground their way through black slaty rocks which offered the climber less secure footing and presented a quite different, more forbidding face.

But Muir knew what he was looking for. He found a Joaquin Canyon at the meeting place of the glaciers on the slopes of Ritter, and others that had drained the ice-melt from the many chambers of the Minarets. Lakes, thunderstorms, the Milky Way, evergreen groves, and flowered meadows occupied his thoughts. He had em- barked on a series of trips which were his longest and hardest to that time, and Linnie Marsh Wolfe observes that his journal-writing this year was his most prolific.

August 13 [?], 1873

I set out from the foot of Red Mountain, August 11. Camped the first evening in the bottom of the West Fork double canyon. Then crossed the Merced Divide the evening of the twelfth, weary and heavy-laden, and camped at the bottom of one of the San Joaquin canyons between two lakes, on a narrow isthmus of rock upon which grew one living tree, a clumpy and well-developed *Pinus albicaulis*. A large dead one lay by it which I used for fuel. This canyon is broad and basiny, con- taining at least ten lakes, separated by bosses of bright gleaming rock, and rich forests of *Pinus albicaulis, Pinus contorta* and spruce,[1] and fine meadows, garden-like both in shape and flowers. I found here a new plant, *Chaenactis*. And a new butterfly; also a hungry wood rat. He

[1] Muir's "spruce" is probably mountain hemlock (*Tsuga mertensiana*).

stole my spectacles and barometer during the night, from beneath a heavy stone. I recovered the barometer, the case much gnawed, but not the spectacles. Also the same animal may have stolen the lid of my teapot. At least here it disappeared.

This morning, I climbed out of this into another yet grander canyon of the Joaquin, with noble side canyons adorned by all kinds of gardens and groves. The rock is slaty and granitoid, much veined and mixed and seamed like marble where cut smooth by the ice. I saw where a snow avalanche in the west-side canyon had broken off about as many pine trees as it had uprooted. Also it had slid over some young ones and left a few standing marked in such a way as to show the avalanche depth at that place to have been about twenty feet. Broken pines, two and a half feet in diameter, and sound, were broken off close to the ground. One was broken five or six feet from the ground, which grew again.

Noble mountains rise close about me, and far southward are the highest of the range with glaciers on their sides. A stream sings lonely.

Storm, thunder, hail on water, grasses wincing. Rush of new-made cascades.

August 14 [?]

Bright after rain. The sun is stealing down the opposite wall, touching every boss and cove in turn, now dyeing to the bottom every rock and meadow. The mountains are wet, washed, reeking. The birds are late; they do not care to come from their snug nooks in leafy cedars and pine, and dry places in the rocks. The butterflies are late, too; their wings are damp. How fresh every mountain, every flower! The sun is not an hour high, yet the gentians are open . . . No sign of injury from hail—only here and there a petal lip hanging low. The cascade by my side sings with a new voice . . . Raindrops and hailstones as well as glaciers and snowbanks are heard in it now. The huge canyon like one life seems born again.

An hour later: A hard climb up the canyonside among wet bushes. I am now near the top of the cascade. A white sun-stained cloud glows in the notch at the top of the mountain—the sun just over it . . . The sun-silvered stream seems the cloud itself coming down, leaping glad from boulder to boulder, often high enough to break into smoke-like spray. About the base is a fringe of willows and tall purple spikes of epilobium. Trees grow on the wall above on both sides.

Garnet Lake, Mt. Ritter (left), and Banner Peak, Minarets Wilderness Area

When I first came in sight of the various glacial fountains of this region, I said there must be a very deep and slaty-walled canyon at their meeting place—a kind of slaty yosemite—and I feared it might be difficult to cross in going to the Minarets. I was right, for certainly this Joaquin Canyon is the most remarkable in many ways of all I have entered. An astonishing number of separate meadows, rich gardens, and groves are contained in the canyon, and it is a composite-slate yosem-ite valley with huge black slate rocks that overlean, and views reaching to the snowy summits. I knew not what most to gaze at—the huge black precipices above me, the beds of white violets and ferns about me, or the grand hemlock and fir groves with the young Joaquin (thirty feet wide, two feet deep, with current of three miles per hour) flowing through them. "Surely," said I, as I snuggled myself away among the roots of my juniper, "this has been a big feast day. Plants, animals, birds, rocks, gardens, magnificent clouds, thunderstorms, rain, hail—all, all have blessed me!"

August 15 [?]

During the night a rascal wood rat (neotoma) tried to steal my hatchet . . . (Strange what frightening capabilities small creatures have in the night. The Englishmen at Lyell were afraid.) Before I went to bed I examined the various rooms in the big cedar, but discovered no nest of mouse or squirrel. However, in the night I was awakened from sound sleep by something about or on or under my head. After the per-formances of the light-pawed or -jawed rat that stole my teapot lid and spectacles and barometer, I kept my barometer in my bosom and made a pillow of my provisions, but did not think the hatchet in any danger. Yet, after repeatedly waking and watching, I caught sight of a large wood rat trying to drag it from beneath the tree by a buckskin string with which the handle was tied. I thumped with it on the tree trunk to frighten him, but in a minute he would return, chattering his teeth in a way provokingly like a rattlesnake.

On starting down the canyonside this morning, I was surprised to find the largest of the four Sierra gentians standing about carelessly in the bush as if quite at home . . . Found it very abundant all the way to the bottom, and all over the bottom, and up the other side, in all kinds of soil and company and climates. Although one of the commonest plants, I had seen it but once before this side the Sierra.

Also, an hour before sunset, I discovered a noble anemone (*Anemone occidentalis,* not before found south of Lassen Peak), gone to seed, and

silky heads of akenia an inch and a half in diameter. The flower must
have been at least two inches. Growing in among rough slate avalanche
blocks on the east side of the canyon at an elevation of eighty-four hundred feet, just above the entrance of the big lower Ritter Cascade, I
found this, my first anemone, in California. The sight sent me bounding
to a certain hillside in Wisconsin where the *Anemone nuttalliana* came
in clouds in spring, and a dozen species of goldenrods and asters gathered and added gold to gold, and purple to purple in autumn.

August 16 [?]

Last night I camped between a close pair of lakes. Had a glorious
thunderstorm.

Saw a boulder fall a thousand feet down the mountainside this afternoon, loosened by rain.

Watching the raindrops plashing and breaking upon the polished surfaces of the rocks near my camp, I could not but admire their wonderful
strength to bear all this direct hammering together with that of the hail,
and all the corroding fogs and dews, and long-lying snows for thousands
of years. Yet their polish is as brilliant as the tranquil surface of a sunny
crystal lake.

Two days before, when I crossed the Merced Divide, I felt I was going
to a strange land, yet not so, only turning over a new page; and a blessed
page it was, engraved with ten lakes and forests and sculptured rocks
uncountable . . .

I never saw such a meeting of lowland and alpine plants of all kinds—
trees, sedges, grasses, ferns—as in this Joaquin composite-slate yosemite.
Perhaps it is because streams descending directly from the summit mountains on both sides, bring down all higher seeds, making a kind of
natural botanical garden.

This day I found *Primula suffrutescens* gone to seed (altitude ninety-
five hundred feet). Had glorious thunder and rain close up at the foot
of Ritter and the Minarets! Oh, how they rose above their resting stature
when the rain bathed them and the lightning played among their black
spires! What tempest waves of air dashed and surged among these rocks
of the great air ocean! After the storm I heard a grouse calling her young
on the meadowside close by. I was sheltered from rain in a clump of
Williamson spruce.[2] Will ascend Minarets tomorrow . . .

The higher we go in the mountains, the milkier becomes the Milky
Way.

[2] Probably the mountain hemlock (*Tsuga mertensiana*).

August 17 [?]

Set out early for the glaciers of the Minarets, and whatsoever else they had to give me. The morning was bright and bracing. I walked fast, for I feared noon rains. Besides, the Minarets have been waited for a long time . . . I saw six woodchucks[3]—high livers all of them, at an altitude of ten thousand, seven hundred feet—on a sloping moraine meadow. They were fine burly sufficient-looking fellows, in every way equal to the situation.

Water ouzels in a lake diving . . . This day I found *Primula suffrutescens* abundant nearly everywhere on my way, up to eleven thousand feet, one place in flower.

On the very summit of one of the passes of the Minarets, standing in the stiff breeze at an altitude of eleven thousand six hundred feet, I found two currant bushes new to me in species, and two half-benumbed bumblebees upon them, and a fly or two. The big *Gentiana* I found yet higher. Saw one with its corolla split down as if a hailstone had fallen into it.

I never before saw rocks so painted with yellow and red lichens as are the sides of the passes among the Minarets.

My camp last night was in the uppermost grove of a canyon running nearly south from one of the many deep recesses of Mount Ritter. I knew that the glacial canyon that drained away the ice from the many chambers of the Minarets ran parallel to this, and was separated from it by a huge wall impassable opposite my camp, but I hoped to be able to cross higher up. Was soon on top and crossed without difficulty. The Minarets were now fairly in my grasp. I had been crossing canyons for five days. This was certainly the last. Their appearance from here was impressively sublime because of their great height, narrow bases, linear arrangement, and dark color. They are the most elaborately carved on the edges of any slate summits I have seen. Four lakes lie like open eyes below the ample clouds of *névé* that send them water. These *névé* slopes are large, and wonderfully adapted in form and situation for picturesque effects among the black angular slate slabs and peaks. I observed the lines of the greatest declivity upon several of these slopes, no doubt due to the slipping and avalanching of dry winter snow upon their steeply inclined surfaces . . . Wind streaks snow, but not thus . . .

I thought of ascending the highest Minaret, which is the one farthest south, but, after scanning it narrowly, discovered it was inaccessible.[4]

[3] Yellow-bellied marmots (*Marmota flaviventris*).

[4] Clyde Minaret, 12,281 feet, inaccessible from the west. It was first ascended from the other side in 1928.

There is one small glacier on the west side near the south which I set out to examine. On the way I had to ascend or cross many *névés* and old moraines and rock bosses, domish in form, with which the bottom of the wide canyon is filled. At the foot of a former moraine of this west glacier is a small lake not one hundred yards long, but grandly framed with a sheer wall of *névé* twenty feet high . . .

Beautiful caves reached back from the water's edge; in some places granite walls overleaned and big blocks broke off from the main *névé* wall, and, with angles sharp as those of ice, leaned into the lake. Undermined by the water, the fissures filled with blue light, and water dripped and trickled all along the white walls. The sun was shining. I never saw so grand a setting for a glacier lake. The sharp peaks of Ritter seen over the snow shone with splendid effect.

The ascent from this rare lakelet to the foot of the moraine of the present glacier is about one hundred feet. This glacier has the appearance of being cut in two by a belt of avalanche rock reaching from the first of the cliffs above the glacier to its terminal moraine. This avalanche is quite recent, probably sent down by the Inyo earthquake of a year ago last twenty-sixth of March. Slate is able to stand earthquake action in much slimmer forms than granite . . . This is the first instance I have discovered of a large avalanche on a glacier.

I wished to reach the head of this glacier, and after ascending a short distance came to where the avalanche by which I was making the attempt was so loosened by the melting of snow and ice beneath that it constantly gave way in small slides that rattled past with some danger. I therefore tried the glacier itself, but the surface was bare of snow, and steps had to be cut. This soon became tedious, and I again attempted to thread my way cautiously among the ill-settled avalanche stones . . . At length I reached the top, examined the wall above the glacier, and thought it possibly might be scaled where avalanches descended. I worked cautiously up the face of the cliff above the ice, wild-looking and wilder every step. Soon I was halted by a dangerous step, passed it with knit lips, again halted, made a little foothold, with my hatchet. Again stopped, made a horizontal movement and avoided this place. Again I was stopped by fine gravel covering the only possible foot- or hand-holds. This I cleared away with the hatchet, holding on with one hand the while. It is hard to turn back, especially when the danger is certain either way. But now the sky was black as the rocks, and I saw the rain falling on the peaks of the Merced group. Besides, the rocks in the shapes they took seemed to be determined to baffle me. I decided to attempt return. After most delicate caution in searching for and making

steps, I reached the head of the glacier. Cut steps again, and began to
work my way down. Now the first lightning shot was fired among the
crags overhead. The wind hissed and surged among the spires. Ritter
was capped with cloud, yet loomed aloft higher. Oh, grandly the black
spires came out on the pale edges of the storm cloud heavy behind
them! . . . More and more lightning, but as yet no rain fell here,
although I saw it falling about Lyell. I ran down the avalanche excitedly,
half enjoying, half fearing. Clad free as a Highlander, I cared not for a
wetting, yet thought I should endeavor to reach camp at once. I started,
but, on passing along the face of the grand spire, made a dash for the
summit of a pass nearly in the middle of the group of Minarets. I
reached the top by careful climbing. The pass is exceedingly narrow,
some places only a few feet wide, made by water and snow acting on
dissoluble seams in the slate . . . Walls of the pass were vertical, and
grand beyond all description. A glorious view broke from the top—
another glacier, of which I could see a strip through a yet narrower
gorge pass of the east side, volcanoes of Mono, a section of a fine lake,
also a good portion of the Inyo Mountains. A splendid irised cloud sallied
overhead, the black clouds disappeared, while the wind played wild
music on the Minarets as on an instrument.

I began to descend the east side of the glacier, which reached to the
top of the pass. I had to cut my steps very carefully in the hard, clear
ice, as a slip of one step would ensure a glissade of half a mile at death
speed. I wedged myself most of the way through the lane-like gorge
between the ice and wall, all the time cutting steps. Came out at last
after many a halt for consideration of the position of my steps, and to
look back upward at the wild, wild cliffs, and wild, wild clouds rushing
over them. It was a weird unhuman pathway, and as I now look back
from my campfire, it seems strange I should have dared its perils.

August 19 [?]

On again reaching the main portion of the glacier I was delighted with
its beauty, its instructive crevasses and ice cataracts, and with the noble
landscape reaching far south and west. This glacier is a perfect mass of
yawning crevasses on the right side, as if its bed had been suddenly
heaved up in the center. It ought not to be set foot upon by solitary
explorers, as many of the most dangerous of the crevasses are slightly
snow-covered even this late in the season . . .

I descended the left side after deliberating whether I should not attempt
the right in order to look down into the wide gaping crevasses—some

four or six feet deep—but on reaching the terminal moraine discovered that I had narrowly escaped some crevasses that reached nearly to my track.

I sketched, and then ran northwestward around the great wall that formed the left bank of the glacier. Here I discovered another glacier, not so wildly broken and shattered, but exceedingly beautiful in its fine swooping curves, its splendidly sculptured walls, and its moraines and lakes and general scenery. In form it is nearly triangular, much crevassed near the head, and finely barred with curved dark-stained lines at the foot. I attempted the ascent up the middle of the glacier to the head, but it was so bare and hard I was compelled to cut every step in the most careful manner. Wearied of this I cut my way over to the snow-covered portion on the right side, which is steeper in its curves, yet much safer. I thought its crevasses all too narrow to be dangerous, but on looking into one was startled to find myself on the brink of one wide enough to take me in. The snow bridge was not more than six inches thick above it. The ice was clear below a depth of four feet, but I could not see down more than ten feet owing to the curve of the walls. All these marginal crevasses have convex sides uppermost. I walked carefully, sounding with my hatchet, and reached the top safely. From here, on looking down the opposite side of the main Minaret wall, I was glad to see I should be able to get over to the west side, and so home to camp. The Minaret Pass is eleven thousand three hundred feet, and the glacier about five hundred yards wide by three or four hundred long . . . I reached camp early, unwet, unwearied, unhurt, after a rich day whose duties domineered me.

August 20 [?]

In descending the canyonside of the Joaquin slate yosemite, I could see the young river beneath flowing from grove to grove and through meadows with here and there a strip of white that marked a cascade, but, in trying to follow it up among the mountains at its head, I lost it entirely. In vain I tried to discover its course by some green forest or willow strip. It appeared to sink. Only dry, empty canyons were seen, excepting the long distant strip of white water which came from the great west glacier of Ritter. In following up the river two days later, which is a favorite pursuit with me, I discovered the cause of my difficulty. The west dip of the slate is so developed at the upper end of the canyon that the stream is huddled up and made to flow out of sight, as if on its edge.

Sixty Lakes Basin,
Kings Canyon National Park

Three miles above the mouth of the Minaret tributary on the main stream there is a beautiful fall, forty or fifty feet wide. It is approached through a fine tall grove, and has the sublime background of the mountains . . .

The first grand cascades on the San Joaquin are five miles above the Minaret tributary and flow from one small lake basin to another lake basin, showing how ice rises in passing the lips of basins.

Camp at head of main
Joaquin Canyon.
Altitude 9800 feet.

Here the river divides, one fork coming in from the north and the other from Ritter. The Ritter fork comes down the mountainside here in a network of cascades, wonderfully woven, as are all slate cascades of great size near summits, when the slate has a cleavage well pronounced. The mountains rise in a circle, showing their grand dark bosses and delicate spires on the starry sky. Down the canyon a company of sturdy, long-limbed mountain pines show nobly. All the rest of the horizon is treeless, because moraineless. How fully are all the forms and languages of waters, winds, trees, flowers, birds, rocks, subordinated to the primary structure of the mountains ere they were ice-sculptured! When all was planned and ready, snow-flowers were dusted over them, forming a film of ice over the mountain plate. And so all this development—the photography of God . . .

Ursa Major nearly horizontal, and has gone to rest. So must I. I am in a small grove of mountain hemlock. Their feathery boughs are extended above my head like hands of gentle spirits. Good night to God and His stars and mountains.

August 21 [?]

Clouds, dense and black, come from the southwest, over the black crests and peaks of Ritter, the lowest torn and raked to shreds. The cold wind is tuned to the opaque, somber sky. Now a little rain, snow, and hail.

I wish to cross to the east side of Ritter today, visiting the main north glacier on my way. I have never crossed these summits, and fear to try on so dark a day . . . At noon, the clouds breaking, I decide to make the attempt, climbing up the fissured and flowery edge of the rock near Ritter Cascade. At the top of the Cascade I find a grand amphitheater, where glaciers from Ritter and peaks to the north once congathered—now meadow and lake and red and black walls with wild undressed falls and rapids and a few hardy flowers. From the rim of this I have a glorious view of high fountain glaciers and *nèvès,* with pointed spears and tapering towers and spires innumerable. Here, too, I find a white stemless thistle, larger than the purple one of Mono.

Yet higher, following the wild streams and climbing around inaccessible gorges, at length I am in sight of the lofty top crest of Ritter and know I am exactly right. The clouds grow dark again and send hail, but I know the rest of my way too well to fear. I can push down to the treeline if need be, in any kind of storm . . .

I come in sight of the main North Ritter Glacier, its snout projecting from a narrow opening gap into a lake about three hundred yards in diameter. Its waters are intensely blue. The basin was excavated by the Ritter Glacier and those of Banner Peak to the north at the time of their greater extension. The glacier enters on the east side. On the west is a splendid frame of pure white *névé,* abounding in deep caves with arched openings. One of these has a span of forty feet, and a height of thirty. This frame of *névé* comes down to the water's edge and in places reaches out over the lake. Most of its face is made precipitous by sections breaking off into the lake after the manner of icebergs. These are snowbergs. The strength of the glacier itself is so nearly spent ere it reaches the lake, it does not break off in bergs, but melts with many a rill, giving a network of sweet music.

Wishing to reach the head of this glacier, I follow up the left lateral moraine that extends from the flank of the mountain to the lake until I reach the top. Then I try to cross the glacier itself where it is not so steep. But I find it bare, unwalkable ice. The least slip would send me down a slope of thirty-five degrees, a distance of three hundred yards, into the lake. I begin to cut steps, but the snout of the glacier is so hard, and every step has to be so perfect, that I make slow and wearisome progress with blankets on my back. I soon realize it will be dark ere I succeed in crossing, therefore I resolve to retrace my steps and attempt crossing at the foot of the glacier close to the lake where it is narrower, and if I find that too dangerous from crevasses, to go around the lake, which last alternative, from the roughness of its shore, would be no easy thing. I find the ice on the end of the glacier softer and cross, then push rapidly up the right moraine to where the glacier becomes much more easily accessible on account of the lowness of its slope and because its surface is roughened with ridges and rocks.

In going up between the edge of the glacier and the moraine I discover the main surface stream of the glacier has cut a large cave, which
I enter and find is made of clear-veined ice—a very unhuman place,
with strange water gurgles and tinkles.

The lower steep portion of the glacier is alive with swift-running rills.
A larger stream begins its course at the head of the glacier, and runs in
a westerly direction along near the right side. It has cut for itself a
strangely curved and scalloped channel in the solid green ice, in which it
glides with motions and tones and gestures I never before knew water
to make.

The glacier receives its snow from the north side of Ritter. It has two
motions, one nearly north, the other W. 10° N. In flowing north it is
soon stopped by the steep wall of Banner Peak, and its course is then
westward down the canyon. In grating along the right bank, pressed
hard against it by the northward thrust, it grinds the stones of its moraine
in a way that crushes off their angles, and gives them forms that I never
before could account for. It also gives to the bank thus crushed a finish
I have often observed without knowing its cause. It is similar to that of
a gorge down which earthquakes have sent stone avalanches. I have been
noting for some time the curved dirt lines on the snouts of glaciers. It is
well seen here, apparent in sections made by the stream, and in some
which I made with an ax, that this surface marking consists of the
weathered ends, or edges rather, of the successive layers of which the
whole glacier is made up by the seasons' snows. Wherever a line with
greater quantity of dirt appears, a section of the clean ice beneath always shows that the greater dirtiness is correspondent with a seam or
layer of harder, bluer ice. These layers of ice are curved more or less
in a vertical direction—some places being nearly on edge. This bending
of the layers proves a bending of the whole glacier—always most bent
where most opposed in its motion . . .

This handsome glacier is not much crevassed, but has a large, conspicuous schrund, and is finely curved, both from slip of winter snow
and from the swedging of its flow. Reckoning the long and much-cre-
vassed glacier between the Minarets and Ritter on the east slope as
belonging to Ritter, and also those of the large half separate crest on the
north of Ritter, then the glaciers of Ritter number six together, having
many large *névés* with feeble glacial motion. All of these glaciers are in
picturesque basins, and are exceedingly beautiful in their edges, which
comply in most graceful lateral curves to all of the salient and re-enter-
ing angles of the black basin rock, and in the vertical curves of the bottom.

When my observations on this most interesting glacier (the main North Ritter Glacier) were finished, it was near sunset, and I had to make haste down to the treeline. Yet I lingered reveling in the grandeur of the landscape. I was on the summit of the pass, looking upon Ritter Lake with its snowy crags and banks, and many a wide glacial fountain beyond, rimmed with peaks, the wind making stern music among their thousand spires, the sky with grand openings in the huge black clouds— openings jagged, walled, and steep like the passes of the mountains beneath them. Eastward lay Islet Lake[5] with its countless little rocky isles; to the left, the splendid architecture of Mammoth Mountain,[6] and in the distance range on range of mountains yet unnamed, with Mono plains and the magnificent lake and volcanic cones, sunlit and warm, between. To the eastward over the Great Basin swelled a range of alabaster cumuli, presenting a series of precipices deeply cleft with shadowy canyons, the whole fringed about their bases with a grand talus of the same alabaster material. Here and there occurred black masses with clearly defined edges like metamorphic slate in granite. Beneath these noble cloud mountains were horizontal bars and feathery touches of rose and crimson with clear sky between, of that exquisite spiritual kind that is connected in some way with our other life, and never fails, wherever we chance to be, to produce a hush of all cares and a longing, longing, longing . . .

My feet soon awakened to their work—a mile of rock-leaping on slopes of water-washed moraines—and I soon came in sight of a wind-bent *Pinus albicaulis* that ensured fire for the night. I walked on soft cushions of carex, and I saw here and there a daisy and a stone fringed with bryanthus. I descended a long, icy *névé,* felt weary, and halted in the first dwarf-pine thicket I came to. The wind blew wildly all through the night. I hedged myself and fire roundabout with boughs to deaden the blows of the wind that came down in craggy avalanches. The outlet of a little glacier sends down its stream over a precipice nearby, making music that is heard in the pauses of the wild wind . . .

August 22 [?]

Morning clear and lovely. The stony isles of Islet Lake are lighted as if the sun arose for them alone. The finely curved mountainfronts to the north show forth their arches and pillars to fine advantage with the

[5] Thousand Island Lake.

[6] Mrs. Wolfe suggests that Muir refers here to "the mass which includes Electra and Foerster peaks on the Merced-San Joaquin watershed."

splendid arrangement of light and shade. The sun silvers the cascade as
if getting its waters ready for the spangles of the lake. The glaciers are
tinted with rose, but ever and anon comes a black, foggy cloud down-
sweeping from the western summits, and applies its chill, somber folds
to the surface in every part, filling also all the chambers and vaults
of the black walls around them.

I moved over into a valley belonging to a cluster of glaciers nearer
Lyell, ready to ascend Matterhorn,[7] and camped on the edge of a
glacial lake in the protecting lee of a clump of *Pinus albicaulis* at an
altitude of ten thousand four hundred and fifty feet.

August 23 [?]

Wildly came the wind all through the half-lighted night, clouds black
and cold hanging about the summits. But will attempt the Matterhorn.
Coffee, and away free-legged as any Highlander. Arrived at the summit
after a stiff climb over *névés* and glaciers and loose, rocky taluses, but
alack! the Matterhorn was yet miles away and fenced off from the
shattered crest I was on, by a series of jagged, unscalable crests and
glaciers that seemed steeper and glassier than any I had seen. After
studying the situation like a chessboard, narrowly scanning each spiky
wall and its glacier-guarded base, I made up my mind to the unhappy
opinion that it would be wrong to incur so many dangers in seeking a
way from this direction to the peak of the Matterhorn. I concluded to
spend the day with three glaciers to the left towards Ritter, and seek the
Matterhorn again next day by ascending a canyon leading up from the
north.

Yet, in order to make sure of the practicability of even that route,
I scaled the peak next me on the left[8] to get a wider view of the jagged
zigzag topography. On reaching the top (twelve thousand feet), I saw it
was possible to descend to one of the glaciers which before seemed to
threaten so much, and that at its top it was not only snow-covered but
less steeply inclined, and that on its shattered, precipitous head wall
there was a narrow slot, three or four feet wide, which I could reach
from the head of the glacier, and possibly descend on the south side
into what promised to be a canyon leading up to the highest *névés* of
Matterhorn, towards which I could see a long, easy spur coming down
from the summit.

[7] Probably Rodgers Peak, 12,978 feet; the Sierra Club credits Robert M. Price
with the first ascent in 1897.
[8] Probably Mount Davis, 12,311 feet.

It is hard to give up a brave mountain, like the Matterhorn, that you have counted on for years, and the upshot of this new view was that I began to scramble down towards the first glacier that lay beneath me, reached it, struck my ax into its snow, and found it in good condition— crisp, yet not too hard. There were some crevasses that threatened, and in some places the schrund yawned in what is called a cruel and infernal manner, but I escaped all these, passing the schrund by a snow bridge, and reached the narrow gap (eleven thousand seven hundred feet altitude). There I found, to my delight, I could clamber down the south side, and that after I reached the edge of a little lake in which snowbergs were drifting, the rest of the way to the Matterhorn peak was nothing but simple scrambling over snow slopes, over the snout of the Matterhorn glacier, across moraines, down the faces of fissured precipices, up couloirs, threatened with avalanches of loose stones, on up higher, higher, peaks in crowds rising all around—Dana, Hoffmann, Ritter, pinnacles of the Minaret group—and I could see the Merced group clouded with ice and snow, and glaciers near and far, and a score of lake gems. With many a rest for breath and for gazing upon the sublimity of the ever-changing landscape, and without any fierce effort or very apparent danger, I reached the topmost stone.

I take bearings of a few peaks and glaciers, and give myself up to the glorious landscape until night draws nigh. Then down again. I discover a narrow avalanche spout or channel in the northeast shoulder which leads to Matterhorn Lake, a gem at the foot of the vertical north face of Matterhorn. This lake is one of the highest in the range (altitude twelve thousand feet) . . . The Matterhorn breaks away at the top in huge rough-edged faulted precipices, and is approachable by the way I came up from the canyon of the San Joaquin. This is easy to find, but outlandish for civil travel. It is also approachable via the Rush Creek Canyon, which was the way of my descent, but this is hard to find.

The Matterhorn is built of black slate, blacker slate, and gray granite, mingled and interfused and belted and conglomerated, making a strange-appearing section on the north side. In some places the granite penetrates the slate in crack-like seams. In other places it appears to have got into large solid slate masses, like plums into a pudding. In some places the slate and granite seem to be about equal in quantity, and even mixed in the form of boulders, but planes of cleavage run unbrokenly through both slate and granite. In Matterhorn and adjacent mountains I observed some instances of curved dome cleavage which is not common at this elevation. The granite of the Matterhorn partakes of all the forms in its crumbling and disintegrated condition that the neighboring slate does—all highly metamorphic.

The glacier of the north side that is nearly inactive has been long dying, as evidenced by its terminal moraines reaching for two hundred yards from the lake, draggled out or heaped irregularly according to periods of weakness or strength. Northwesterly is another glacier, emptying into a lake, three hundred yards in diameter—a rare gem in color and setting (altitude eleven thousand five hundred feet). The water of Matterhorn Lake flows into this, and the waters of both, after descending in cascades three hundred and fifty feet, enter a long, picturesque, islanded lake, one thousand yards long. This last lake receives the drainage of three glaciers, and its outlet is a fine stream forming one of the feeders of the Middle Fork of San Joaquin. The second of these three lakes is nobly surrounded by mountain peaks and glaciers and clouds of pure white *névé*. Its south shore has many precipices of icy *névé* rising from the water's edge. Not a plant grows there, but the north shore has sedges, and on one place where a high wall-faced rock reflects the sun heat is a garden containing . . . gooseberries . . . one goldenrod, a noble thistle, and the bush epilobium, fringes of which are in flower, of as rich a purple as ever worn by highbred plant of the tropics. Besides there are nodding carices in clumps, and senecio, and hairy lupines and spraguea—all this at an altitude of eleven thousand five hundred feet, with a circumference of snowy mountains looking at it, and a chill, icy lake clashing its frosty waves at its foot.

The outlet of these three lakes, on its way down the mountainside to the big open valley that goes straight to the east or Thousand-Mile branch of the San Joaquin, cuts itself a passage beneath a narrow but deep *névé*. The entrance of this is imposing, the roof splendidly sculptured and arched. The glad and bold stream enters this gateway at a bound. In crossing the *névé* I narrowly escaped falling into a crevasse twenty or thirty feet deep and three feet wide.

Had a glorious walk home, reaching gardens yet richer and richer. I reached camp on the lakeside, sifted full of mountain air, rich, happy, and weary . . .

Sierra juniper, San Joaquin River near
Long Creek, Minarets Wilderness Area

August 24 [?]

Wild, unweariable wind all the night and day. Crossed over to the Tuolumne Valley . . . The air on the divide is full of insects, and when seen in the sunlight with the eyes protected by the crest of the mountain they appear like transparent flecks of silver. So also do the rocks and bushes. A stiff wind blows the insects, driving them like chaff. Some with fluttering wings fly against the wind . . . I have observed the air full of silvered cobwebs above the summit of Lyell. None of these insects or webs are at all visible under other circumstances.

August 25 [?]

I camped for the night near the right Lyell Glacier on a steep mountainside at an elevation of eleven thousand two hundred and fifty feet. It was cold and windy, and difficult getting wood, and even more so getting water. I climbed up the mountain and brought down a hatful of snowballs, enough for coffee night and morning. Then I built up a place for a fire with rocks, to keep the wood from rolling down the slope, and also for a bed. It is a wild, loud, frosty night. Bread about gone. Home tomorrow or next day.

John of the Mountains

Yosemite Valley
September 3rd, 1873

Dear Sister Sarah:[9]

I have just returned from the longest and hardest trip I have ever made in the mountains, having been gone over five weeks. I am weary, but resting fast; sleepy, but sleeping deep and fast; hungry, but eating much. For two weeks I explored the glaciers of the summits east of here, sleeping among the snowy mountains without blankets and with but little to eat on account of its being so inaccessible. After my icy experiences it seems strange to be down here in so warm and flowery a climate.

I will soon be off again, determined to use all the season in prosecuting my researches—will go next to Kings River a hundred miles south, then to Lake Tahoe and adjacent mountains, and in winter work in Oakland with my pen.

The Scotch are slow, but some day I will have the results of my mountain studies in a form in which you all will be able to read and judge of them . . . The mountains are calling and I must go . . .

The Life and Letters of John Muir

[9] Sarah Muir Galloway, at Fountain Lake farm, Wisconsin.

3. GRAND CANYONS AND ICY SUMMITS

Two weeks after returning from his exhausting journey to the Minarets, Muir answered the mountains' call and set off on his most ambitious trip south of Yosemite. This time he sought company. Dr. Albert Kellogg, botanist, and William Simms, artist, went with him to Wawona. There, after a day's delay, they enlisted Galen Clark, pioneer guide and innkeeper, hoping he would be a climbing companion for Muir. There were also horses and mules. Muir fretted about the slow going.

Nine days out, the icy summits proved irresistible. Muir took a supply of food and started alone for the Evolution basin. It was late September. He had a memorable encounter with a band of wild sheep, and climbed at least one of the Evolution peaks and saw the gothic panorama of the Sierra crest—"a mass of ice sculpture."

Galen Clark, who had made some high-country excursions in the Yosemite region, was evidently unprepared for what lay ahead. When Muir returned and showed him the view from a divide, we are told, Clark "groaned," remembered his obligations at Clark's Station, left the little party and went home.

The route was formidable, indeed, in those days before engineers, rangers, and trail crews established the modern network which includes the John Muir Trail. Muir and his companions traveled the divide between the North and Middle forks of the Kings, crossed the main river below their confluence, and climbed back up by way of Mill Creek to the Big Trees of the present Grant Grove and the divide between the Kings and the Kaweah. Leaving the others in the great South Fork canyon, Muir made his way to the peaks of either the Kings-Kern Divide or the Mount Brewer massif. It was necessary to double his steps back to the canyon and up again over Kearsarge Pass to find the nervous Kellogg and Simms, whom he then left in the Owens Valley to await his return from Mount Whitney.

The nation's highest mountain was "causing some stir in the newspapers," as Muir commented to Mrs. Carr. Clarence King had

just hastened to the summit, attempting to retrieve the honors of the first ascent he had erroneously claimed in 1871. On his arrival at the top King found the lucky half-dollar left there thirteen days earlier by a local fisherman. Muir climbed the true Mount Whitney more than five weeks after King, but he was the first to ascend the relatively difficult east face.

When he completed this tour of the range and returned to Yosemite via Lake Tahoe, as W. F. Badé points out, Muir had "traveled over a thousand wilderness miles, climbed numerous peaks, and discovered many glaciers and new yosemites." "It is astonishing," Muir wrote, "how high and far we can climb in mountains that we love."

Clark's Station
September 13th, 1873

Dear Mrs. Carr:

We have just arrived from the Valley, and are now fairly off for the ice in the highest and broadest of the Sierras. Our party consists of the blessed Doctor [Kellogg] and Billy Simms, *Artist,* and I am so glad that the Doctor will have company when I am among the summits. We hoped to have secured Clark also, a companion for me among the peaks and snow, but alack, I *must* go alone. Well, I will not complain a word, for I shall be overpaid a thousand, thousand fold. I can give you no measured idea of the time of our reaching Tahoe, but I will write always on coming to stations if such there be in the rocks and sage where letters are written . . .

Now for God's glorious mountains . . .

The Life and Letters of John Muir

*San Joaquin River below Long Creek,
Minarets Wilderness Area*

On divide between Chiquito
Creek and South Fork Merced
September 19

In descending the sandy slope of the divide, Clark got a glimpse of a frightened bear beating a hasty flight from the open hillside to the dense chaparral that filled the bottom of the gulch. At noon, we lunched on the edge of a beautiful brown and yellow meadow spread with many a bay projecting into a forest of fir and pine (altitude seventy-one hundred feet).

From the divide we obtained a glorious view of all the heads of the San Joaquin River excepting the north forks. Through the haze and smoke we could see Mount Gabb and Mount Abbot, and Red Slate Peak. Chiquito Buttes were on our left. These are a cluster of domes, not well developed, which have been laid bare by the great Joaquin Glacier.

Camp on Chiquito Creek
September 20

After a long, weary search through many miles of dry tamarack[1] flats, we camped in the deep picturesque channel of Chiquito Joaquin. This is the head of a fine forest basin, with rocks marvelously colored. We saw deer . . .

The wild cherry is abundant on the rough hillsides at an elevation of six thousand to eight thousand feet. The berries are bitter, but beautiful, and droop gracefully.

No pine in the forest compares with *Pinus contorta* in gracefulness of habit and airy, feathery lightness. I have seen many specimens as graceful in motion and in form as the fairest grasses. It is badly named.

Nooned upon a delightful untrodden meadow, over which insects joyous and busy hummed in the sunshine . . .

Camp on Middle Fork,
San Joaquin, Boulder Valley
September 22

Made tedious progress, horses and mules tending constantly to roll down canyon . . . The average slope of San Joaquin Canyon, Middle Fork, is twenty-three degrees for a height of seventy-five hundred feet . . . Aldery gulches, cool water, crimson and yellow sand.

[1] Lodgepole pine (*Pinus contorta*).

The glowing sunset beams fall in bars through the forest, touching with marvelous power the hushed waiting firs, yellow ferns, and glistening grass stems that grow in sandy moraines, and the asters and goldenrods along our camp meadow . . .

Two large bucks with branched antlers like dead pine roots are splendidly framed in willows as they stand in grasses over their backs—noble inhabitants of this wild forest.

September 23

In the morning we ascended four hundred feet to a magnificent basin containing groves of fir and *Pinus contorta* and yellow meads and lakes, with gray, rocky, sparsely feathered ridges around. Then a long ride over a succession of sandy flats, some well chaparraled, others remarkably open with bars of light and shade purely divine. No track but that of the deer . . .

At noon we come to a lava plateau. Granite is now breaking into a labyrinth of rocks of every conceivable form, with ponds and winding meads innumerable. We arrive at a large tributary of the South Fork about noon, and at Mono Creek at 3 P.M. . . . Gentians a meadowful, one foot high. Many roses and linosyris.

We pass a lake lovely with ducks and rippling glassy dark mountains nobly sculptured, sheer to the water. Pines and junipers stand picturesquely on the rock headlands . . . Hum of bees, and dragonflies . . . Altitude seventy-one hundred feet.

Camp. September 24

In this poor rocky wilderness are wild roses with scarlet hips, yarrow and goldenrod, also mint, monardella, and asters . . .

The direction of the striae in this section is about N. 33° W. Mount Gabb and Mount Abbot in the distance . . .

Camp in South Fork, Joaquin Canyon
September 25

View very grand and universal. Ritter the noblest and most ornate of all. Red Slate Peak very noble—black, white, and red. Then Mount Gabb and Mount Abbot and an inseparable field of high peaks at the head of Joaquin. One is castle-shaped and gray. Another towers dark on the right side of the canyon as we look. Snowy peaks loom yet beyond at the head of Kings River Forest. It grows dusk . . . shadows are stealing over the many meads and groves of Joaquin Canyon . . .

South Fork, San Joaquin
September 26. Night.

I am camped at the head of this San Joaquin yosemite this ninth day, in a small oval dry lake basin, with a rocky wall fifty feet above the river. The basin here is filled with fallen trees, and fringed with willow. I set out this noon for the icy summits, leaving Clark, Billy, and Doctor Kellogg in camp on a moraine with the animals. I have a week's provisions.

My fire cannot be seen far, hid as it is in willows and rocks. No Indians will find me. I shall be too high for them tomorrow evening. I hear the river rushing. It is a fine, calm, starry, soothing night. Many goldenrods and gentians grow in the meads of this yosemite.

September 27. Dawn.

A calm Indian-summery morning; a hazy light wrapping all the high mountains, shadows creeping, barred with lights, summits tipped with the first spirit of dawn.

At San Joaquin Cascades.

The river forks here, the left valley being deeper and in every way larger, but far the greater portion of water comes from the right cascades in vertical short leaps . . . Here granite meets slate—slate on the south side, granite in the north . . . Mostly the granite and slate, however mixed, yet are separate and meet sharply, but in some places they seem to blend. However, in all cases every crack and seam and joint belonging to one is continued on through the other. Granite has essentially the same physical structure as slate . . .

This San Joaquin Canyon all the way up from the lowest to the highest yosemite is very rough. One is constantly compelled to ascend knobs and buttresses that rise sheer or steeply inclined from the water's edge . . . The scenery from the first main fork is very grand. The walls are steep and close, fold on fold, rising to a height of three thousand to four thousand feet . . .

I saw a fine band of mountain sheep, light gray in color, white on the backs of hips, with black tails. All horned, they seemed strong and moved with great deliberation, led by the largest. They crossed the river between the steps of the cascade where the channel was blocked and bridged with big boulders. On level ground they were close together, but in ascending the steep mountain wall were far apart in single file, zigzag. They were in full sight at first, only forty yards distant, and seemed to have been scattered; two or three were on my left on the opposite side of the cascades. Had they been tame sheep, they would have run off to destruction. This first lovely fellow studied the intentions of the flock, and met them by making leaps on glacial bosses that made me hold my breath. They first had to cross loose angular blocks of granite, which they did splendidly; then they leaped up the face of the mountain just where I thought they wouldn't, and perhaps couldn't, go. I could have scaled the same precipice, but not where they did. I could have followed in most places only by being barefooted.

Like the true mountaineers they are, they never seemed to hurry. They went up over the polished bosses in admirable order and with no noise, each showing a separate will, some lingering to look back at me, some hastening on to the front. Each individual crossed the river, unlike tame sheep. Tame sheep often jump at a rock face and fall back, but here was not one false step. These are clean and elegant, the others dirty and awkward. These are guarded by the great Shepherd of us all, those by erring money-seekers. They passed in review before me; so also did deer—the sheep for the rocks and rough mountain work, the deer for the forest and green grassy meadows.

Looking at them I often cried out, 'That was good!' . . . I exulted in the power and sufficiency of Nature, and felt like saying aloud to God as to a man, 'Well done!' Our horses roll end over end, and our much-vaunted mules, so surefooted and mountain-capable, roll like barrels. I must so often judge for my horse, and, considering him as a kind of machine, I know the slope he can bear and how he will be likely to come off in making various rock steps . . . These noble fellows—I would like their company! Where are the alp-loving ibex or chamois that can outleap them? Not long ago I saw their tracks on the Matterhorn.[2] Clark said one must kill mountain sheep. But I'm glad these were not killed. They were as fearless of water and the roar of foaming cascades as the ouzel that sang for me today . . .[3]

September 28.

I camped last night in a wide valley above the uppermost (San Joaquin) yosemite in full view of Mount Humphreys . . .[4]

[2] Rodgers Peak.

[3] Muir gave a more extended version of this encounter in his essay on the wild sheep (see pages 122–127).

[4] Not the present Humphreys; Mrs. Wolfe says it was probably Mount Darwin, 13,830 feet.

I saw three dead wild sheep that had been snowbound . . . Lake Millar, fourteen hundred yards long, fifty to one hundred and fifty yards wide, has waters of a bright green, and lies along the gothic front of Mount Millar[5] on the south side . . .

In ascending the main Mount Millar fork of Joaquin, the first tributary of any size is on the right south side about one mile above the first meadow. It is a bright active stream coming down in a foamy cascade of one thousand feet . . .

Mount Millar.

. . . Had a glorious view from the top of Mount Millar of the Owens River and Valley, and of the Sierra, one broad field of peaks upon no one of which can the eye rest. They are gothic near the axis—a mass of ice sculpture. Mount Emerson[6] is imposing with its evenly balanced crest and far-reaching snowy wings. Emerson and Millar are each about thirteen thousand five hundred feet high.

Millar is planted with ivesia to the top, also with polemonium and with yellow compositae. At the base grow larkspurs, columbine, spiraea, dodecatheon. Birds on top and bees. Bush epilobium far up and ferns cystopteris and pellaea.

Camp at Big Meadows.
September 29.

The direction of the slate cleavage is nearly vertical where it meets the granite at the fork of the river . . .

A bright white silver strip cascade comes into the south South Fork just above its junction with the east South Fork on the west side . . .

Deer, grouse, squirrels . . .

Camp on South Fork, San Joaquin.
September 30.

In camp again with the main party. Up early and went with Clark to a point on the divide to view the landscape and plan the route. The view is awful—a vast wilderness of rocks and canyons. Clark groaned and went home.

John of the Mountains

[5] One of the Evolution peaks.
[6] Not the present Emerson. Perhaps Mount Fiske?

Camp on South Fork, San Joaquin, near
divide of San Joaquin and Kings River,
September 27th[7]

Dear Mrs. Carr:

We have been out nearly two weeks. Clark is going to leave us. Told me five minutes ago. Am a little nervous about it, but will of course push on alone.

We came out through the Mariposa Grove, around the head of the Chiquito Joaquin, across the canyon of the North Fork of San Joaquin, then across the canyon of Middle Fork of San Joaquin, and up the east side of the South Fork one day's journey. Then picked our wild way across the canyon of the South Fork and camped up one day's journey on the west side of the canyon; there we made a camp for four days. I was anxious to see the head fountains of this river, and started alone, Clark not feeling able to bear the fatigue involved in such a trip. I set out without blankets for a hard climb; followed the Joaquin to its *glaciers*,[8] and climbed the highest mountain I could find at its head, which was either Mount Humphreys or the mountain next south. This is a noble mountain, considerably higher than any I have before ascended. The map of the Geological Survey gives no detail of this wild region.

I was gone from camp four days; discovered fifteen glaciers, and yosemite valleys "many O."[9] The view from that glorious mountain (13,500 feet high?) is not to be attempted here. Saw over into Owens River valley and all across the fountains of Kings River. I got back to camp last evening. This morning after breakfast Clark said that he ought to be at home attending to business and could not feel justified in being away, and therefore had made up his mind to leave us, going home by way of the valley of the main Joaquin.

We will push over to the Kings River region and attempt to go down between the Middle and South forks. Thence into the canyon of the South Fork and over the range to Owens Valley, and south to Mount Whitney if the weather holds steady, then for Tahoe, etc. As we are groping through unexplored regions our plans may be considerably modified. I feel a little anxious about the lateness of the season. We may be at Tahoe in three or four weeks.

We had a rough time crossing the Middle Fork of the Joaquin. Browny rolled down over the rocks, not sidewise but end over end. One of the

[7] The date is questionable, as the letter apparently was written the same day as the previous journal entry.

[8] Muir's emphasis. He was riding his glaciological hobby hard.

[9] "Many O" is apparently a familiar verse refrain.

mules rolled boulder-like in a yet more irregular fashion. Billy went forth
to sketch while I was among the glaciers, and got lost—was thirty-six
hours without food.

I have named a grand *wide-winged* mountain on the head of the Joaquin Mount Emerson. Its head is high above its fellows and wings are
white with ice and snow.

This is a dear bonnie morning, the sun rays lovingly to His precious
mountain pines. The brown meadows are nightly frosted browner and the
yellow aspens are losing their leaves. I wish I could write to you, but
hard work near and far presses heavily and I cannot. Nature makes huge
demands, yet pays a thousand, thousand fold. As in all the mountains
I have seen about the head of Merced and Tuolumne this region is a song
of God . . .

The Life and Letters of John Muir

North Fork, Kings River.
October 1.

Our tenth camp was on a small grass meadow, on the edge of the North
Fork of Kings River (altitude eighty-seven hundred feet). From the divide
of Kings River and the San Joaquin we entered a long straight valley
remarkable for its many domes on the east side, from whose curved
bases had come many avalanches of snow, cutting gaps in the timber and
making hillocks on the west side. Some of these hillocks of former avalanches had crops of trees two feet in diameter . . . The middle portion
of this valley is blocked up and roughened in a remarkable way by rock-
heaps swept down by avalanches. When a valley stream is dammed by
debris, it sorts out the finer material if it has not too much velocity,
and thus sand-heaps are formed, as at Big Tuolumne Meadows. If the
valley be narrow, then the force of the stream carries all things away and
sorts them out at long distances . . .

October 2.

Our twelfth camp is in a very interesting yosemite valley of North Fork
Kings River, nearly circular at the bottom and timbered with sugar and
yellow pines of rare beauty, some very large. Most of the bottom surface
is oversown with boulders, and washed and spread by flood water. The

upper end has a few acres of sandy flats on which are grouped pines and oaks . . .

A small mirror-lake occupies the extreme head of the valley where the river issues from a narrow and tortuous gorge in cascades. So narrow and tortuous is it that the upper end seems to be completely closed, and it is impossible to know the course of the river above for a single mile.

The walls of the valley begin at the head in a distinct yosemite style, but they extend without any marked change far below the bottom. At the head on the west side is an El Capitan rock, about one thousand feet high, and all the rocks which circle around the head are separate from the general wall. They give evidence of great glacial force, are still bright and polished, and present many precipitous fronts with level tablets on which are grouped small pines and live oaks . . .

The lake of this valley is a perfect mirror. Its banks, or rather those of the calm deep lagoon-like outlet, are willowed and flowered superbly and banked with old logs, leaning oaks, and noble pines . . .

As night came on, the gray starry sky, meeting the moonlit wall of El Capitan, seemed to blend with it. The granite was luminous, as ethereal as the sky. A noble company of pines reared their brown columns and spread their curving boughs above us in impressive majesty. Only the trees nearby were in the circle of our campfire sun. Beyond was another circle entirely distinct and distant—a black sharp-angled line of tree-writing along the base of the sky. Who shall read it for us? . . . Roar of the river in the night . . .

Camp on divide between North and Middle Fork, Kings River. October 4.

Our camp last night was in dense fir, on the edge of a small sloping meadow. This morning we ascended the ridge, and, following it, found a trail descending near the junction of the North Fork and main stream . . . Camped fifteen hundred feet above the river . . . The view is lovely from this dark, rocky ridge nobly designed . . . Before us lies the river canyon with innumerable folds and groves sweeping down to it in front, swell over swell, boss over boss, oak-dotted below, pine-feathered above, all hazed with the atmosphere of Indian summer.

John of the Mountains

Camp in dear Bonnie Grove where
the pines meet the foothill oaks.
About eight or ten miles southeast
from the confluence of the
North Fork of Kings River with
the trunk.
October 2d [?]

Dear Mrs. Carr:

After Clark's departure a week ago we climbed the divide between
the South Fork of the San Joaquin and Kings River. I scanned the vast
landscape on which the ice had written wondrous things. After a short
scientific feast I decided to attempt entering the valley of the west
branch of the North Fork, which we did, following the bottom of the
valley for about ten miles, then were compelled to ascend the west side
of the canyon into the forest. About six miles farther down we made out
to re-enter the canyon where there is a yosemite valley, and by hard
efforts succeeded in getting out on the opposite side and reaching the
divide between the North Fork and the Middle Fork. We then followed
the top of the divide nearly to the confluence of the North Fork with
the trunk, and crossed the main river yesterday, and are now in the
pines again, over all the wildest and most impracticable portions of our
journey.

In descending the divide to the main Kings River we made a descent
of near seven thousand feet, "down derry down" with a vengeance, to
the hot pineless foothills. We rose again and it was a most grateful resur-
rection. Last night I watched the writing of the spiry pines on the sky
gray with stars, and if you had been here I would have said, Look! etc.

Last evening when the Doctor and I were bed-building, discussing as
usual the goodnesses and badnesses of boughy mountain beds, we were
astonished by the appearance of two prospectors coming through the
mountain rye. By them I send this note.

General Grant Tree,
General Grant Grove,
Kings Canyon National Park

Today we will reach some of the Sequoias near Thomas' Mill (*vide* Map of Geological Survey), and in two or three days more will be in the canyon of the South Fork of Kings River. If the weather appears tranquil when we reach the summit of the range I may set out among the glaciers for a few days, but if otherwise I shall push hastily for the Owens River plains, and thence up to Tahoe, etc.

I am working hard and shall not feel easy until I am on the other side beyond the reach of early snowstorms. Not that I fear snowstorms for myself, but the poor animals would die or suffer . . .

The Life and Letters of John Muir

Camp at Thomas Mills.
Altitude 5700 feet.
October 6.

Coming here we had a long weary uphill climb. Up from the valley over a hill five hundred feet, then down two thousand feet, to the wide-open, level-bottomed, oak-dotted valley of Mill Creek, past an Indian town, then up the valley six miles to a ranch and wagon road and six miles more to the mills.[10] Beautiful valleys, brown as the plains.

The ice action is not clear in the foothills. Did the ice sculpture these sharp ridges just before the breaking up of the ice winter, as it sculptured the summits which they resemble? . . .

October 7.

Sunrise beams pouring through gaps in the rocky crest, warm level beams brushing across the shoulders in so fitting a way they seem to have worn channels for themselves as glaciers do. The oaks' stems are set aglow. The ground is colored purple with gilia, and gray with *Plantago patagonica,* and red-brown with buckeye, dark live oak, and sycamore.

Among the Big Trees.
Altitude 6500 feet.

The girth of "General Grant" is one hundred and six feet near the ground. It is a tree much like the "Grizzly Giant" of Mariposa. I saw a great many fine trees, fifteen to twenty-five feet in diameter, bulging

[10] The Thomas Mill was situated west of Grant Grove, near where Miramonte now stands.

moderately at the base, and holding their diameter in noble simplicity and symmetry. The "General Grant" is burned near the ground on the east side, and bulges in huge gnarly waves and crags on the north and west. Its bole above the base thirty or forty feet is smooth and round.

The grand old tree has been barbarously destroyed by visitors hacking off chips and engraving their names in all styles. Men residing in the grove, shingle-making, say that in the last six weeks as many as fifty visitors have been in the grove. It is easy of access by a wagon road between Thomas Mills and the Big Trees.

The great Kings River Canyon is just a few days beyond, with all that is most sublime in the mountain scenery of America, and as the Southern Pacific Railroad is completed beyond Visalia, this whole region is now comparatively accessible to tourists.

The general appearance of the grove is so like that of Mariposa that one familiar with the latter grove can hardly know that this Kings River grove is not the Mariposa. I could not choose between the two. The trees are the same in size and general form, so also the firs and yellow and sugar pine are mingled with them in the same proportions. Underbrush of *Cornus* and willow grow along the streams, *Rubus* and a few ferns on the hillside. This grove on both sides is quite small, and grows on granite debris and moraine material well rotted, the soil not having been much removed from the roots since growth. In many places quite near the trees I observed the granite bedrock fast crumbling.

The Big Sequoias are always near the big yosemite canyons. A man told me he had seen an old barkless stump forty feet in diameter north of this grove . . . Also another man told of another "old snag," "bigger'n Grant," he said. Many fine groves grow about Kaweah's streams . . .

Camp on top of divide between
Kaweah and Kings River Basins.

We camp on top of the divide between Kaweah and Kings River water, by the first large stream above Thomas Mills, in a lovely grove of *Pinus amabilis* and *P. grandis*.[11] We are fairly free in the mountains once more. The weather all gold.

[11] The generic name is now *Abies,* and the trees were probably the white fir and red fir, *A. concolor* and *A. magnifica.*

> Camp where the trail crosses
> the south fork of the South Fork
> of Kings River. Altitude 6550 feet.
> October 8.

The scenery from the top of the divide between Kaweah and Kings River is sublime on both sides, the canyons of Kaweah showing beyond and yet beyond, till blue and faint in the distance . . . On the left, the yosemite scenery about the many forks of Kings River presents sublime combinations of cliff and canyon and bossy dome, with high, sharp boulder peaks in the distance. A high conic peak, black with a small snow patch, towards the head of Joaquin was well seen from the trail today. Was it Goddard? . . .

> Camp in Yosemite,
> South Fork, Kings River.
> October 10

We camped opposite the first Tissiack[12] on a large mead . . . Delight- ful river reaches, picturesquely treed and bushed and flowered and ferned . . .

The Frémont pine[13] is common in the valley. Glacial polish on the walls in many places . . . The south wall from the fall[14] to the upper end of the valley is very picturesque, more so than any portion of the Merced yosemite wall of equal extent. Gothic peaks are well developed. Tissiack is very impressive and like that of the other yosemite in general form . . .

Still another Tissiack, a magnificent rock, rises higher where the large north tributary equivalent to Tenaya Fork comes in.[15] The view up this North Fork from the trail is exactly like the view up Tenaya Canyon. A Washington Column is much grander than that of Yosemite. Thus this Kings River yosemite has two Washington Columns and nearly two North Domes, but no lakes and few meadows. The main portion is filled with gravel, washed boulders, and sandy flats, well groved. It has not many acorn-bearing oaks, therefore is not a favorite place with Indians. They find more and better acorns below, also fish. No Indian camps here . . .

[12] Tissiack was the Indian name of Yosemite's Half Dome. This camp must have been at Zumwalt Meadow, below the Grand Sentinel.

[13] The one-leaved nut pine, *Pinus monophylla*.

[14] Roaring River Falls.

[15] Later named by Muir the Glacier Monument; the "large north tributary" is the South Fork itself, emerging from Paradise Valley.

> At mouth of first tributary
> of South Fork Kings River.
> October 11.

Set out for Mount Tyndall alone, leaving Billy and Dr. Kellogg at camp[16] with the animals . . .

It is hard traveling along this portion of the stream, the avalanche material having been planted with poplars and all kinds of chaparral. Even the bears seem at times to be at fault in making their trails. The colors of the poplars and epilobium and mountain ash are glorious in combination. The light rain and snow of the previous days brightened all colors. The dogwood does most of the red, the aspen the yellow, and the sedges and a multitude of smaller plants the other tints. The bracken is splendidly colored now, and is in great size and abundance.

The falls on the North Fork are only a series of moderately inclined cascades, far inferior in power to those of Tuolumne. The South Fork rises fast but steadily, not doing or saying anything specially emphatic . . .

At an elevation of ninety-seven hundred feet, the South Fork divides into many branches that run up to the glaciers and *névés* of a noble amphitheater of lofty mountains, forming fountains for the brave young river . . .[17]

I ascended two peaks in the afternoon. Clouds gathered about the brows, now dissolving, now thickening and shooting down into and filling up the canyons with wonderful rapidity. A great display of cloud motion about and above and beneath me.

Hurrying down from amid a thicket of stone spires to the treeline and water, I reached both at dark. A grand mountain towers above my camp. A rushing stream brawls past its base. Willows are on one side, dwarf *flexilis* on the other. The moon is doing marvels in whitening the peaks with a pearly luster, as if each mountain contained a moon. I have leveled a little spot on the mountainside where I may nap by my fireside. The altitude of my camp is eleven thousand five hundred feet and I am blanketless.

> October 12.

Set out early for Mount Tyndall and reached the summit about 9 A.M.[18] Had grand views of the valley of the Kern and the Green-

[16] Perhaps at the junction of Bubbs Creek and the South Fork.

[17] Vidette Meadows, and Center Basin?

[18] Not the present Mount Tyndall; perhaps one of the peaks on the Kings-Kern Divide.

horn Mountains[19] and north and south along the axis of the range, and out over the Inyo Range and the Great Basin. Descended and pushed back to the main camp. Arrived about noon to find Billy and Dr. Kellogg gone, though they promised to wait three days for me. They left me neither horse nor provisions. I pushed on after them, following their tracks on the trail towards Kearsarge Pass, by long stretches of dry meadows and many lakes, surrounded by savage and desolate scenery. The pass is over twelve thousand feet high.[20] *Primula suffrutescens* is abundant on the granite sand up to the head of the pass. The scenery of the summit is grand. *Pinus flexilis* abundant. I overtook the runaway train at sunset, a mile over the divide, just as they were looking for a camping ground. When asked why they had left me, they said they feared I would not return. Strange that in the mountains people from cities should so surely lose their heads.

October 13.

We descended the long pass, which is one steep declivity scarce broken from top to bottom. In a few hours we passed from ice and snow to the torrid plain. I took some provisions and my horse and left the party at the foot of the pass to make an excursion to Mount Whitney, while the rest of the party went to Independence to wait for me there. I skirted the base of the range past Lone Pine, and over into the valley of the Kern by the Hockett Trail. My horse got mired in a floating bog. Thought I should lose him, but got him out, though he sank over his back. He whinnied with joy at his escape. I camped on the edge of a sedge meadow. A cold, windy night; the wind blew the coals out of my fire, overturned my dishes, and took my hat.

October 15.

I left my horse on the meadow, and set out for the summit afoot. Soon I gained the top of old Mount Whitney, about fourteen thousand feet high.[21] Found a mule trail to the summit. I leveled to another summit, five or six miles north and five hundred feet higher, and set out to climb it also. The way was very rough, up and down canyons. I reached the base of the highest peak near sunset at the edge of

---

[19] The Great Western Divide.
[20] 11,823 feet.
[21] Mount Langley, 14,042 feet.

a small lake. No wood was within four or five miles. Therefore, though tired, I made up my mind to spend the night climbing, as I could not sleep. I took bearings by the stars. By midnight I was among the summit needles.[22] There I had to dance all night to keep from freezing, and was feeble and starving next morning.

October 16.

I had to turn back without gaining the top. Was exhausted ere I reached horse and camp and food.

October 17 and 18.

Set out for Independence and reached it at night. Ate and slept all next day.[23]

John of the Mountains

Independence
October 16th

Dear Mrs. Carr:

All of my season's mountain work is done. I have just come down from Mount Whitney and the newly discovered mountain five miles northwest of Whitney,[24] and now our journey is a simple saunter along the base of the range to Tahoe, where we will arrive about the end of the month, or a few days earlier.

I have seen a good deal more of the high mountain region about the heads of Kings and Kern rivers than I expected to see in so short and so late a time. Two weeks ago I left the Doctor and Billy in the Kings River yosemite, and set out for Mount Tyndall and adjacent mountains and canyons. I ascended Tyndall and ran down into the Kern River canyon and climbed some nameless mountains between Tyndall and Whitney, and thus gained a pretty good general idea of the region.[25] After crossing the range by the Kearsarge Pass, I again left the Doctor and Billy and pushed southward along the range and northward and

[22] Mrs. Wolfe says Muir was on the crest near what is now known as Mount Muir, 14,015 feet.

[23] Dates are confused, but it was apparently at this time that Muir wrote his letter to Mrs. Carr, deciding afterward to try again for the summit of Mount Whitney.

[24] Actually, the present Mount Langley and Mount Muir.

[25] Muir probably did not go farther than the Kings-Kern Divide.

Mt. Brewer, Kearsarge Pinnacles from Kearsarge Pass, Kings Canyon National Park

up Cottonwood Creek to Mount Whitney; then over to the Kern Canyon again and up to the new "highest" peak which I did not ascend, as there was no one to attend to my horse.

Thus you see I have rambled this highest portion of the Sierra pretty thoroughly, though hastily. I spent a night without fire or food in a very icy windstorm on one of the spires of the new highest peak, by some called Fisherman's Peak.[26] That I am already quite recovered from the tremendous exposure proves that I cannot be killed in any such manner. On the day previous I climbed two mountains, making over ten thousand feet of altitude. It seems that this new Fisherman's Peak is causing some stir in the newspapers. If I feel writeful I will send you a sketch of the region for the "Overland."

I saw no mountains in all this grand region that appeared at all inaccessible to a mountaineer. Give me a summer and a bunch of matches and a sack of meal and I will climb every mountain in the region.

I have passed through Lone Pine and noted the yosemite and local subsidences accomplished by the earthquakes. The bunchy bush compositae of Owens Valley are glorious. I got back from Whitney this P.M. How I shall sleep! My life rose wave-like with those lofty granite waves. Now it may wearily float for a time along the smooth flowery plain . . .

The Life and Letters of John Muir

October 19.

Set out afoot for the summit by direct course up the east side. Camped in the sage at a small spring the first night.

October 20.

I pushed up the canyon which leads past the north shoulder of the mountain. Camped at the timberline . . .

October 21.

I climb to the summit by 8 A.M., sketch and gain glorious views, and descend to the foot of the range.[27]

[26] Because the first ascent, August 18, 1873, was made by three local fishermen, this name was favored by people in Owens Valley. It did not survive, and the name of Whitney was transferred to it as the highest peak.

[27] Muir was the first person to ascend Whitney by an eastern approach route. Farquhar tells the story of early climbs in his *History of the Sierra Nevada* (University of California Press, 1965).

Independence,
October 22.

I found *Pinus flexilis* at an elevation of ten thousand feet, forty feet high, ten inches in diameter at base, with cones three to four inches long, tapered and opening.

It is almost one unbroken slope from the Owens plain to the top of Fisherman's Peak. First, the canyon is narrow and precipitous, walled at the bottom, then opens gradually. Halfway to the top the canyon forms and, of course, gives birth to a yosemite with high, bare walls. The canyon is filled with birch and willow and yellow pine and boulders from the sleepiness of streams. Higher still is a lake, and walls yet higher and exceedingly bare are planted with lichens and primula, bush epilobium, sedges and ferns (*Pellaea Brewerii*). Hush of stream.

October 23. Sunrise.

Orange on the sky. Mountains beyond of different shades of blue, then crimson, the near granite being chocolate-colored from the thick air of the desert . . .

John of the Mountains

4. MULE TRAIN SOUTH; CLIMBING MOUNT WHITNEY

It was nearly two years before Muir returned to the region south of Yosemite. During that time he made repeated trips to Mount Shasta, freezing his feet severely on one of them, and found adventure in storms and trees on the Feather and Yuba rivers. He revisited Yosemite, and spent laborious months in San Francisco and Oakland becoming a writer. When he started south from Yosemite with three friends in June 1875 he was a public figure, "John Muir, the Naturalist," writing regularly for the San Francisco Daily Evening Bulletin. *His column-length articles were headlined, "Summering in the Sierra."*

The first three "letters" of this series took the party (including William Keith, John Swett, and J. B. McChesney) via Tuolumne

*Meadows to Mono Lake. They intended to go on to Mount Whitney,
but apparently turned back after reaching the Owens Valley. Muir's
published notes contain an enthusiastic comment on the "second
big valley south of Red Slate Mountain." Keith later produced an
epic painting, "The California Alps."*

*Then came a more serious expedition, occupying most of July.
With two vigorous companions, a packer and mules, Muir left the
Valley and Clark's Station for "the wild untrampled kingdoms of
the Sierra." Three* Bulletin *articles, published in August and September, recount the excitement of another visit to the sequoia groves
and "Kings River Valley," an ascent of Mount Whitney, and the
return through the lava floods and dead lakes of the Owens and
Mono valleys.*

Yosemite Valley
August 5, 1875

. . . I have just returned from an extended excursion to the summit
of Mount Whitney, in the course of which I passed through the Kings
River yosemite, which is larger, and in some respects more interesting
than the yosemites of the Tuolumne and Merced. This magnificent valley
is situated upon the South Fork of Kings River, about forty-five miles
from Visalia in a straight line. It measures about nine miles in length from
east to west, and has an average width at bottom of about half a mile.
The walls are quite as precipitous as those of Yosemite, so-called, and
are about 3000 feet in height, and sculptured into the same noble forms
that characterize all the yosemites of the Sierra. The bottom of the
valley is about 5000 feet above the level of the sea, and its level surface
is diversified with meadows and groves, through which the river pours its
crystal floods in lavish abundance—now calmly and with scarce a ripple
over brown pebbles and sheets of yellow sand, now in rushing rapids over
beds of mossy boulders and dams of avalanche debris.

We set out from here on the 9th of July, our party consisting of
George Bayley of San Francisco, Charles Washburn, a student of the
State University, with "Buckskin Bill" as mule master, all well mounted
on tough, obstinate mules. Right gladly we pushed our way into the
wild untrampled kingdoms of the Sierra, inspired with the thousand
indefinite joys of the green summer woods; past Clark's Station and
the Mariposa Grove of Big Trees; through the luxuriant forests of the

Upper Fresno, fairly dripping with balsam and gum; climbing many a hill and dale bestrewn with brown burrs, and fording many a bright dashing brook hedged with tangled alders and willows; making a devious trail, yet tending ever southward, independent in our course as birds in the calm cloudless air. Soon we found ourselves among the heated foothills of the San Joaquin, and on the edge of the strangely dappled plains.

At Centerville we crossed the wide stately current of Kings River, still transparent and sparkling as if fresh from the high alpine snows, then facing eastward climbed to the piney woods again, and meandered like a headless river through the magnificent groves of King Sequoias that still flourish in cool glens and hollows from Kings River southward to the Kaweah, and yet beyond. Here we heard the sound of axes, and soon came upon a group of busy men engaged in preparing a butt section of a giant sequoia they had felled for exhibition at the Quaker Centennial.[1] This tree was twenty-five feet in diameter at the base, and so fine was the taper of the trunk that it still measured ten feet in diameter at a height of two hundred feet from the ground. According to the testimony of the annual wood-rings, counted by three different persons, this tree at the time of its death was from 2125 to 2317 years old. The section cut for exhibition is sixteen feet long, split into eight immense staves, the heartwood being removed by splitting and hewing until the staves measure about eight inches in thickness inside the bark. When, therefore, the section is set up for exhibition it will appear as a huge tub cut from a hollow log. The speculative genius who planned and is executing this sequoia enterprise is Martin Vivian of Helena, Montana, and in order to make the most of it, he purposes placing his rustic tub on exhibition during the coming winter at St. Louis. A wagon road has been graded into the grove, and the staves are now almost ready for transportation to the railroad.

Many a poor, defrauded town dweller will pay his dollar and peep, and gain some dead arithmetical notion of the bigness of our Big Trees, but a true and living knowledge of these tree gods is not to be had at so cheap a rate. As well try to send a section of the storms on which they feed.

Out of this solemn ancient forest we climbed, still upward and eastward, into the cool realms of the alpine pines, and at length caught a long, sweeping view of the beetling cliffs and rock brows that form the walls of the glorious yosemite, for which we were so eagerly looking.

[1] The Philadelphia "Centennial Exposition" in 1876.

The trail by which we descended to the bottom of the valley enters at the lower or west end, zigzagging in a wild independent fashion over the South Lip, and corresponding in a general way both in position and direction to the Mariposa trail of the Merced Yosemite, and like it, affording a series of enchanting views up the valley, over the groves and meadows between the massive granite walls. Indeed, so fully and radically were these views a yosemite in all their leading features it was difficult to realize that we were not entering the old Yosemite by Inspiration Point. Bayley's joy usually finds expression in a kind of explosive Indian war whoop, and wild echoes were driven rudely from cliff to cliff, as the varied landscapes revealed themselves from the more commanding points along the trail.

In about two hours after beginning the descent, we found ourselves among the sugar pine groves at the lower end of the valley, through which we rode in perfect ecstasy, for never did pines seem so noble and religious in all their gestures and tones. The sun pouring down mellow gold, seemed to be shining only for them, and the wind gave them voice, but the gestures of their outstretched arms appeared wholly independent of the winds, and impressed one with a solemn awe that overbore all our knowledge of causes and brought us into the condition of beings new-arrived from some other far-off world. The ground was smoothly strewn with dead, clean leaves and burrs, making a fine brown surface for shadows, many a wide, even bar, from tapering trunk columns, and rich mosaic from living leaf and branch. There amid the groves we came to small openings without a tree or shadow, wholly filled with the sun, like pools of glowing light . . .

Beginning at the lower end of the valley, the first two miles of the walls are leveled off at the tops, and are so broken and soil-besprinkled they support quite a number of trees and shaggy bushes, but farther up the granite speedily assumes yosemite forms and dimensions, rising in stupendous cliffs, angular and sheer from the level flats and meadows. On the north wall there is an El Capitan and group of Three Brothers. Farther up on the same side there is an Indian Canyon and North Dome and Washington Column. On the south wall counterparts of the Sentinel and Cathedral Rocks occur in regular order bearing the same relative position to one another that they do in the old Yosemite, for the simple reason that like causes produce like effects, both valleys being in general terms simple pieces of erosion accomplished by the ancient glaciers that flowed through them.

With regard to waterfalls, those of the old Yosemite are more striking and impressive in their forms and in the songs they sing, although the whole quantity of water that pours over the walls is considerably less and comes from lower sources. The waters of the new valley effect their descent by a series of comparatively short leaps and inclines, which, according to the vague classification in vogue in these dark, pretentious days, would mostly be brought under the head of cascades. These, however, are exceedingly beautiful, more beautiful than vertical falls, and belong to a higher type of water beauty. Nevertheless, it may be long ere waterfalls have their beauty measured in any other way than by plumblines and tapelines.

Our ride up the valley was perfectly enchanting, every bend of the river presenting reaches of surpassing loveliness, sunbeams streaming through its border groves, or falling in broad masses upon the white rapids or calm, deep pools. Here and there a dead pine that had been swept down in flood time reached out over the current, its green mosses and lichens contrasting with the crystal sheen of the water, and its gnarled roots forming shadowy caves for speckled trout where the current eddies slowly, and protecting sedges and willows dip their leaves. Among these varied and ever-changing river reaches the appreciative artist may find studies for a lifetime.

The deeply sculptured walls presented more and more exciting views, calling forth the unbounded admiration of the whole party. Bold sheer brows standing forth into a full blaze of light, deep shadowy side gorges and canyons inhabited by wild cascades, groups of gothic gables, glacier-polished domes, coming into view in ever-changing combinations, and with different foregrounds. Yet no individual rock in the valley equals El Capitan or Half Dome, but, on the other hand, from no position on the Yosemite walls could a section five miles in length be selected equal in downright beauty and grandeur to five miles of the middle portion of the south wall of the new valley.

We camped for the night at the foot of the new Washington Column, where the ferns and lilies reached to our heads, their rich, lavish exuberance contrasting strikingly with the massive, naked walls.

The summer day died in purple and gold, and we lay watching the growing shadows and the fading sunglow among the heights. Each member of the party made his own bed, like birds building nests. Mine was made of fern fronds, with a sprinkling of mint spikes in the pillow, thus combining luxurious softness with delicate fragrance, in which one sleeps not only restfully but deliciously, making the down beds of palaces and palace hotels seem poor and vulgar by contrast.

The full moon rose just after the night darkness was fairly established. The dim gray cliff at the foot of which we lay was crowned with an arch of white, cold light long before the moon's disc appeared above the opposite wall. Down the valley one rockfront after another caught the silvery glow, and came out from the gray and dusky shadows in long, imposing ranks, like very spirits, forming altogether one of the most impressive scenes I ever beheld. The tranquil sky was also intensely lovely, blooming with stars like a meadow, and the thickets and groves along the riverbank were masses of solid darkness. It was too surpassingly beautiful a night for sleep, and we feasted long upon the rare scene ere the weariness of enjoyment closed our eyes. Next morning we rode up the valley in the sunshine, following the north bank of the river to where it forks at the head. The glacier-polished rocks glowed in the slant sunbeams in many places as if made of burnished steel. All the glacial phenomena of the new valley, the polished surfaces, *roches moutonnées,* and moraines, are fresher and less changed than those of the old. It is evidently a somewhat younger valley, a fact easily explained by its relations to the fountains of the ancient glaciers lying above it in the snowy alps. Like the old valley, this also is a favorite summer resort of Indians, because it produces acorns and its streams abound in trout, and, no doubt, they have names for all the principal rocks and cascades, and possess numerous grotesque and ornamental legends, though as yet I have not been able to learn any of them.[2] A good mountain trail conducts out of the head of the valley, across the range by the Kearsarge Pass to Owens Valley, which we followed, and reached Independence in two days, where we made up our outfit for the ascent of Mount Whitney, the loftiest peak in the range . . .

San Francisco *Daily Evening Bulletin,*
August 13, 1875

Independence, Inyo County
August 17, 1875

. . . We set out from the little village of Independence with plenty of excelsior determination, Bayley, as usual, rejoicing in warwhoops, much to the wonderment of sober passers-by. The massive sun-beaten Sierra rose before us out of the gray sagebrush levels like one vast

[2] Two years earlier, Muir's journal had indicated a different opinion about the use of the South Fork canyon by Indians (see page 37). Certainly there were bands of Yokuts who inhabited the lower reaches of the river, and there was a trade route across the Sierra which passed through the canyon.

wall 9000 feet high, adorned along the top with a multitude of peaks that seem to have been nicked out in all kinds of fanciful forms for the sake of beauty. Mount Whitney is one of those wall-top peaks, having no special geological significance beyond the scores of nameless peaks amid which it stands, and possessing so little appreciable individuality that we did not meet a single person living here who was able to point it out. Where is Mount Whitney? we would ask the teamsters and farmers we met between Independence and Lone Pine. "Don't know exactly," was the common reply. "One of them topmost peaks you see yonder," at the same time waving their hands indefinitely toward the wilderness of summits.

For those travelers who dislike climbing, the proper way to the top of Whitney lies from Lone Pine around the southern extremity of the high Sierra to the Upper Kern River valley, by way of Cottonwood Creek. The mountain is thus approached from the west where the slopes are lowest, and where one may easily ride to an elevation of 12,000 feet above sea level, leaving only a light foot scramble of between 2500 and 3000 feet to be made in reaching the utmost summit; whereas, by the quick direct route discovered by me two years ago, leading up the east flank of the range opposite Lone Pine, the elevation to be overcome by foot climbing amounts to about 9000 feet.

THE ASCENT[3]

With the exception of our one young student, our party were mountaineers, and we chose the eastern route, the mountain influences bearing us buoyantly aloft without leaving us any gross weight to overcome by ordinary conscious effort. On the first day we rode our mules some eighteen miles, through a fine, evenly planted growth of sagebrush to the foot of the range, immediately west of Lone Pine. Here we "found *a man*," a whole-souled Welshman, by the name of Thomas, with whom we camped for the night, and where all was made ready for an early start up the mountain next morning. Each carried a loaf of bread, a handful of tea and a tin cup, and a block of beef about four inches in diameter, cut from the lean heartwood of a steer; the whole compactly bundled in half a blanket, and carried by a strap passed over the shoulder, and besides these common necessaries, Bayley carried a small bottle of spirits for healing, sustaining, and fortifying uses, in case of

[3] Subheadings presumably were added by the *Bulletin*.

encounters with triangular headed snakes, bears, Indians, mountain rams, noxious night airs, snowstorms, etc.; and in case of vertigo and difficult breathing at great heights, together with broken bones, flesh wounds, skin erosions, abrasions, contusions. For in prudence, is it not well to realize that "something might happen," and well to have a helpful spirit—a guardian angel in a bottle ever near?[4]

The highway by which we ascended was constructed by an ancient glacier that drew its sources from the eastern flank of Mount Whitney and the adjacent summits, and poured its icy floods into Owens Valley, which during the glacial epoch was a sea of ice. Of this mighty, rock-crushing ice river, scarce a vestige remains, and its channel is now occupied by a dashing crystal stream that kept us good company all the way to the summit. The day was warm, and many were the delicious lavings we enjoyed among its pools beneath the cooling shadows of its leafy border groves. The great declivity of the canyon gives rise to numerous rapids and cascades, along the edges of which, soil of sufficient depth for the best wild gardens and thickets cannot be made to lie; but small oval flats of rich alluvium occur between the rocky inclines, rising one above another in almost regular order like stairs. Here the alder and the birch grow close together in luxuriant masses, crossing their topmost branches above the streams, and weaving a bowery roof.

A MINOR YOSEMITE

At an elevation of about 8000 feet above the sea we come to a fine yosemite valley, where a large tributary glacier from the southwest had united with the main trunk. The sheer granite walls rise loftily into the pure azure to the height of from two to three thousand feet, sculptured in true yosemite style, and presenting a most lavish abundance of spires and gothic gables along the top, with huge buttresses and free and interlacing arches down the face, with numerous caves and niches for ornamental groups of pines. Nor is there any lack of white falling water, nor of tender joyous plant beauty, to complement every manifestation of stern, enduring rockiness. For a distance of two or three miles above the head of this wild yosemite the ascent is rather steep and difficult, because the canyon walls come sheer down in many places to the brink of the rushing stream, leaving no free margin for a walk, and in many places a dense growth of alder and willow, crushed and felted with the pressure of winter snow, renders the gorge all but

[4] This is a rare allusion to the use of liquor, perhaps unique in Muir's writings about the Sierra.

impassable, the dead limbs all sloping downward, meeting the up-strug-gling mountaineer like clusters of presented bayonets.

The difficulties I encountered in forcing my way through this portion of the gorge during my first ascent caused me to scan the gaps and terraces of the south wall, with a view to avoiding the bottom of the gorge altogether. Coming to the conclusion that the thing was at least practicable, I led the party over a rough earthquake talus, beneath an overhanging cliff, and up an extremely steep and narrow gully to the edge of the main canyon wall.

AN ACCIDENT   GLACIER MEADOWS
A GLIMPSE OF WHITNEY

Here occurred the only accident worth mentioning connected with the trip. Washburn, who climbs slowly, was soon a considerable distance in the rear, and I sat down at the head of the narrow gully to wait for him. Bayley soon came up somewhat breathless with exertion, and with-out thinking of consequences, loosened a big boulder that went bounding down the narrow lane with terrible energy, followed by a train of small stones and dust. Washburn was about a hundred feet below, and his destruction seemed inevitable, as he was hemmed in between two sheer walls not five feet apart. We shouted to give him warning, and listened breathlessly until his answering shout assured us of his escape. On coming up weary and nerve-shaken with fright, he reported that the dangerous mass shot immediately over him as he lay crouched in a slight hollow. Falling rocks, single or in avalanches, form the greatest of all the perils that beset the mountaineer among the summit peaks.

By noon we reached a genuine glacier meadow, where we disturbed a band of wild sheep that went bounding across the stream and up the precipitous rocks out of sight. We were now 10,000 feet above sea level, and were in the Alps; having passed in half a day from the torrid plains of Owens Valley to an Arctic climate, cool and distant in all its sounds and aspects as Greenland or Labrador.

Here we caught our first fair view of the jagged, stormworn crest of Mount Whitney, yet far above and beyond, looming gray and ruin-like from a multitude of shattered ridges and spires. Onward we pushed, unwearied, waking hosts of new echoes with shouts of emphatic excelsior. Along the green, plushy meadow, following its graceful margin curves, then up rugged slopes of gray boulders that had thundered from the shattered heights in an earthquake, then over smooth polished glacier pavements to the utmost limits of the timberline, and our first day's climbing was done.

CAMPING ON THE MOUNTAIN

Our elevation was now eleven thousand five hundred feet, and as the afternoon was less than half done, we had ample time to prepare beds, make tea, and gather a store of pitchy pine for our night fire. We chose the same camping ground I had selected two years before on the edge of a sedgy meadow enameled with buttercups and daisies, near a waterfall and snowbank, and surrounded with ranks of majestic alps. There were the withered pine tassels on which I had slept, and circling heap of stones built as a shelter from the downrushing night wind, and the remains of my woodpile gathered in case of a sudden snowstorm. Each made his own tin cupful of tea, and dinner was speedily accomplished. Then bed-building was vigorously carried on, each selecting willow shoots, pine tassels or withered grass with a zeal and naturalness whose sources must lie somewhere among our ancient grandfathers, when "wild in wood," etc. I have experimented with all kinds of plant pillows with especial reference to softness and fragrance, and here I was so happy as to invent a new one, composed of the leaves and flowers of the alpine dodecatheon,[5] elastic, fragrant and truly beautiful. Here we rested as only mountaineers can. The wind fell to soft whispers, keen spiky shadows stole over the meadow, and pale rosy light bathed the savage peaks, making a picture of Nature's repose that no words can ever describe. Darkness came, and the night wind began to flow like a deep and gentle river; the cascade nearby sounded all its notes with most impressive distinctness, and the sky glowed with living stars. Then came the moon, awakening the giant peaks that seemed to return her solemn gaze. The grand beauty of our chamber walls came out in wonderfully clear relief, white light and jet shadows revealing their wild fountain architecture, divested of all distracting details.

[5] Shooting star, *Dodecatheon jeffreyi.*

Summer snow near Forester Pass,
Kings Canyon National Park

STILL UPWARD   GLACIER LAKES   VEGETATION

We rose early and were off in the first flush of dawn, passing first over a rounded ice-polished brow, then along the north shore of a glacier lake whose simple newborn beauty enchanted us all. It lay imbedded in the rocks like a dark blue-green—a perfect mountain eye. Along its northern shore we sped joyously, inspired with the fresh unfolding beauties of the morning, leaping huge blocks of porphyry laid down by an ancient earthquake, and over morainal embankments and slopes of crystalline gravel; every muscle in harmonious accord, thrilled and toned and yielding us the very highest pleasures of the flesh. Speedily we met the glances of another crystal lake, and of our dearest alpine flowers; azure daisies and primulas, cassiope and bryanthus, the very angels of mountain flora. Now the sun rose, and filled the rocks with beamless spiritual light. The Clark crow was on the wing, and the frisky tamias and marmot came out to bask on favorite boulders, and the daisies spread their rays and were glad. Above the second lake basin we found a long upcurving field of frozen snow, across which we scampered, with our breasts filled with exhilarating azure, leaping with excess of strength and rolling over and over on the clean snowground, like dogs.

SCALING THE DIVIDING RIDGE   AT THE SUMMIT

We followed the snow nearly to its upper limit, where it leaned against the dividing axis of the range, placing our feet in hollows melted by radiated heat from stones shot down from the crumbling heights. To scale the dividing ridge in front was impossible, for it swept aloft in one colossal wave with a vertical shattered crest. We were therefore compelled to swerve to the north; then carefully picking our way from ledge to ledge, gained the summit about 8 A.M. There stood Mount Whitney now without a single ridge between; its spreading base within a stone's throw; its pointed, helmet-shaped summit 2000 feet above us. We gazed but a moment on the surrounding grandeur: the mighty granite battlements; the dark pine woods far below, and the glistening streams and lakes; then dashed adown the western slope into the valley of the Kern. On my first ascent I pushed direct to the summit up the north flank, but the memories of steep slopes of ice and snow over which I had to pick my way, holding on by small points of stones frozen more or less surely into the surface, where a single slip would result in death, made me determine that no one would ever be led by me through the same dangers. I therefore led around the north base of the mountain to the westward, much to Bayley's disgust, who declared that he could, or at least *would* follow wherever I was able to lead. Cautious Washburn wisely gave in his adhesion for the longer and safer route, and I remained firm in avoiding the dangerous ice slopes. We passed along the rocky shores of a lake whose surface was still (July 21st) covered with cakes of winter ice, around the edges of which the color of the water was a beautiful emerald green. Beyond the lake we gradually climbed higher, mounting in a spiral around the northwest shoulder of the mountain, crossing many a strong projecting buttress and fluting hollow, then bearing to the left urged our way directly to the summit. Higher, higher, we climbed with muscles in excellent poise, the landscape becoming more and more glorious as the wild Alps rose in the tranquil sky. Bayley followed closely, lamenting the absence of danger, whenever in this attenuated air he could command sufficient breath. Washburn seldom ventured to leap from rock to rock, but moved mostly on all fours, hugging projecting angles and boulders in a sprawled, outspread fashion, like a child clinging timidly to its mother, often calling for directions around this or that precipice, and careful never to look down for fear of giddiness, yet from first to last evincing a most admirable determination and persistence of the slow and sure kind. Shortly after 10 o'clock A.M. we gained the utmost summit—a fact duly announced by Bayley as soon as he was rested into a whooping condition, and before any note was taken of the wilderness of landscapes by which we were zoned. Undemonstrative Washburn examined the records of antecedent visitors, then remarked with becoming satisfaction, "I'm the first and only student visitor to this highest land in North America."[6]

SUCCESSIVE ASCENTS   CLARENCE KING'S MISTAKE

This mountain was first ascended in the summer of 1873, by a party of farmers and stock raisers from Owens Valley, who were taking exercise. It was ascended a few weeks later by Clarence King, myself and a few others, and this summer by one party besides our own.

The first climbers of the mountain named it Fisherman's Peak. The mountain climbed by Clarence King several years previous, and supposed by him to be the highest in the range, and on which he then bestowed the name of Whitney, lies some six or seven miles to the south of the present Mount Whitney, alias Fisherman's Peak. The old Mount Whitney,[7] though upward of 14,000 feet in height, may easily be as-

[6] Thousands of students and others, from the very young to the very old, have since visited the summit. Mount McKinley, 20,320 feet, is North America's highest.
[7] Mount Langley.

cended to the very summit on horseback, and, in general, every mountain in the range may easily be ascended by climbers of ordinary nerve and skill.[8] Mount Whitney has not yet been accurately measured, although fair approximations have been reached, making its height about 14,800 feet above the sea.[9] Mount Shasta, situated near the northern extremity of the range, is a few hundred feet lower; yet its individual height, measured from its own proper base, is from nine to eleven thousand feet, while that of Whitney is only from two to three thousand. The former is a colossal cone rising in solitary grandeur and might well be regarded as an object of religious worship; the latter is one of the many peaks of an irregular and fragmentary form. Shasta was built *upward* by fire, Whitney was built *downward* by ice. I would gladly try to write a few words concerning the landscapes that lay manifest in all their glory beneath and around us, but there is no room here. We left the summit about noon and swooped to the torrid plains before sundown, as if dropping out of the sky.

San Francisco *Daily Evening Bulletin,*
August 24, 1875

Black's Hotel,
Yosemite, California
July 31st, 1875

Dear Mrs. Carr:

I have just arrived from our long excursion to Mount Whitney, all hale and happy, and find your weary, plodding letter, containing things that from this rocky standpoint seem strangely mixed—things celestial and terrestrial, cultivated and wild. Your letters set one a-thinking, and yet somehow they never seem to make those problems of life clear, and I always feel glad that they do not form any part of my work, but that my lessons are simple rocks and waters and plants and humble beasts, all pure and in their places, the Man beast with all his complications being laid upon stronger shoulders.

I did not bring you down any sedum roots or cassiope sprays because I had not then received your letter, not that I forgot you as I passed the blessed Sierra heathers, or the primulas, or the pines laden with fragrant, nutty cones. But I am more and more made to feel that my gardens and herbariums and woods are all in their places as they grow, and I know

[8] There are significant exceptions; see *A Climber's Guide to the High Sierra,* edited by Hervey H. Voge (Sierra Club, revised edition, 1965).
[9] 14,495 feet.

them there, and can find them when I will. Yet I ought to carry their poor dead or dying forms to those who can have no better.

The Valley is lovely, scarce more than a whit the worse for the flower-crushing feet that every summer brings . . . I am not decided about my summer. I want to go with the sequoias a month or two into all their homes from north to south, learning what I can of their conditions and prospects, their age, stature, the area they occupy, etc. But John Swett, who is brother now, papa then, orders me home to booking. Bless me, what an awful thing town duty is! I was once free as any pine-playing wind, and feel that I have still a good length of line, but alack! there seems to be a hook or two of civilization in me that I would fain pull out, yet *would not pull out*—O, O, O!!! . . .

The Life and Letters of John Muir

5. HUNTING BIG TREES

Alone once more, except for a tough little brown mule, Muir set off in August 1875 for his longest sojourn in the southern Sierra. His goal was to see the Big Trees in their splendor all the way from Yosemite's Mariposa Grove to the forests of the Kings, Kaweah, and Tule rivers. For two months he "drifted" south in his energetic way, wrangling poor Brownie up and down steep mountainsides and through deep woods and brush until the starving mule gave voice to legitimate grievances and won a recuperative leave in the foothills. His master, of course, went back to complete his tour of the sequoias.

The story of this journey is full of human interest. Muir tells of meeting John Nelder, the pathetic retired gold-miner for whom Nelder Grove is named; Hale Tharp, pioneer rancher from Three Rivers, in his one-log cabin near Crescent Meadow; and two Indian sheepherders who were disappointingly not as wild as their wilderness-loving guest. We have a close-up picture of the ardent botanist pursuing his biggest game, Sequoia gigantea, *to the limits of its range regardless of hunger, hardship, and fatigue.*

Most significantly, in these excerpts, we feel the impact of his observation of timber-cutting and milling operations and a forest fire on Muir's developing concepts of conservation. Within a few months he was to write his trumpet call to battle in the letter to the Sacramento Record-Union, *"God's First Temples; How Shall We Preserve Our Forests?" It was the beginning of a lifelong fight. Among the victories were the creation of Sequoia and General Grant national parks in 1890 and the Sierra Forest Reserve in 1893.*

Emerging from the mountains at the time, however, Muir expressed his feelings in a letter to Mrs. Carr:

"I've had a glorious season of forest grace, notwithstanding the hundred canyons I've crossed, and the innumerable gorges, gulches, and avalanchal corrugations . . . It seems a whole round season since I saw you, but have I not seen the King Sequoia in forest glory?"

Fresno Grove of Big Trees, Sept. 1875

A few days ago while camped in the fir woods on the head of one of the southmost tributaries of the Merced, I caught sight of a lofty granite dome, called Wa-mello by the Indians, looming into the free sky far above the forest, and though now studying trees, I soon found myself upon its commanding summit. Here I obtained glorious views of the wide fertile valleys of the Fresno, filled with forests; innumerable spires of yellow pines towering above one another on the sloping heights; miles of sugar pine with feathery arms outstretched in the sunshine; and toward the southwest I beheld the lofty dome-like crowns of the sequoia, rising here and there out of the green slopes and levels of the pines, singly or densed together in imposing congregations.

. . . I came drifting through the gorges and woods, arriving here when the grove was full of noon sunshine, and in sauntering from tree to tree, making my way through hazel and dogwood and over huge brown logs, I came suddenly upon a handsome cottage with quaint, old-fashioned chimney and gables, every way uncommon, and so new and fresh that it still smelled of balsam and rosin like a newly felled tree. Strolling forward, wondering to what my strange discovery would lead, I found an old, gray-haired man, sitting at the door upon a bark stool, weary-eyed and unspeculative and seemingly surprised that his fine forest hermitage had been discovered. After drinking at the burn that trickles past the door,

I sat down beside him and bit by bit he gave me his history, which, in the main, is only a sad illustration of early California life during the gold period, full of intense experiences, now up in exciting success, now down in crushing reverses, the day of life waning meanwhile far into the afternoon, and long shadows turning to the east; health gone and gold; the game played and lost; and now, creeping into this solitude, where he may at least maintain independence, he awaits the coming of night . . . The name of my hermit friend is John A. Nelder, a man of broad sympathies, and a keen intuitive observer of nature. Birds, squirrels, plants all receive loving attention, and it is delightful to see how sensitively he feels the silent influences of the woods. How his eye brightens as he gazes upon the grand sequoia kings that stand guard around his cabin. How he pets and feeds the wild quails and Douglas squirrels, and how tenderly he strokes the sapling sequoias, hoping that they will yet reach the full stature of their race and rule the woods.

Tomorrow I will push on southward along the sequoia belt, making special studies of the species and visiting every grove as far as its southernmost limit.

San Francisco *Daily Evening Bulletin,*
September 21, 1875

Pluno, Calif., October 19, 1875

The motto, "Where there isn't a way, make a way," slips lightly over the tongue of teacher or scholar where no way is needed, but to the traveler in these mountain woods it is soon loaded with meaning. There are ways *across* the range, old ways graded by glaciers and followed by men and bears, but not a single way, natural or artificial, has yet been constructed *along* the range; and the traveler who will thus move in a direction at right angles to the course of the ancient ice rivers must make a way across canyons and ridges laid side by side in endless succession, and all roughened with gorges, gulches, landslips, precipices, and stubborn chaparral almost impenetrable to wolves and bears. Such is the region in which I have been making ways during the last month in pursuit of *Sequoia gigantea.* My own ways are easily made, for my mountaineering has heretofore been almost wholly accomplished on foot, carrying a minimum of every necessary, and lying down by any streamside whenever overtaken by weariness and night. But on this occasion I have been prevailed upon to take a tough, brown mule to carry a pair of blankets and saddlebags; and many a time while the little hybrid was

East Lake, Kings Canyon National Park

wedged fast in the rocks, or was struggling out of sight in a wilderness of thorny bushes I have wished myself once more wholly free, notwithstanding the hunger days and cold nights that would follow.

. . . Going southward from Fresno, not a single sequoia is found until we reach Dinkey Creek, a tributary of the North Fork of Kings River. Here is a small grove of about two hundred trees growing upon coarse flood soil. The largest specimen measures thirty-two feet in diameter, four feet above the ground. This little isolated grove was discovered a few years ago by a couple of bear hunters, but on account of its remoteness from traveled roads and trails is hardly known.[1]

San Francisco *Daily Evening Bulletin,*
October 22, 1875

. . . I was greatly interested to find a vigorous company of sequoias near the northern limit of the grove growing upon the top of a granite precipice thinly besprinkled with soil, and scarce at all changed since it came to the light from beneath the ice sheet toward the close of the glacial period—a fact of great significance in its bearings on sequoia history in the Sierra.

One of the most striking of the simpler features of the grove is a waterfall, made by a bright little stream that comes pouring through the woods from the north, and leaps a granite precipice. All the canyons of the Sierra are embroidered with waterfalls, yet each possesses a character of its own, made more beautiful by each other's beauty, instead of suffering by mere vulgar arithmetical contrast. The booming cataract of Yosemite, half a mile high, is one thing; this little woodland fairy is another. Its plain spiritual beauty is most impressively brought forward by the gray rocks and the huge brown trees, several of which stand with wet feet in its spray; and then it is decked with goldenrods that wave overhead, and with ferns that lean out along its white wavering edges, the whole forming a bit of pure picture of a kind rarely seen amid the sublimities of sequoia woods.

"The New Sequoia Forests of California,"
Harper's Monthly, November 1878

[1] McKinley Grove, now on the road between Shaver Lake and Wishon Reservoir.

. . . I spent two weeks among the canyons of the San Joaquin, exploring every forest where the sequoia was likely to be, without discovering a single specimen, or any traces of their former existence. This remarkable gap in the belt is nearly fifty miles wide. Leaving the secluded colony of Dinkey Creek I led my mule down the canyon of the North Fork of Kings River, forded the stream, and climbed to the summit of the dividing ridge between the North and Middle forks.[2] Here in pushing my way southward I was compelled to make a descent of 7000 feet at a single swoop. Every pine and fir disappeared from the woods long ere I reached the bottom of the main canyon. Oaks with bark as white as milk cast their shadows on the sunburned ground, and not a mountain flower was left me for company.

San Francisco *Daily Evening Bulletin,*
October 22, 1875

. . . Here the river is broad and rapid, and when I heard it roaring I feared my short-legged mule would be carried away. But I was so fortunate as to strike a trail near an Indian rancheria that conducted to a regular ford about ten miles below the Kings River yosemite, where I crossed without the slightest difficulty, and gladly began climbing again toward the cool spicy woods. The lofty ridge forming the south wall of the great Kings River Canyon is planted with sugar pine, but through rare vistas I was delighted to behold the well-known crowns of sequoia once more swelling grandly against the sky only six or seven miles distant.

"The New Sequoia Forests of California,"
Harper's Monthly, November 1878

. . . In a day and a half we reached the sequoia woods in the neighborhood of the old Thomas Mill Flat. Thence striking off northeastward I found a magnificent forest nearly six miles long by two in width, composed mostly of Big Trees, with outlying groves as far west as Boulder Creek. Here five or six days were spent, and it was delightful to learn from countless trees, old and young, how comfortably they were settled down in concordance with climate and soil and their noble neighbors.

Imbedded in these majestic woods there are numerous meadows, around the sides of which the Big Trees press close together in beautiful lines,

[2] By his later account, this was when Muir "first saw" Tehipite Valley. Apparently it was a distant view of the canyon from Rodgers Ridge or Spanish Mountain.

Vidette Meadow,
Kings Canyon National Park

showing their grandeur openly from the ground to their domed heads in the sky. The young trees are still more numerous and exuberant than in the Fresno and Dinkey groves, standing apart in beautiful family groups, or crowding around the old giants. For every venerable lightning-stricken tree, there is one or more in all the glory of prime, and for each of these, many young trees and crowds of saplings . . .

On a bed of sandy ground fifteen yards square, which had been occupied by four sugar pines, I counted ninety-four promising seedlings, an instance of sequoia gaining ground from its neighbors. Here also I noted eighty-six young sequoias from one to fifty feet high on less than half an acre of ground that had been cleared and prepared for their reception by fire. This was a small bay burned into dense chaparral, showing that fire, the great destroyer of tree life, is sometimes followed by conditions favorable for new growths. Sufficient fresh soil, however, is furnished for the constant renewal of the forest by the fall of old trees without the help of any other agent,—burrowing animals, fire, flood, landslip, etc., for the ground is thus turned and stirred as well as cleared, and in every roomy, shady hollow beside the walls of upturned roots many hopeful seedlings spring up.

The largest, and as far as I know the oldest, of all the Kings River trees that I saw is the majestic stump . . . about a hundred and forty feet high, which above the swell of the roots is thirty-five feet and eight inches inside the bark, and over four thousand years old. It was burned nearly half through at the base, and I spent a day in chopping off the charred surface, and cutting into the heart, and counting the wood-rings with the aid of a lens. I made out a little over four thousand without difficulty or doubt, but I was unable to get a complete count, owing to confusion in the rings where wounds had been healed over. Judging by what is left of it, this was a fine, tall, symmetrical tree nearly forty feet in diameter before it lost its bark. In the last sixteen hundred and seventy-two years the increase in diameter was ten feet.[3] . . . I found a scattered growth of Big Trees extending across the main divide to within a short distance of Hyde's Mill, on a tributary of Dry Creek. The mountain ridge on the south side of the stream was covered from base to summit with a most superb growth of Big Trees. What a picture it made! In all my wide forest wanderings I had seen none so sublime . . .

In this glorious forest the mill was busy, forming a sore, sad center of destruction, though small as yet, so immensely heavy was the growth. Only the smaller and most accessible of the trees was being cut. The logs,

[3] Muir's count may have been erroneous. Accurate ring counts of logged trees in recent years indicate the oldest tree to be about 3200 years.

from three to ten or twelve feet in diameter, were dragged or rolled with long strings of oxen into a chute and sent flying down the steep mountainside to the mill flat, where the largest of them were blasted into manageable dimensions for the saws. And as the timber is very brash, by this blasting and careless felling on uneven ground, half or three-fourths of the timber was wasted.

I spent several days exploring the ridge and counting the annual wood-rings on a large number of stumps in the clearings, then replenished my bread sack and pushed on southward. All the way across the broad rough basins of the Kaweah and Tule rivers sequoia ruled supreme, forming an almost continuous belt for sixty or seventy miles, waving up and down in huge massy mountain billows in compliance with the grand glacier-plowed topography.

Day after day, from grove to grove, canyon to canyon, I made a long, wavering way, terribly rough in some places for Brownie, but cheery for me, for Big Trees were seldom out of sight. We crossed the rugged, picturesque basins of Redwood Creek, the North Fork of the Kaweah, and Marble Fork gloriously forested, and full of beautiful cascades and falls, sheer and slanting, infinitely varied with broad curly foam fleeces and strips of embroidery in which the sunbeams revel. Thence we climbed into the noble forest of the Marble and Middle Fork divide. After a general exploration of the Kaweah basin, this part of the sequoia belt seemed to me the finest and I then named it "the Giant Forest."[4] It extends, a magnificent growth of giants grouped in pure temple groves, ranged in colonnades along the sides of meadows, or scattered among the other trees, from the granite headlands overlooking the hot foothills and plains of the San Joaquin back to within a few miles of the old glacier fountains at an elevation of 5000 to 8400 feet above the sea.

. . . Bogs and meadows are rare or entirely wanting in the isolated groves north of Kings River; here there is a beautiful series of them lying on the broad top of the main dividing ridge, imbedded in the very heart of the mammoth woods as if for ornament, their smooth, plushy bosoms kept bright and fertile by streams and sunshine.

Resting awhile on one of the most beautiful of them when the sun was high, it seemed impossible that any other forest picture in the world could rival it . . . I stood fixed in silent wonder or sauntered about shifting my points of view, studying the physiognomy of separate trees . . . giving free expression to my joy, exulting in Nature's wild immortal vigor and

[4] This was the only name in the Kern and Kaweah region for which Muir took credit. Douglas Strong says it seems to have existed before this visit.

beauty, never dreaming any other human being was near. Suddenly the spell was broken by dull bumping, thudding sounds, and a man and horse came in sight at the farther end of the meadow, where they seemed sadly out of place. A good big bear or mastodon or megatherium would have been more in keeping with the old mammoth forest. Nevertheless, it is always pleasant to meet one of our own species after solitary rambles, and I stepped out where I could be seen and shouted, when the rider reined in his galloping mustang and waited my approach. He seemed too much surprised to speak until, laughing in his puzzled face, I said I was glad to meet a fellow mountaineer in so lonely a place. Then he abruptly asked, "What are you doing? How did you get here?" I explained that I came across the canyons from Yosemite and was only looking at the trees. "Oh then, I know," he said, greatly to my surprise, "you must be John Muir." He was herding a band of horses that had been driven up a rough trail from the lowlands to feed on these forest meadows. A few handfuls of crumb detritus was all that was left in my bread sack, so I told him that I was nearly out of provision and asked whether he could spare me a little flour. "Oh yes, of course you can have anything I've got," he said. "Just take my track and it will lead you to my camp in a big hollow log on the side of a meadow two or three miles from here. I must ride after some strayed horses, but I'll be back before night; in the meantime make yourself at home." He galloped away to the northward, I returned to my own camp, saddled Brownie, and by the middle of the afternoon discovered his noble den in a fallen sequoia hollowed by fire—a spacious loghouse of one log, carbon-lined, centuries old yet sweet and fresh, weatherproof, earthquake-proof, likely to outlast the most durable stone castle, and commanding views of garden and grove grander far than the richest king ever enjoyed. Brownie found plenty of grass and I found bread, which I ate with views from the big round, ever-open door. Soon the good Samaritan mountaineer came in, and I enjoyed a famous rest listening to his observations on trees, animals, adventures, etc., while he was busily preparing supper.[5] In answer to inquiries concerning the distribution of the Big Trees he gave a good deal of particular information of the forest we were in, and he had heard that the species extended a long way south, he knew not how far. I wandered about for several days within a radius of six or seven miles of the camp, surveying boundaries, measuring trees, and climbing

[5] The mountaineer was Hale D. Tharp, then forty-seven, who first visited Giant Forest with two Indians in 1858. Tourists still go to see his unusual cabin at Log Meadow.

the highest points for general views. From the south side of the divide I saw telling ranks of sequoia-crowned headlands stretching far into the hazy distance, and plunging vaguely down into profound canyon depths foreshadowing weeks of good work. I had now been out on the trip more than a month, and I began to fear my studies would be interrupted by snow, for winter was drawing nigh . . . Bidding good-by to the kind sequoia cave-dweller, we vanished again in the wilderness, drifting slowly southward, sequoias on every ridgetop beckoning and pointing the way.

Our National Parks, 1901

At the time of my visit this forest[6] was on fire, and as fire, whether occurring naturally by lightning or through the agency of man, is the great master scourge of forests, and especially of sequoia, I was glad of the opportunity presented to study the methods of its destruction.

Between the river and the west end of the forest there was a heavy growth of cherry, manzanita, and ceanothus, combined into one continuous sheet of chaparral, through which I had to pass on my way into the burning sequoia woods. But this chaparral also was on fire, and the flames were racing up the shaggy hillside as fast at times as a horse could gallop. Now bending forward and feeding on the green leaves with a passionate roar, devouring acres at a breath, then halting and shooting far into the sky, with flapping edges fringed and hacked like a dandelion leaf.

It was interesting to notice how much faster these wild fires can run up hill than down. If the wind be not among the conditions, then the steeper the better for speed; but when driven by the wind, a certain slope is required for the attainment of the maximum velocity, which slope varies with the wind and the character of the chaparral.

Passing through the smoke and ashes which these wildfire billows had given for beauty, I pushed up the mountainside into the burning forest as far as consistent with safety. One is in no danger of being chased and hemmed in by sequoia fires, because they never run fast, the speeding winds flowing only across the treetops, leaving the deeps below calm, like the bottom of a sea. Furthermore, there is no generally distributed fire food in sequoia forests on which fires can move rapidly. Fire can only creep on the dead leaves and burrs, because they are solidly packed. Besides the general leaf stratum on which running fires mostly depend

[6] Between the Middle and East forks of the Kaweah.

for food, there are a good many dead branches that become available here and there. And when aged sequoias fall, their crowns are smashed as if made of glass, making perfect woodpiles, limb piled on limb, broken into lengths of two or three feet, and mingled with the dense leaf tassels. The trunks, also, are broken straight across as if sawed into logs, and when the forest fire comes creeping forward into those grand woodpiles, a most sublime blaze is produced, booming and roaring like a waterfall. But all flame and noise speedily disappear, leaving only the great logs two hundred feet long, and from twenty-five to ten feet thick, lying among the gray ashes like bars of red-hot iron, enveloped in one equal, rich, ruby, flameless glow. Sequoia fire is more beautiful in color than that of any other species I ever noticed. And now fancy a forest hillside strewn with those majestic trunks straight as arrows, smooth, and perfect in taper and roundness, and covered with a plush of flameless, enthusiastic fire, gorgeous in color as the bars of a sunset cloud. Get this picture clearly before your mind, and you have one of the most perfectly glorious fire spectacles to be found on the face of the earth.

Sequoia smoke is also surpassingly beautiful; not muddy with resiny lampblack, like that of the pine, but fine brown and purple when well lighted.

Although the fallen trunks burn on the outside for days in succession, they never lose much of their bulk in this way. Strange to say, however, although perfectly undecayed, they burn *inside* for months, and in so methodical a manner that they are at length bored into regular tubes, as if by some huge auger. For it must be understood that all those far-famed hollow trunks, into which horsemen may gallop, are hollowed, after falling, through the agency of fire. No sequoia is made hollow by decay; and even supposing it possible that in rare instances they *should* become hollow, like oaks, while yet standing, they would inevitably smash into small fragments when they fell.

. . . Hence into the basin of the Tule the sequoia forests become still more extensive and interesting, and I began to doubt more than ever my ability to trace the belt to its southern boundary before the fall of winter snow. My mule became doubly jaded, and I had to drag him wearily from canyon to canyon, like a fur trader making tedious portages in his canoe, and to further augment my difficulties, I got out of provisions, while I knew no source of supply nearer than the foothills far below the sequoia belt. I began to calculate how long I would be able, or how long it would be right, to live on manzanita berries, so as to save time that was extremely precious at this critical period of the year, by obviating the necessity of descending to the inhabited foothills only to return again.

"Sequoia Woods on
Kings River Oct 21st

"Have been studying the age of the giants here yesterday & today.
Push eastward into the South Fork Canyon, thence over the divide
into Middle Fork & down far as possible.

"Cloudy—no snow as yet. Rec'd yrs just before leaving San Fran.
Will write on return in two or three weeks. Hard work ahead but
glorious.

"Ever cordially yrs
J M"

The promised letter, addressed to General John Bidwell, California pioneer and landowner who was one of Muir's good friends,
tells of a series of river adventures, beginning with a float trip down
the Sacramento and ending with another down the Merced and
San Joaquin. In between was the mountaineer's extraordinary walk
from Visalia to the Kaweah and Kings sequoias, across country to
the South Fork canyon, over the divide to the head of the main
Middle Fork Kings canyon, down the length of the Middle Fork
past Tehipite Valley, climbing the canyon wall below the confluence
of the Middle and South forks, and back to Converse's, Hyde's
Mill, and Visalia.

Details are tantalizingly scarce. The letter to Bidwell doesn't mention a young man named John Rigby who is said to have been
with Muir on the hike down the Middle Fork. This was the final
act of Muir's great work of exploration south of Yosemite during
the 1870s, but his mind was already busy with the strategy that
would bring his message to the reading public. Pure travel narratives
were not the thing, he seemed to judge, and we know little of this
hard journey and what rewards it brought. Fourteen years later,
when Muir next visited the Kings, he had neither the time nor
perhaps the stamina to go again to the Middle Fork.

One scrap of journal, possibly written on the Monarch Divide
or Cirque Crest, gives us a glimpse of the poetry of dawn after
storm on those heights. A new climate, a new world, and the falling
waters rejoiced . . .

San Francisco
December 3, 1877

My Dear General:

I arrived in my old winter quarters here a week ago, my season's field
work done, and I was just sitting down to write to Mrs. Bidwell when

your letter of November 29th came in. The tardiness of my Kings River postal is easily explained. I committed it to the care of a mountaineer who was about to descend to the lowlands, and he probably carried it for a month or so in his breeches' pocket in accordance with the well-known business habits of that class of men. And now since you are so kindly interested in my welfare I must give you here a sketch of my explorations since I wrote you from Sacramento.

I left Snag-Jumper[1] at Sacramento in charge of a man whose name I have forgotten. He has boats of his own, and I tied Snag to one of his stakes in a snug out-of-the-way nook above the railroad bridge. I met this pilot a mile up the river on his way home from hunting. He kindly led me into port, and then conducted me in the dark up the Barbary Coast into the town; and on taking leave he volunteered the information that he was always kindly disposed toward strangers, but that most people met under such circumstances would have robbed and made away with me, etc. I think, therefore, that leaving Snag in his care will form an interesting experiment on human nature.

I fully intended to sail on down into the bay and up the San Joaquin as far as Millerton, but when I came to examine a map of the river deltas and found that the distance was upwards of three hundred miles, and learned also that the upper San Joaquin was not navigable this dry year even for my craft, and when I also took into consideration the approach of winter and danger of snowstorms on the Kings River summits, I concluded to urge my way into the mountains at once, and leave the San Joaquin studies until my return.

Accordingly, I took the steamer to San Francisco, where I remained one day, leaving extra baggage, and getting some changes of clothing. Then went direct by rail to Visalia, thence pushed up the mountains to Hyde's Mill on the Kaweah, where I obtained some flour, which, together with the tea Mrs. Bidwell supplied me with, and that piece of dried beef, and a little sugar, constituted my stock of provisions. From here I crossed the divide, going northward through fine sequoia woods to Converse's on Kings River. Here I spent two days making some studies on the Big Trees, chiefly with reference to their age. Then I turned eastward and pushed off into the glorious wilderness, following the general direction of the South Fork a few miles back from the brink until I had crossed three tributary canyons from 1500 to 2000 feet deep. In the eastmost and middle one of the three I was delighted to

[1] A homemade skiff, built at the Bidwell ranch, in which Muir rowed and floated down the Sacramento River from Chico.

discover some four or five square miles of sequoia, where I had long guessed the existence of these grand old tree kings.

After this capital discovery I made my way to the bottom of the main South Fork Canyon down a rugged side gorge, having a descent of more than four thousand feet. This was at a point about two miles above the confluence of Boulder Creek. From here I pushed slowly on up the bottom of the canyon, through brush and avalanche boulders, past many a charming fall and garden sacred to nature, and at length reached the grand yosemite at the head, where I stopped two days to make some measurements of the cliffs and cascades. This done, I crossed over the divide to the Middle Fork by a pass 12,200 feet high,[2] and struck the head of a small tributary that conducted me to the head of the main Middle Fork Canyon, which I followed down through its entire length, though it has hitherto been regarded as absolutely inaccessible in its lower reaches. This accomplished, and all my necessary sketches and measurements made, I climbed the canyon wall below the confluence of the Middle and South forks and came out at Converse's again; then back to Hyde's Mill, Visalia, and thence to Merced City by rail, thence by stage to Snelling, and thence to Hopeton afoot.

Here I built a little unpretentious successor to Snag out of some gnarled, sun-twisted fencing, launched it in the Merced opposite the village, and rowed down into the San Joaquin—thence down the San Joaquin past Stockton and through the tule region into the bay near Martinez. There I abandoned my boat and set off cross lots for Mount Diablo, spent a night on the summit, and walked the next day into Oakland. And here my fine summer's wanderings came to an end. And now I find that this mere skeleton finger board indication of my excursion has filled at least the space of a long letter, while I have told you nothing of my gains. If you were nearer I would take a day or two and come and report, and talk inveterately in and out of season until you would be glad to have me once more in the canyons and silence. But Chico is far, and I can only finish with a catalogue of my new riches, setting them down one after the other like words in a spelling book.

1. Four or five square miles of sequoias.
2. The ages of twenty-six specimen sequoias.
3. A fine fact about bears.
4. A sure measurement of the deepest of all the ancient glaciers yet traced in the Sierra.

[2] If Muir was that high, he may have crossed Cirque Crest or Windy Ridge. Windy Canyon descends into the main canyon above Simpson Meadow.

5. Two waterfalls of the first order, and cascades innumerable.
6. *A new yosemite valley!!!*
7. Grand facts concerning the formation of the central plain of California.
8. A picturesque cluster of facts concerning the river birds and animals.
9. A glorious series of new landscapes, with mountain furniture and garniture of the most ravishing grandeur and beauty.

Here, Mrs. Bidwell, is a rose leaf from a wild briar on Mount Diablo whose leaves are more flowery than its petals. Isn't it beautiful? That new yosemite valley is located in the heart of the Middle Fork Canyon, the most remote, and inaccessible, and one of the very grandest of all the mountain temples of the range.[3] It is still sacred to Nature, its gardens untrodden, and every nook and rejoicing cataract wears the bloom and glad sun-beauty of primeval wildness—ferns and lilies and grasses over one's head. I saw a flock of five deer in one of its open meadows, and a grizzly bear quietly munching acorns under a tree within a few steps.

The cold was keen and searching the night I spent on the summit by the edge of a glacier lake twenty-two degrees below the freezing point, and a storm wind blowing in fine hearty surges among the shattered cliffs overhead, and, to crown all, snow-flowers began to fly a few minutes after midnight, causing me to fold that quilt of yours and fly to avoid a serious snowbound. By daylight I was down in the main Middle Fork in a milder climate and safer position at an elevation of only seventy-five hundred feet. All the summit peaks were quickly clad in close unbroken white.

I was terribly hungry ere I got out of this wild canyon—had less than sufficient for one meal in the last four days, and this, coupled with very hard nerve-trying cliff work was sufficiently exhausting for any mountaineer. Yet strange to say, I did not suffer much. Crystal water, and air, and honey sucked from the scarlet flowers of zauschneria, about one-tenth as much as would suffice for a hummingbird, was my last breakfast—a very temperate meal, was it not?—wholly ungross and very nearly spiritual. The last effort before reaching food was a climb up out of the main canyon of five thousand feet. Still I made it in fair time—only a little faint, no giddiness, want of spirit, or incapacity to observe and enjoy, or any nonsense of this kind. How I should have liked to have then tumbled into your care for a day or two!

[3] Tehipite Valley.

My sail down the Merced and San Joaquin was about two hundred and fifty miles in length and took two weeks, a far more difficult and less interesting [trip], as far as scenery is concerned, than my memorable first voyage down the Sacramento. Sandbars and gravelly riffles, as well as snags, gave me much trouble, and in the tule wilderness I had to tether my tiny craft to a bunch of rushes and sleep cold in her bottom with the seat for a pillow. I have gotten past most of the weariness but am hungry yet notwithstanding friends have been stuffing me here ever since. I may go hungry through life and into the very grave and beyond unless you effect a cure, and I'm sure I should like to try Rancho Chico—would have tried it ere this were you not so far off.

I slept in your quilt all through the excursion, and brought it here tolerably clean and whole. The flag I left tied to the bushtop in the bottom of the third F Canyon. I have not yet written to Gray, have you? Remember me to your sister, I mean to write to her soon. I must close. With lively remembrances of your rare kindness, I am

Ever very cordially yours

JOHN MUIR

The Life and Letters of John Muir

Middle Fork Kings River.
(October 1877)

At midnight the storm songs of the wind began to sound on the mountaintops, and, looking up twenty-five hundred feet, I saw a cloud ragged with streamers on the edges. In a few moments snow-flowers began to fly with the awful deliberation . . . of a mountain storm. The gray light of the coming dawn began to mingle with the dull starlight. Then a thin metallic white clearness appeared on the canyon cliffs, below which the storm wrapped the peaks in gray . . . Then a yet stranger light came on. The cliffs here and there caught a glow of yellow, changing the white gradually to rose. One beheld a thousand views of clouds—a new climate, a new world. The mighy pines glowed like flames, and the falling waters rejoiced as if conscious of the treasures being heaped in their fountains . . . A grand reproduction of Egypt's Sphinx on the south wall . . . its head turned north.

Shafts of glad, warm sunlight came streaming through the pines . . .

John of the Mountains

THE STUPENDOUS ROCKS

. . . a wilderness of crumbling spires and battle-
ments, built together in bewildering combi-
nations, and glazed in many places with a thin
coating of ice . . .

OVERLEAF: *Kearsarge Pass, Kings Canyon National Park*

1. THE BIG KINGS RIVER CANYON

Muir's years of freedom ended with his foray into the Kings Middle Fork in 1877. Courtship and marriage, the responsibilities of authorship, ranching and family life, and his career as advocate of the public interest in park and forest conservation, now restricted his time and his style of travel. Even when he broke out to explore Alaskan glaciers, home ties and cares pursued him. But his passion for the Sierra Nevada did not dim, and he was single-minded in his efforts to protect its scenic character. Robert Underwood Johnson wrote of him, "The 'dreamer' proved to be a propagandist of the most practical sort."

Muir met Johnson, an editor of the Century, *in 1889, and took him to Yosemite where their hikes and campfire talks helped to shape history. Armed with maps and information which Muir provided, reinforced by two Muir articles on Yosemite published in the magazine in August and September 1890, Johnson launched a nation-wide movement and successfully lobbied for the creation of a Yosemite National Park. Sequoia and General Grant Grove entered what was to become the national park system through legislation enacted at the same time. Neither man was satisfied with the boundaries, however, and from 1890 until Muir died in 1914 they worked together to perfect the two great Sierra parks which exist today as Yosemite and Kings-Sequoia.*

As soon as he had written the Yosemite articles, Muir made plans to revisit what he called the Kings River yosemite to "gather fresh facts" for a third Century *piece. In it he intended to describe the South Fork canyon and the surrounding forests and peaks from the Whitney crest on the east to the Kings and Kaweah sequoias on the west. All this should be contained in "one grand national park." He was arranging for others to go with him, including artists to provide illustrations and a lawyer to help describe the proposed reservation.*

*The illness and death of Mrs. Muir's father, and then the lateness
of the season, delayed the trip for more than six months. Finally,
during the first two weeks of June 1891, with the artist Charles D.
Robinson, the guide John Fox, and another companion, Muir
camped on the South Fork, studied elevations and renewed his acquaintance with the terrain. Back at home in Martinez, he wrote
to Johnson that he was "bending and stretching at the oar in this
Kings River article hard as I can." He told his friend:*

*"Had a good trip but a little hard. Had to walk in to the yosemite
from the Sequoia Park. Rain, sleet, snow, & flooded streams. Slid
2 miles on dead avalanche. Mule with all our grub went down the
river but was caught on a grand jam . . ."*

*Again, he complained of interruptions "a hundred times a day
. . . This 3rd yosemite article will I fear be a rough piece of writing.
My stock of cliff & cascade adjectives are all used up & I am too
dull to invent new ones. Still it will have a good deal of topography
& timber in it & may answer the purpose of a park argument . . ."*

*The result of this travail was the following article, "A Rival of
the Yosemite," which was published in the* Century *in November.
(Its concluding paragraph appears in the last section of this book.)
Although the one grand park Muir proposed was to be another
half-century in the making and the South Fork canyon and Tehipite
were excluded until 1965, this was his prophetic and definitive
description of the features now protected in Kings Canyon and
Sequoia national parks.*

In the vast Sierra wilderness far to the southward of the famous
Yosemite Valley, there is a yet grander valley of the same kind. It is
situated on the South Fork of Kings River, above the most extensive
groves and forests of the giant sequoia, and beneath the shadows of the
highest mountains in the range, where the canyons are deepest and the
snow-laden peaks are crowded most closely together. It is called the
Big Kings River Canyon, or Kings River yosemite, and is reached by way
of Visalia, the nearest point on the Southern Pacific Railroad, from
which the distance is about forty-five miles, or by the Kearsarge Pass
from the east side of the range. It is about ten miles long, half a mile
wide, and the stupendous rocks of purplish gray granite that form the
walls are from 2500 to 5000 feet in height, while the depth of the valley
below the general surface of the mountain mass from which it has been

carved is considerably more than a mile. Thus it appears that this new yosemite is longer and deeper, and lies embedded in grander mountains, than the well-known Yosemite of the Merced. Their general characters, however, are wonderfully alike, and they bear the same relationship to the fountains of the ancient glaciers above them.

As to waterfalls, those of the new valley are far less striking in general views, although the volume of falling water is nearly twice as great and comes from higher sources. The descent of the Kings River streams is mostly made in the form of cascades, which are outspread in flat plume-like sheets on smooth slopes, or are squeezed in narrow-throated gorges, boiling, seething, in deep swirling pools, pouring from lin to lin, and breaking into ragged, tossing masses of spray and foam in boulder-choked canyons—making marvelous mixtures with the downpouring sun-beams, displaying a thousand forms and colors, and giving forth a great variety of wild mountain melody, which, rolling from side to side against the echoing cliffs, is at length all combined into one smooth, massy sea-like roar.

The bottom of the valley is about 5000 feet above the sea, and its level or gently sloping surface is diversified with flowery meadows and groves and open sunny flats, through the midst of which the crystal river, ever changing, ever beautiful, makes its way; now gliding softly with scarce a ripple over beds of brown pebbles, now rushing and leaping in wild exultation across avalanche rock-dams or terminal moraines, swaying from side to side, beaten with sunshine, or embowered with leaning pines and firs, alders, willows, and tall balsam poplars, which with the bushes and grass at their feet make charming banks. Gnarled snags and stumps here and there reach out from the banks, making cover for trout which seem to have caught their colors from rainbow spray, though hiding mostly in shadows, where the current swirls slowly and protecting sedges and willows dip their leaves.

From this long, flowery, forested, well-watered park the walls rise abruptly in plain precipices or richly sculptured masses partly separated by side canyons, displaying wonderful wealth and variety of architectural forms, which are as wonderful in beauty of color and fineness of finish as in colossal height and mass. The so-called war of the elements has done them no harm. There is no unsightly defacement as yet; deep in the sky, inviting the onset of storms through unnumbered centuries, they still stand firm and seemingly as fresh and unworn as newborn flowers.

From the brink of the walls on either side the ground still rises in a series of ice-carved ridges and basins, superbly forested and adorned with many small lakes and meadows, where deer and bear find grateful homes; while from the head of the valley mountains other mountains rise beyond in glorious array, every one of them shining with rock crystals and snow, and with a network of streams that sing their way down from lake to lake through a labyrinth of ice-burnished canyons. The area of the basins drained by the streams entering the valley is about 450 square miles, and the elevation of the rim of the general basin is from 9000 to upward of 14,000 feet above the sea; while the general basin of the Merced yosemite has an area of 250 square miles, and its elevation is much lower.

When from some commanding summit we view the mighty wilderness about this central valley, and, after tracing its tributary streams, note how every converging canyon shows in its sculpture, moraines, and shining surfaces that it was once the channel of a glacier, contemplating this dark period of grinding ice, it would seem that here was a center of storm and stress to which no life would come. But it is just where the ancient glaciers bore down on the mountain flank with crushing and destructive and most concentrated energy that the most impressive displays of divine beauty are offered to our admiration. Even now the snow falls every winter about the valley to a depth of ten to twenty feet, and the booming of avalanches is a common sound. Nevertheless the frailest flowers, blue and gold and purple, bloom on the brows of the great canyon rocks, and on the frosty peaks, up to a height of 13,000 feet, as well as in sheltered hollows and on level meadows and lake borders and banks of streams.

At the head of the valley the river forks, the heavier branch turning northward, and on this branch there is another yosemite, called from its flowery beauty Paradise Valley; and this name might well be applied to the main canyon, for notwithstanding its tremendous rockiness, it is an Eden of plant-beauty from end to end.

THE TRIP TO THE VALLEY[1]

Setting out from Visalia we ride through miles and miles of wheat-fields,[2] and grassy levels brown and dry and curiously dappled with

[1] Subheadings are from the *Century*.

[2] This was in the period of which Frank Norris wrote in *The Octopus;* wheat is no longer the crop, and you will see citrus, other fruits, and a diversified agriculture.

low oval hillocks with miniature hollows between them called "hog-wallows"; then through tawny, sun-beaten foothills, with here and there a bush or oak. Here once roamed countless droves of antelope, now utterly exterminated. By the end of May most of the watercourses are dry. Feeble bits of cultivation occur at long intervals, but the entire foothill region is singularly silent and desolate-looking, and the traveler fondly turns his eyes to the icy mountains looming through the hot and wavering air.

From the base of the first grand mountain plateau we can see the outstanding pines and sequoias 4000 feet above us, and we now ascend rapidly, sweeping from ravine to ravine around the brows of subordinate ridges. The vegetation shows signs of a cooler climate; the golden-flowered fremontia, manzanita, ceanothus, and other bushes show miles of bloom; while great beds of blue and purple bells brighten the open spaces, made up chiefly of brodiaea, calochortus, gilia of many species, etc., the whole forming a floral apron of fine texture and pattern, let down from the verge of the forest in graceful, flowing folds. At a height of 3000 feet we find here and there a pine standing among the bushes by the wayside, lonely and far apart, as if it had come down from the woods to welcome us. As we continue to ascend the flower mantle thickens, wafts of balsam come from the evergreens, fragrant tassels and plumes are shaken above us, cool brooks cross the road, till at length we enter the glorious forest, passing suddenly out of the sun glare into cooling shadows as if we had entered some grand inclosed hall.

We have now reached an elevation of 6000 feet, and are on the margin of the main forest belt of the Sierra. Looking down we behold the central plain of California outspread like an arm of the sea, bounded in the hazy distance by the mountains of the coast, and bathed in evening purple. Orange groves and vineyards, fields, towns, and dusty pastures are all submerged and made glorious in the divine light. Finer still is the light streaming past us through the aisles of the forest.

Down through the shadows we now make our way for a mile or two in one of the upper ravines of Mill Creek. Stumps, logs, and the smashed ruins of the trees cumber the ground; the scream of saws is heard; a lumber village comes in sight, and we arrive at the Moore and Smith Mills, the end of the stage line. From here the distance to the valley in a direct line is only about eighteen miles, and two trails lead to it, one of which traces the divide between the waters of the Kaweah and Kings rivers, while the other holds a more direct course across the basins of Big and Little Boulder creeks, tributaries of Kings River. Both ways are fairly good as mountain trails go, inasmuch as you are seldom compelled to travel more than two miles to make an advance of one, and less than half of the miles are perpendicular. A stout walker may make the trip to the valley in a day. But if instead of crossing every ridge wave of these broad boulder basins a good carriage road were built around the brows and headlands of the main river canyon, the valley could be reached in less than half a day, and with the advantage of still grander scenery. The lower trail is the one commonly traveled, and upon the whole it is the more interesting, for it leads all the way through glorious forests, amid which the stately shafts and domes of sequoia are frequently seen.[3] Climbing a steep mile from the mill, we enter the General Grant National Park of Big Trees, a square mile in extent, where a few of the giants are now being preserved amid the industrious destruction by ax, saw, and blasting powder going on around them.[4] Still ascending we pass the little flowery Round Meadow, set in a superb growth of silver firs, and gain the summit of the ridge that forms the west boundary of Little Boulder Creek Basin, from which a grand view of the forest is obtained—cedar, sugar pine, yellow pine, silver fir, and sequoia filling every hollow, and sweeping up the sides and over the top of every ridge in measureless exuberance and beauty, only a few gray rock brows on the southern rim of the basin appearing in all the sylvan sea.

We now descend to Bearskin Meadow, a sheet of purple-topped grasses enameled with violets, gilias, larkspurs, potentillas, ivesias, columbine, etc.; parnassia and sedges in the wet places, and majestic trees crowding forward in proud array to form a curving border, while Little Boulder Creek, a stream twenty feet wide, goes humming and swirling merrily through the middle of it. Here we begin to climb again; ever up or down we go, not a fairly level mile in the lot. But despite the quick, harsh curves, vertical or horizontal, and the crossing of bogs and boulder-choked gullies, the sustained grandeur of the scenery keeps weariness away. The air is exhilarating. Crisp and clear comes the bold ringing call of the mountain quail, contrasting with the deep blunt bumping of the grouse, while many a small singer sweetens the air along the leafy fringes of the streams.

The next place with a name in the wilderness is Tornado Meadow. Here the sequoia giants stand close about us, towering above the firs and

[3] An excellent highway has replaced the old stage road; it not only connects Fresno and Visalia with Grant Grove and Giant Forest but also with Cedar Grove and Copper Creek.

[4] Grant Grove is no longer a separate park, as it was made a part of Kings Canyon National Park in 1940.

sugar pines. Then follows another climb of a thousand feet, after which we descend into the magnificent forest basin of Big Boulder Creek. Crossing this boisterous stream as best we may, up again we go 1200 feet through glorious woods, and on a few miles to the emerald Horse Corral and Summit Meadows,[5] a short distance beyond which the highest point on the trail is reached at Grand Lookout, 8300 feet above the sea. Here at length we gain a general view of the great canyon of Kings River lying far below, and of the vast mountain region in the sky on either side of it, and along the summit of the range. Here too we see the forest in broad dark swaths still sweeping onward undaunted, climbing the farther mountain slopes to a height of 11,000 feet. But King Sequoia comes not thus far. The grove nearest the valley is on one of the eastern branches of Boulder Creek, five miles from the lower end.

CHIEF FEATURES OF THE CANYON

Going down into the valley we make a descent of 3500 feet, over the south shoulder, by a careless crinkled trail which seems well-nigh endless. It offers, however, many fine points of view of the huge granite trough, and the river, and the sublime rocks of the walls plunging down and planting their feet on the shady level floor.

At the foot of the valley we find ourselves in a smooth spacious park, planted with stately groves of sugar pine, yellow pine, silver fir, incense cedar, and Kellogg oak. The floor is scarcely ruffled with underbrush, but myriads of small flowers spread a thin purple and yellow veil over the brown needles and burrs beneath the groves, and the gray ground of the open sunny spaces. The walls lean well back and support a fine growth of trees, especially on the south side, interrupted here and there by sheer masses 1000 to 1500 feet high, which are thrust forward out of the long slopes like dormer windows. Three miles up the valley on the south side we come to the Roaring Falls and Cascades. They are on a large stream called Roaring River, whose tributaries radiate far and wide and high through a magnificent basin back into the recesses of a long curving sweep of snow-laden mountains. But though the waters of Roaring River from their fountains to the valley have an average descent of nearly five hundred feet per mile, the fall they make in getting down into the valley is insignificant in height as compared with the similarly

[5] Horse Corral Meadow, site of a pack station, is a road and trail head for travel into the back country of Kings Canyon National Park.

situated Bridal Veil of the old Yosemite. The height of the fall does not greatly exceed its width. There is one thundering plunge into a dark pool beneath a glorious mass of rainbow spray, then a boisterous rush with divided current down a boulder delta to the main river in the middle of the valley. But it is the series of wild cascades above the fall which most deserves attention. For miles back from the brow of the fall the strong, glad stream, five times as large as the Bridal Veil Creek, comes down a narrow canyon or gorge, speeding from form to form with most admirable exuberance of beauty and power, a multitude of small sweet voices blending with its thunder tones as if eager to assist in telling the glory of its fountains. On the east side of the fall the Cathedral Rocks spring aloft with imposing majesty. They are remarkably like the group of the same name in the Merced yosemite and similarly situated though somewhat higher.

Next to Cathedral Rocks is the group called the Seven Gables,[6] massive and solid at the base, but elaborately sculptured along the top and a considerable distance down the front into pointed gothic arches, the highest of which is about three thousand feet above the valley. Beyond the Gable group, and separated slightly from it by the beautiful Avalanche Canyon and Cascades, stands the bold and majestic mass of the Grand Sentinel, 3300 feet high, with a split vertical front presented to the valley, as sheer, and nearly as extensive, as the front of the Yosemite Half Dome.

Projecting out into the valley from the base of this sheer front is the Lower Sentinel, 2400 feet high; and on either side, the West and East sentinels, about the same height, forming altogether the boldest and most massively sculptured group in the valley. Then follow in close succession the Sentinel Cascade, a lace-like strip of water 2000 feet long; the South Tower, 2500 feet high; the Bear Cascade, longer and broader than that of the Sentinel; Cave Dome, 3200 feet high; the Sphinx, 4000 feet, and the Leaning Dome, 3500. The Sphinx,[7] terminating in a curious sphinx-like figure, is the highest rock on the south wall, and one of the most remarkable in the Sierra; while the whole series from Cathedral Rocks to the Leaning Dome at the head of the valley is the highest, most elaborately sculptured, and the most beautiful series of rocks of the same extent that I have yet seen in any yosemite in the range.

[6] Some of these names were never commonly used and have not survived in Kings Canyon.

[7] One of Muir's names, established from the time of this article.

Turning our attention now to the north wall, near the foot of the valley a grand and impressive rock presents itself, which with others of like structure and style of architecture is called the Palisades. Measured from the immediate brink of the vertical portion of the front, it is about two thousand feet high, and is gashed from top to base by vertical planes, making it look like a mass of huge slabs set on edge. Its position here is relatively the same as that of El Capitan in Yosemite, but neither in bulk nor in sublime boldness of attitude can it be regarded as a rival of that great rock.

The next notable group that catches the eye in going up the valley is the Hermit Towers, and next to these the Three Hermits, forming together an exceedingly picturesque series of complicated structure, slightly separated by the steep and narrow Hermit Canyon. The Hermits stand out beyond the general line of the wall, and in form and position remind one of the Three Brothers of the Yosemite Valley.

East of the Hermits a stream about the size of Yosemite Creek enters the valley, forming the Booming Cascades.[8] It draws its sources from the southern slopes of Mount Hutchings and Mount Kellogg, 11,000 and 12,000 feet high, on the divide between the Middle and South forks of the Kings River.[9] In Avalanche Canyon, directly opposite the Booming Cascades, there is another brave bouncing chain of cascades, and these two sing and roar to each other across the valley in hearty accord. But though on both sides of the valley, and up the head canyons, water is ever falling in glorious abundance and from immense heights, we look in vain for a stream shaken loose and free in the air to complete the glory of this grandest of yosemites. Nevertheless when we trace these cascading streams through their picturesque canyons, and behold the beauty they show forth as they go plunging in short round-browed falls from pool to pool, laving and plashing their sun-beaten foam bells; gliding outspread in smooth shining plumes, or rich ruffled lacework fold over fold; dashing down rough places in wild ragged aprons, dancing in upbulging bosses of spray, the sweet brave ouzel helping them to sing, and ferns, lilies, and tough-rooted bushes shading and brightening their gray rocky banks—when we thus draw near and learn to know these cascade falls, which thus keep in touch with the rocks, and plants, and birds, then we admire them even more than those which leave their channels and fly down through the air.

[8] Granite Creek.
[9] Mount Hutchings, 10,785 feet, and Goat Mountain, 12,207 feet.

Meadow in Bubbs Creek Canyon,
Kings Canyon National Park

Above the Booming Cascades, and opposite the Grand Sentinel, stands the North Dome, 3450 feet high. It is set on a long bare granite ridge, with a vertical front like the Washington Column in Yosemite. Above the Dome the ridge still rises in a finely drawn curve, until it reaches its culminating point in the pyramid, a lofty symmetrical rock nearly 6000 feet above the floor of the valley.

A short distance east of the Dome is Lion Rock, a very striking mass as seen from a favorable standpoint, but lower than the main rocks of the wall, being only about 2000 feet high. Beyond the Lion, and opposite the East Sentinel, a stream called Copper Creek comes chanting down into the valley. It takes its rise in a cluster of beautiful lakes that lie on top of the divide between the South and Middle forks of Kings River, to the east of Mount Kellogg. The broad, spacious basin it drains abounds in beautiful groves of spruce and silver fir, and small meadows and gardens, where the bear and deer love to feed, but it has been sadly trampled by flocks of sheep.[10]

From Copper Creek to the head of the valley the precipitous portion of the north wall is comparatively low. The most notable features are the North Tower, a square, boldly sculptured outstanding mass two thousand feet in height, and the Dome arches, heavily glaciated, and offering telling sections of domed and folded structure. At the head of the valley, in a position corresponding to that of the Half Dome in Yosemite, looms the great Glacier Monument, the broadest, loftiest, and most sublimely beautiful of all these wonderful rocks. It is upward of a mile in height, and has five ornamental summits, and an indescribable variety of sculptured forms projecting or countersunk on its majestic front, all balanced and combined into one symmetrical mountain mass.[11]

THE VALLEY FLOOR

The bottom of the valley is covered by heavy deposits of moraine material, mostly outspread in comparatively smooth and level beds, though four well-characterized terminal moraines may still be traced stretching across from wall to wall, dividing the valley into sections. These sections, however, are not apparent in general views. Compared with the old Yosemite this is a somewhat narrower valley, the meadows

[10] Grouse Lake, 10,473 feet, from which Copper Creek originates, lies southwest of the summit of Goat Mountain.

[11] Glacier Monument, 11,165 feet, was named by Muir in the course of writing this article; the artist, Robinson, had wanted to call it "The White Woman."

are smaller, and fewer acres if cultivated would yield good crops of fruit or grain. But on the other hand the tree growth of the new valley is much finer; the sugar pine in particular attains perfect development, and is a hundred times more abundant, growing on the rough taluses against the walls, as well as on the level flats, and occupying here the place that the Douglas spruce[12] occupies in the old valley. Earthquake taluses, characteristic features of all yosemites, are here developed on a grand scale, and some of the boulders are the largest I have ever seen— more than a hundred feet long, and scarcely less in width and depth.

With the exception of a small meadow on the river bank, a mile or more of the lower end of the valley is occupied by delightful groves, and is called Deer Park.[13] Between Deer Park and the Roaring Fall lies the Manzanita Orchard, consisting of a remarkably even and extensive growth of manzanita bushes scarcely interrupted by other bushes or trees. Beyond the Roaring Fall the soil beds are rather rocky, but smooth sheets occur here and there, the most notable of which is Blue Flat, covered with blue and fragrant lupines; while all the boulder beds are forested with noble pines and firs.

The largest meadow in the valley lies at the foot of the Grand Sentinel.[14] It is noted for its fine growth of sweet-brier rose, the foliage of which as well as the flower is deliciously fragrant, especially in the morning when the sun warms the dew. At the foot of the South Tower, near the Bear Cascades, there is a notable garden of mariposa tulips, and above this garden lies Bear Flat, extending to the head of the valley. It is a rather rough, bouldery space, but well planted, and commands glorious views of all the upper end of the valley.

On the north side of the valley the spaces that bear names are the Bee Pasture, Gilia Garden, and Purple Flat, all lavishly flowery, each with its own characteristic plants, though mostly they are the same as those of the south side of the river, variously developed and combined; while aloft on a thousand niches, benches, and recesses of the walls are charming rock ferns, such as adiantum, pellaea, cheilanthes, allosorus, etc., and brilliant rugs and fringes of the alpine phlox, Menzies pentstemon, bryanthus, cassiope, alpine primula, and many other small floral mountaineers.

In passing through the valley the river makes an average descent of about fifty feet per mile. Down the canyon below the valley the descent is 125 feet per mile for the first five miles, and of course the river is here

---

[12] Douglas fir.
[13] Cedar Grove.
[14] Zumwalt Meadow.

one continuous chain of rapids. And here too are several beautiful falls on streams entering the canyon on both sides, the most attractive of which is on Boulder Creek, below a fine grove.

TYNDALL CANYON

At the head of the valley in front of the Monument the river divides into two main branches, the larger branch trending northward through Paradise Canyon,[15] the other eastward through Tyndall Canyon,[16] and both extend back with their wide-reaching tributaries into the High Sierra among the loftiest snow mountains of the range, and display scenery along their entire courses harmoniously related to the grand gorge. Tracing the Tyndall Canyon we find that its stream enters the valley in a most beautiful and enthusiastic cascade, which comes sweeping around the base of the Monument, and down through a bower of maple, dogwood, and tall leaning evergreens, making a fall of nearly eight hundred feet. A few miles above the valley the declivity of the canyon is moderate, and nowhere does it expand into meadows of considerable width, or levels of any kind, with the exception of a few small lake basins. But the walls are maintained in yosemite style, and are striped with cascades and small sheer falls from 1000 to 2500 feet in height. In many places the canyon is choked with the boulders of earthquake avalanches, and these, being overgrown with tangled bushes, make tedious work for the mountaineer, though they greatly enhance the general wildness. Pursuing the upper south

[15] Paradise Valley, on the South Fork of Kings River.

[16] Bubbs Creek, which arises in Center Basin; Muir's Mount Tyndall is not the present one.

Falls on Bubbs Creek
above Junction Meadows,
Kings Canyon National Park

fork of the canyon past Mount Brewer, the scenery becomes more and more severely rocky, and the source of the young river is found in small streams that rise in the spacious snow fountains of Mount Tyndall and the neighboring peaks.[17]

PARADISE CANYON

Returning now to the main valley and ascending the Paradise Canyon we find still grander scenery, at least for the first ten miles. Beneath the shadow of the Glacier Monument, situated like Mirror Lake beneath the Half Dome of Yosemite, is a charming meadow with magnificent trees about it, and huge avalanche taluses tangled with ceanothus and manzanita and wild cherry, a favorite pasture and hiding place for bears; while the river with broad, stately current sweeps down through the solemn solitude. Pursuing our savage way through the stubborn underbrush, and over or beneath boulders as large as hills,[18] we find the noble stream beating its way for five or six miles in one continuous chain of roaring, tossing, surging cascades and falls. The walls of the canyon on either hand rise to a height of from 3000 to 5000 feet in majestic forms, hardly inferior in any respect to those of the main valley. The most striking of these on the west wall is the Helmet, four thousand feet in height; and on the east side, after the Monument, Paradise Peak. Of all the grand array only these have yet been named.[19] About eight miles up the canyon we come to Paradise Valley, where the walls, still maintaining their lofty yosemite characters, especially on the east side, stand back and make space for charming meadows and gravelly flats, while one grand fall not yet measured, and several smaller ones, pouring over the walls, give voice and animation to the glorious mountain solitude.

DESTRUCTIVE TENDENCIES

At first sight it would seem that these mighty granite temples could be injured but little by anything that man may do. But it is surprising to find how much our impressions in such cases depend upon the delicate

---

[17] Not Tyndall, but the peaks of the Kings-Kern Divide where it meets the main Sierra crest.

[18] Modern trails avoid such hazards.

[19] These names seem not to have survived.

bloom of the scenery, which in all the more accessible places is so easily rubbed off. I saw the Kings River valley in its midsummer glory sixteen years ago, when it was wild, and when the divine balanced beauty of the trees and flowers seemed to be reflected and doubled by all the onlooking rocks and streams as though they were mirrors, while they in turn were mirrored in every garden and grove. In that year (1875) I saw the following ominous notice on a tree in the Kings River yosemite:

We, the undersigned, claim this valley
for the purpose of raising stock.
MR. THOMAS, MR. RICHARDS, HARVEY & CO.

and I feared that the vegetation would soon perish. This spring (1891) I made my fourth visit to the valley, to see what damage had been done, and to inspect the forests. Besides, I had not yet seen the valley in flood, and this was a good flood year, for the weather was cool, and the snow on the mountains had been held back ready to be launched. I left San Francisco on the 28th of May, accompanied by Mr. Robinson, the artist. At the new Kings River Mills we found that the sequoia giants, as well as the pines and firs, were being ruthlessly turned into lumber. Sixteen years ago I saw five mills on or near the sequoia belt, all of which were cutting more or less of "big-tree" lumber. Now, as I am told, the number of mills along the belt in the basins of the Kings, Kaweah, and Tule rivers is doubled, and the capacity more than doubled. As if fearing restriction of some kind, particular attention is being devoted to the destruction of the sequoia groves owned by the mill companies, with the view to get them made into lumber and money before steps can be taken to save them. Trees which compared with mature specimens are mere saplings are being cut down, as well as the giants, up to at least twelve to fifteen feet in diameter. Scaffolds are built around the great brown shafts above the swell of the base, and several men armed with long saws and axes gnaw and wedge them down with damnable industry. The logs found to be too large are blasted to manageable dimensions with powder. It seems incredible that Government should have abandoned so much of the forest cover of the mountains to destruction. As well sell the rain clouds, and the snow, and the rivers, to be cut up and carried away if that were possible. Surely it is high time that something be done to stop the extension of the present barbarous, indiscriminating method of harvesting the lumber crop.

At the mills we had found Mr. J. Fox, bear-killer and guide, who owns a pack train and keeps a small store of provisions in the valley for the convenience of visitors. This sturdy mountaineer we engaged to manage our packs, and under his guidance after a very rough trip we reached our destination late at night.

Arrived in the valley, we found that the small grove (now under Government protection) has been sadly hacked and scarred by campers and sheep-owners, and it will be long before it recovers anything like the beauty of its wildness.

Several flocks of sheep are driven across the river at the foot of the valley every spring to pasture in the basins of Kellogg[20] and Copper creeks. On the south side of the valley, in the basin of Roaring River, more than 20,000 sheep are pastured, but none have ever been allowed to range in the valley.

GAME AND SPORT

After breakfast two anglers with whom we had fallen in on the way set forth to a big jam of flood timber on the south side of the river, and amid its shady swirls and ripples bagged the glittering beauties as fast as sham flies could be switched to them, a hundred trout of a morning being considered no uncommon catch under favorable conditions of water and sky.[21] This surely is the most romantic fishing ground in the world. Nearly all the visitors to the valley are hunters or anglers; they number about four hundred a year, and nearly all come from Owens Valley on the eastern slope of the Sierra, or from the Visalia plains. By means of ropes and log footbridges we got across the three streams of Roaring River, and, passing through the fragrant lupine garden of Blue Flat, which Fox calls the Garden of Eden, we made our permanent camp in a small log cabin on the edge of the meadow at the foot of the Grand Sentinel.

The fauna of the valley is diverse and interesting. The first morning after our arrival I saw the black-headed grosbeak, the Louisiana tanager,[22] and Bullock's oriole, whose bills must still have been stained by the cherries of the lowland orchards. I also noticed many species of woodpeckers, including the large logcock (*Hylotomus pileatus*),[23] and innumerable finches and flycatchers. The mountain quail and grouse also

[20] Granite?
[21] The legal limit, in season, is now ten fish.
[22] Western tanager (*Piranga ludoviciana*).
[23] Pileated woodpecker (*Dryocopus pileatus*).

dwell in the valley, as well as in all the silver-fir woods on the surrounding heights. The large California gray squirrel, as well as the Douglas, is seldom out of sight as one saunters through the groves, and in the cabin we were favored with the company of wood rats. These amusing animals made free with our provisions, bathed in our water bucket, and ran across our faces in the night.

Besides our party there were two other persons in the valley, who had arrived a few days before us: a young student whose ambition was to kill a bear, and his uncle, a tough, well-seasoned mountaineer who had roamed over the greater part of the western wilderness. The boy did kill a bear a few days after our arrival, not so big and ferocious a specimen as he could have wished, but formidable enough for a boy to fight single-handed. It was jet-black, sleek, and becomingly shaggy; with teeth, claws, and muscles admirably fitted for the rocky wilderness. After selecting certain steaks, roasts, and boiling-pieces, the remainder of the lean meat was cut into ribbons and strung about the camp to dry, while the precious oil was put into cans and bottles. Bread at that camp was now made of flour and bear oil, instead of flour and water, and bear muffins, bear flapjacks, and bear shortbread were the order of the day.

The black bear is seldom found to the north of Kings River. Of the other two species—the cinnamon and grizzly—the former is more common.[24] But all the species are being rapidly reduced in numbers. From city hunters bears have little to fear, but many fall before the rifles of the mountaineer and prospector. Shepherds poison, and even shoot, many in the aggregate every year. Pity that animals so good-natured and so much a part of these shaggy wilds should be exterminated. If all the Kings River bears great and small were gathered into this favorite yosemite home of theirs, they would still make a brave show, but they would probably number fewer than five hundred.

EXCURSIONS FROM THE VALLEY

The side and head canyons of the valley offer ways gloriously rugged and interesting back into the High Sierra. The shorter excursions to points about the rim of the valley, such as Mt. Kellogg, Mt. Brewer, the North Dome, the Helmet, Avalanche Peak, and the Grand Sentinel, may be made in one day. Bear trails will be found in all the canyons leading up

[24] Black and cinnamon are color variations of the American black bear (*Ursus americanus*). The grizzly (*U. henshawi*) has been extinct in California for many years.

to these points, and may be safely followed, and throughout them all and on them all glorious views will be obtained.[25]

The excursion to Avalanche Peak by way of Avalanche Canyon and the Grand Sentinel is one of the most telling of the short trips about the valley, and one that every visitor should make, however limited as to time. From the top of the Sentinel the bottom of the valley, with all its groves and meadows and nearly all of the walls on both sides, is seen, while Avalanche Peak commands a view of nearly all the magnificent basin of Roaring River, and of the region tributary to the valley on the north and east. A good bear trail guides you through the cherry brush and boulders along the cascades. A thousand feet above the valley you come to the beautiful Diamond Fall, 200 feet high and 40 feet wide. About a thousand feet higher a small stream comes in from the east, where you turn to the left and scale the side of the canyon to the top of the Grand Sentinel. After gazing up and down into the tremendous scenery displayed here, you follow the Sentinel ridge around the head of the beautiful forested basin, into which the canyon expands, to the summit of the peak. In spring the Avalanche basin and canyon are filled with compact avalanche snow, which lies long after the other canyons are clear. In June last I slid comfortably on the surface of this snow from the peak down nearly to the foot of the Diamond Fall, a distance of about two miles. Of course this can only be done when the surface is in a melting condition or is covered with fresh snow. In April one might slide from the summit to the bottom of the valley, making a fall of a mile in one swift swish above the rocks, logs, and brush that roughen the way in summer.

MTS. TYNDALL, KEARSARGE, AND WHITNEY

The excursion to Mt. Tyndall from the valley and return requires about three days. You trace the east branch of the river from the head of the valley until it forks, then trace the South Fork past the east side of Mt. Brewer until it divides into small streams, then push up eastward as best you can to the summit.[26] The way is rather rough, but the views

[25] Most of these excursions are more ambitious than Muir seems to indicate. Consult Park rangers, maps, and guidebooks.

[26] This was Muir's route in 1873, up Bubbs Creek to climb what he thought was Tyndall. It may have been Junction Peak, 13,888 feet, or a peak on the Kings-Kern Divide.

obtained of the loftiest and broadest portion of the High Sierra are the
most comprehensive and awe-inspiring that I know of. It is here that
the great western spur on Greenhorn Range strikes off from the main
axis to the southwest and south, bearing a noble array of snowy mountains, and forming the divide between the Upper Kern on the east and the
Kaweah and Tule rivers on the west, while the main chain forms the
eastern boundary of the basin of the Kern.[27] Northward the streams fall
into Kings River, eastward into Owens Valley and the dead salt Owens
Lake, lying in the glare of the desert 9000 feet below you. To the
north and south as far as the eye can reach you behold a vast crowded
wilderness of peaks, only a few of which are named as yet. Mt. Kearsarge
to the northward, a broad round-shouldered mountain on the main axis
at the head of the pass of that name; Mt. Brewer, noted for the beauty
of its fluted slopes; Mt. King, an exceedingly sharp and slender peak
a few miles to the eastward of the Glacier Monument; and Mt. Gardiner,
a companion of King. Within two miles of where you stand rises the
jagged mass of Mt. Williamson, a little higher than Tyndall, or 14,300
feet, and seven miles to the southward rises Mt. Whitney, 14,700 feet
high, the culminating point of the range, and easily recognized by its
helmet-shaped peak facing eastward.[28] Though Mt. Whitney is a few
hundred feet higher than Tyndall, the views obtained from its summit
are not more interesting. Still, because it is the highest of all, every climber
will long to stand on its topmost crag. Some eighteen years ago I spent
a November night[29] on the top of Whitney. The first winter snow had
fallen and the cold was intense. Therefore I had to keep in motion to
avoid freezing. But the view of the stars and of the dawn on the desert
was abundant compensation for all that. This was a hard trip, but in
summer no extraordinary danger need be encountered. Almost any one
able to cross a cobblestoned street in a crowd may climb Mt. Whitney.
I climbed it once in the night, lighted only by the stars. From the summit
of Mt. Tyndall you may descend into Kern Valley and make direct for
Mt. Whitney, thus including both of these lordly mountains in one
excursion, but only mountaineers should attempt to go this gait. A much
easier way is to cross the range by way of the Kearsarge Pass, which,
though perhaps the highest traveled pass on the continent, being upward

[27] The western spur is the Kings-Kern Divide, which joins the Great Western
Divide (Muir's Greenhorn Range) south of Mt. Brewer.

[28] Elevations are: Williamson, 14,384 feet; the present Tyndall, 14,018; Whitney,
14,495.

[29] It was in October 1873.

of 12,000 feet above the sea, is not at all dangerous. The trail from the valley leads up to it along extensive meadows and past many small lakes over a broad plateau, and the views from there are glorious. But on the east side the descent to the base of the range is made in one tremendous swoop through a narrow canyon. Escaping from the shadowy jaws of the canyon you turn southward to Lone Pine. Then by taking the Hockett Trail up Cottonwood Canyon you pass over into Kern Valley and approach the mountain from the west, where the slopes are easy, and up which you may ride a mule to a height of 12,000 feet, leaving only a short pull to the summit. But for climbers there is a canyon which comes down from the north shoulder of the Whitney peak. Well-seasoned limbs will enjoy the climb of 9000 feet required by this direct route. But soft, succulent people should go the mule way.

THE TEHIPITE VALLEY

The Kings River Canyon is also a good starting point for an excursion into the beautiful and interesting Tehipite Valley, which is the yosemite of the Middle Fork of Kings River. By ascending the valley of Copper Creek, and crossing the divide, you will find a Middle Fork tributary that conducts by an easy grade down into the head of the grand Middle Fork Canyon, through which you may pass in time of low water, crossing the river from time to time, where sheer headlands are brushed by the current, leaving no space for a passage. After a long rough scramble you will be delighted when you emerge from the narrow bounds of the great canyon into the spacious and enchantingly beautiful Tehipite. It is about three miles long, half a mile wide, and the walls are from 2500 to nearly 4000 feet in height.[30] The floor of the valley is remarkably level, and the river flows with a gentle and stately current. Nearly half of the floor is meadowland, the rest sandy flat planted with the same kind of trees and flowers as the same kind of soil bears in the great canyon, forming groves and gardens, the whole inclosed by majestic granite walls which in height, and beauty, and variety of architecture are not surpassed in any yosemite of the range. Several small cascades coming from a great height sing and shine among the intricate architecture of the south wall, one of which when seen in front seems to be a nearly continuous fall about two thousand feet high. But the grand fall of the valley is on the north side,

[30] Corrected by Muir to "3500 to nearly 4000" in a version which appeared in the *Sierra Club Bulletin* (January 1914).

made by a stream about the size of Yosemite Creek.[31] This is the Tehipite Fall,[32] about 1800 feet high. The upper portion is broken up into short falls and magnificent cascade dashes, but the last plunge is made over a sheer precipice about four hundred feet in height into a beautiful pool.

To the eastward of the Tehipite Fall stands Tehipite Dome, 2500 feet high,[33] a gigantic round-topped tower, slender as compared with its height, and sublimely simple and massive in structure. It is not set upon, but against, the general masonry of the wall, standing well forward, and rising free from the open sunny floor of the valley, attached to the general mass of the wall rocks only at the back. This is one of the most striking and wonderful rocks in the Sierra.

I first saw this valley in 1875 when I was exploring the sequoia belt, and again two years later when I succeeded in tracing the Middle Fork canyon all the way down from its head. I pushed up the canyon of the South Fork in November when the streams were low, through the great canyon, and crossed the divide by way of Copper Creek. The weather was threatening, and at midnight while I lay under a tree on the summit I was awakened by the terribly significant touch of snow on my face. I arose immediately, and while the storm wind made wild music I pushed on over the divide in the dark, feeling the way with my feet. At daybreak I found myself on the brink of the main Middle Fork Canyon, and in an hour or two gained the bottom of it, and pushed down along the river-bank below the edge of the storm cloud. After crossing and recrossing the river again and again, and breaking a way through chaparral and boulders, with here and there an open spot gloriously painted with the colors of autumn, I at length reached Tehipite. I was safe; for all the ground was now familiar. The storm was behind me. The sun was shining clear, shedding floods of gold over the tinted meadows, and fern flats, and groves. The valley was purely wild. Not a trace, however faint, could I see of man or any of his animals, but of nature's animals many. I had been out of provisions for two days, and at least one more hunger day was before me, but still I lingered sketching and gazing enchanted. As I sauntered up to the foot of Tehipite Fall a fat buck with wide branching antlers bounded past me from the edge of the pool within a stone's throw, and in the middle of the valley he was joined by three others, making fine romantic pictures as they crossed the sunny meadow.

[31] Crown Creek.
[32] Silver Spray Falls.
[33] In Muir's revision, "about 3600 feet."

Mt. Brewer, lake below Harrison Pass, Kings Canyon National Park

A mile below the fall I met a grizzly bear eating acorns under one of the large Kellogg oaks. He either heard my crunching steps on the gravel or caught scent of me, for a few minutes after I saw him he stopped eating and came slowly lumbering toward me, stopping every few yards to listen. I was a little afraid, and stole slowly off to one side, and crouched back of a large libocedrus tree. He came on within a dozen yards of me, and I had a good quiet look into his eyes—the first grizzly I had ever seen at home. Turning his head he chanced to catch sight of me; after a long studious stare, he good-naturedly turned away and wallowed off into the chaparral. So perfectly wild and romantic was Tehipite in those days. Whether it remains unchanged I cannot tell, for I have not seen it since.

"A Rival of the Yosemite,"
Century Magazine, November 1891

2. ALONG THE KERN

Muir served as President of the Sierra Club from its founding in 1892 until he died in 1914. He participated in the club's first summer outing based at Yosemite's Tuolumne Meadows in 1901, and the next July joined the second club outing for ten days in the Kings Canyon area. Then, with a horseback party of friends including the artist William Keith, C. Hart Merriam, head of the U. S. Biological Survey, and Henry Gannett, of the U. S. Geological Survey, Muir crossed from Giant Forest to Mount Whitney and back, spending most of August exploring the grand canyon of the Kern and other features of what is now Sequoia National Park.

Although described by a companion as "the leader and mainspring of the entire trip," Muir was now sixty-four. In the climb of Mount Whitney on August 11 he was preceded by three boys, who were on top for half an hour or more before he arrived sedately with four ladies. (One of them, Miss Marian Hooker, a grandniece of J. D. Whitney, was seventy-two, and with proper deference no one touched the precise summit until she had done so.)

On reaching home, Muir told Robert Underwood Johnson in a letter about this "magnificent trip through the highest of the high Sierra." He planned to write an article on the Kern Canyon for the Century, *and to include it as a chapter in the book he thought of as "The Yosemite and Other Yosemites." But he seems to have given up the idea of the article. The most detailed report we have from him of the 1902 trip to the Kern is in the interview he gave to a Visalia newspaper, which quoted him as follows.*

We all had a delightful trip. We went from Giant Forest by way of Panorama Point, Bearpaw Meadow and Timber Gap to Mineral King and from the latter place across Farewell Gap and Coyote Pass to the Kern. We visited the lakes and then went up the canyon for twenty-five miles. The walls for the entire distance will average from 2500 to 3000 feet high on either side and for ten miles on the south wall there is hardly a break in the solid granite. There was not much water in Chagoopa Falls, but we could see where there had been several pretty falls earlier in the season. We camped at the junction for several days and from there had several side trips that were highly enjoyed. We went up the river to where the canyon begins one day and the next took a ride up the Kern-Kaweah, or west branch of the Kern. This is a beautiful country and one well worth visiting.

It is a delightful ride from the Kern to the top of Mt. Whitney. We made our last camp at Crabtree Meadow and started from there to make the ascent of Whitney at 5 o'clock in the morning. We rode to Langley camp and from that point walked the rest of the way. The last one in the party reached the summit by 10 o'clock. We were all agreed that the trip to Whitney and along the Kern was the most enjoyable part of our summer outing. Even Mr. Gannett, the topographer of the geological department, and who has traveled over the Rocky mountain range and over much of the Sierra, said that he enjoyed the trip to Whitney better than any mountain climb he had ever made. He thought it excelled any other portion of the Sierra for magnificent scenery and I agree with him. The sculptured granite rocks from Crabtree Meadow to Whitney surpass in beauty those of the Kings River. There are no individual rocks in the Kern Canyon that equal El Capitan in Yosemite Valley or the Sentinel rock in the Kings, but the very magnitude of the country will make it the most popular resort.

The trip down Whitney (Golden Trout) Creek was highly enjoyed. We had all the golden trout we could eat and the trail was excellent. The natural bridge across Volcano Creek was not made by volcanic action, but by a hot spring. The spring is gone and lava is all around but there is no doubt about how the bridge was made. In the Yellowstone Park the hot springs there are making just such curious things.

The beauty of the trip we have just made is found in the magnificent Giant Forest, the splendid climb out of the forest and among the Balfour pines[1] to the Alta Meadows, the view from Panorama Point where one can see some splendid sculptured granite at the head of the middle fork of the Kaweah and from where the Kaweah peaks loom a mile above and the stream in the canyon glistens three thousand feet below; the blue-gentian meadows and magnificent flowers that are blooming where snow avalanches have destroyed the timber, the Redwood Meadows where the last sequoias are seen, the long ascent to Timber Gap through the Balfour pines and silver fir (*Abies magnifica*), the long zigzag down through one bed of flowers from Timber Gap to Mineral King, then up to Farewell Gap and the beautiful views at the head of the Little Kern, the descent to the lower yosemite of the Kern, the splendid lakes and ride up the canyon with its magnificent walls, the marvelously sculptured granite domes near the base of Whitney and finally the unparalleled view from the summit of our highest mountain—these are some of the things that made our trip so enjoyable.

If one going to the mountains has the time to spare, he should go to Kings Canyon, but if he has to choose between the Kings and the Kern, he should take the latter. I know of no mountain trip in California that surpasses the one to Kern River and to Mt. Whitney.

There is quite a good deal of work needed on your trails, however. The government ought to see to it that a trail is constructed from the Giant Forest to Panorama Point. There should be a trail from the forest to Mineral King that would enable one to avoid climbing to such high altitudes simply to drop down again. The trail out of the Kern towards Crabtree Meadow is monumented a part of the way, where it is the least needed, but when we got onto the hard meadows where a horse cannot make a trail and among the big broken rocks, the monuments are too far apart to be of value to the traveler. A few hundred dollars for making and improving trails could be well spent in this county.

Tulare County Times, Visalia, California,
August 28, 1902

[1] Foxtail pine (*Pinus Balfouriana*).

3. HIGH SIERRA PASSES

*Crossing the Sierra Nevada crest even now, nearly a century
after Muir began his explorations, has an element of adventure. The
abrupt ascent from the east, or the more gradual approach from the
west, past timberline into stark and often snow-covered granite highlands, may be breath-taking in more ways than one, and leads, as
we are told, to a "fine wildness."*

*"The Passes of the Sierra," from which this is an excerpt, was a
magazine article, an extended caption for engravings in the parlor
book edited by Muir,* Picturesque California, *and finally a chapter
in* The Mountains of California.

Between the Sonora Pass and the southern extremity of the Alps, a
distance of nearly 160 miles, there are only five passes through which
trails conduct from one side of the range to the other. These are barely
practicable for animals; a pass in these regions meaning simply any notch
or canyon through which one may, by the exercise of unlimited patience,
make out to lead a mule or sure-footed mustang. Only three of the five
passes may be said to be in use, viz.: the Kearsarge, Mono, and Virginia
Creek, the tracks leading through the others being only obscure Indian
trails, not graded in the least, and scarce at all traceable by white men;
for much of the way is over solid rock pavements and bosses, where the
unshod ponies of the Indians leave no appreciable sign, while only skilled
mountaineers are able to detect the marks that serve to guide the Indians,
such as slight abrasions of the looser rocks, the displacement of stones
here and there, and bent bushes and weeds. A general knowledge of the
topography, however, is the main guide, enabling one to determine where
the trail ought to go—*must* go. One of these Indian trails crosses the

range by a nameless pass between the headwaters of the South and Middle forks of the San Joaquin,[1] the other between the North and Middle forks of the same river, just to the south of the Minarets; this last being about 9000 feet high, the lowest of the five.[2] The Kearsarge is the highest, crossing the summit of the range near the head of the South Fork of Kings River, about eight miles to the north of Mount Tyndall, through the midst of the most stupendous rock scenery to be found anywhere in the Alps. The summit of the pass is over 12,000 feet above sea level;[3] nevertheless, it is one of the safest of the five, and is used every summer, from July to October or November, by hunters, prospectors, and stock owners, and to some extent by enterprising pleasure-seekers, also. For, besides the surpassing grandeur of the scenery about the summit, the trail, in ascending the western flank, conducts through a grove of the giant sequoias, and through the magnificent yosemite valley of the South Fork of Kings River. This is, perhaps, the highest traveled pass on the North American continent.

But, leaving wheels and animals out of the question, the free mountaineer can make his way across the range almost everywhere, and at any time of year. To him nearly every notch between the peaks is a pass, though much patient step-cutting is at times required up and down steeply inclined glaciers, and cautious climbing over precipices, that at first sight would seem hopelessly inaccessible to the lowlander.

In pursuing my studies during the last eight years, I have crossed from side to side of the range at intervals of a few miles all along the highest portion of the chain, with far less real danger than one would naturally count on. And what fine wildness was thus developed—storms and avalanches, lakes and waterfalls, gardens and meadows—only those will ever know who give the freest and most buoyant portion of their lives to climbing and seeing for themselves.

All the passes of the alpine portion of the range make their steepest ascents on the eastern flank. On this side the average rise is not far from a thousand feet to the mile, while on the west it is about two hundred feet. Another marked difference between the eastern and western portions of the passes is that the former begin at the very foot of the range, while the latter can hardly be said to begin until an elevation of from seven to ten thousand feet is reached. Approaching the range from the gray levels of Mono and Owens Valley on the east, the traveler sees before him the steep, short passes in full view, fenced in by rugged spurs that come

[1] Piute Pass, 11,400 feet?
[2] Minaret Summit Pass, 9300 feet?
[3] 11,823 feet.

plunging down from the shoulders of the peaks on either side, the courses of the more direct being disclosed from top to bottom without a single interruption. But from the west one sees nothing of the pass he may be seeking until near the summit, after days have been spent in threading the forests growing on the main dividing ridges between the river canyons.

It is interesting to observe how surely the alp-crossing animals of every kind fall into the same trails. The more rugged and inaccessible the general character of the topography of any particular region, the more surely will the trails of white men, Indians, bears, deer, wild sheep, etc., be found converging into the best passes. The Indians of the western slope venture cautiously over the passes in settled weather to attend dances, and obtain loads of pine nuts and the larvae of a small fly that breeds in Mono and Owens lakes, which, when dried, forms an important article of food; while the Paiutes cross over from the east to hunt the deer and obtain supplies of acorns, and it is truly astonishing to see what immense loads the haggard old squaws make out to carry barefooted through these rough passes, oftentimes for a distance of sixty or seventy miles. They are always accompanied by the men, who stride on unburdened and erect a little in advance, stooping occasionally to pile steppingstones for them against steep rocks, just as they would prepare the way in difficult places for their ponies.[4]

Bears evince great sagacity as mountaineers, but although fond of traveling, they seldom cross the range. I have several times tracked them through Mono Pass, but only in late years after cattle and sheep had passed that way, when they doubtless were following to feed on the stragglers and on those that had been killed by falling over the rocks. Even the wild sheep, the best mountaineers of all, choose regular passes in making journeys across the summits. Deer seldom pass from one side of the range to the other. I have never yet observed a single specimen of the mule deer of the Great Basin west of the summit, and rarely one of the black-tailed species on the eastern slope, notwithstanding many of the latter ascend the range nearly to the summit every summer, to feed safely in the wild gardens and bring forth their young.

The glaciers are the pass-makers, and it is by them that the courses of all mountaineers are predestined. Every pass without exception in the Californian Alps was created by them without the slightest aid or predetermining guidance from any of the cataclysmic agents. We have seen elaborate statements of the amount of drilling and blasting accomplished in the construction of the railroad across the Sierra, above Donner Lake;

[4] Muir shared some frontier prejudices of his day. As hunter and protector, the male Indian had reasons for traveling in advance which observers failed to acknowledge.

but for every pound of rock moved in this way, the glaciers which descended east and west through this same pass, crushed and carried away
more than a hundred tons.

The so-called practicable road passes are simply those portions of the
range more degraded by glacial action than the adjacent portions, and
degraded in such a way as to leave the summits rounded, instead of sharp
and impracticable; while the peaks, from the superior strength and hard-
ness of their rocks, or from more favorable position, having suffered less
degradation, are left towering above the passes as if they had been heaved
into the sky by some force acting from beneath.

The scenery of all the passes, especially at the head, is of the very
wildest and grandest description,—lofty peaks massed together and laden
around their bases with ice and snow; chains of glacier lakes; cascading
streams in endless variety, with glorious views, westward over a sea of
rocks and woods, and eastward over the strange ashy plains and volcanoes and mountain ranges of Mono and Inyo. Every pass, however,
possesses treasures of beauty all its own, and the finding of these is one
of the mountaineer's exceeding great rewards.

"The Passes of the Sierra,"
Scribner's Monthly, March 1879

Split boulder near Lake Ediza,
Minarets Wilderness Area

4. ORIGIN OF THE VALLEYS

To understand the vehemence of Muir's attack on the geological problems of mountain sculpture and mountain building in the Sierra Nevada, one must be reminded of the novelty, in his time, of the teachings of Lyell and Agassiz and the evolutionary philosophy of Darwin. It is also necessary to explain the adversary position in which he found himself in California, where Josiah Dwight Whitney, Harvard professor and since 1860 the State Geologist, had ruled once and for all that a great primeval cataclysm was responsible for the origin of Yosemite Valley and related Sierra land forms. Whitney never retreated from what he had written in the 1868 edition of The Yosemite Book, *published by authority of the California State Legislature:*

"Much less can it be supposed that the peculiar form of the Yosemite is due to the erosive action of ice. A more absurd theory was never advanced, than that by which it was sought to ascribe to glaciers the sawing out of these vertical walls and the rounding of the domes. Nothing more unlike the real work of ice, as exhibited in the Alps, can be found. Besides, there is no reason to suppose, or at least no proof, that glaciers have ever occupied the Valley, or any portion of it . . . so that this theory based on entire ignorance of the whole subject, may be dropped without wasting any more time upon it."

Whitney's own theory was that "the bottom of the Valley sank down to an unknown depth, owing to its support being withdrawn from underneath, during some of those convulsive movements which must have attended the upheaval of so extensive and elevated a chain . . ."

John Muir arrived in Yosemite at the very moment Whitney was expounding this view. He had the impertinence to look at the phenomena with fresh eyes, feel their shape with the hands of a craftsman, and doubt. He wrote to Mrs. Carr in 1870, "Whitney says that the bottom has fallen out of the rocks here—which I most devoutly disbelieve." He searched for evidence to support his counter-theory of glacial action, and found it, even measuring the movement of ice on Mount Lyell. But to convince those who were awed by

Whitney's eminence Muir had to become a crusader and polemicist. The papers he wrote for presentation by Asa Gray before the American Association for the Advancement of Science, and his newspaper and magazine articles of the 1870s, were largely directed to winning friends for glaciological interpretation of the Sierran landscape.

First published in Overland *in 1874, this study of the "Origin of Yosemite Valleys" with its companion articles, seven in all, have been reprinted by the Sierra Club in a volume edited by William Colby,* Studies in the Sierra *(revised edition, 1960). The text confirms that one of Muir's principal reasons for the long trip south in 1873 had been to verify his findings on the Merced and Tuolumne through comparison with the geology of the yosemites of the San Joaquin, Kings, and Kern rivers.*

The greatest obstacle in the way of reading the history of yosemite valleys is not its complexity or obscurity, but simply the *magnitude of the characters* in which it is written. It would require years of enthusiastic study to master the English alphabet if it were carved upon the flank of the Sierra in letters sixty or seventy miles long, their bases set in the foothills, their tops leaning back among the glaciers and shattered peaks of the summit, often veiled with forests and thickets, and their continuity often broken by cross gorges and hills. So also the sculptured alphabet canyons of the Sierra are magnificently simple, yet demand years of laborious research for their apprehension. A thousand blurred fragments must be conned and brooded over with studious care, and kept vital and formative on the edges, ready to knit like broken living bones, while a final judgment is being bravely withheld until the entire series of phenomena has been weighed and referred to an all-unifying, all-explaining law. To one who can leisurely contemplate Yosemite from some commanding outlook, it offers, as a whole, a far more natural combination of features than is at all apparent in partial views obtained from the bottom. Its stupendous domes and battlements blend together and manifest delicate compliance to law, for the mind is then in some measure

Mt. Spencer showing glacial polish, Evolution Valley, Kings Canyon National Park

emancipated from the repressive and enslaving effects of their separate magnitudes, and gradually rises to a comprehension of their unity and of the poised harmony of their general relations.

Nature is not so poor as to possess only one of anything, nor throughout her varied realms has she ever been known to offer an exceptional creation, whether of mountain or valley. When, therefore, we explore the adjacent Sierra, we are not astonished to find that there are many yosemite valleys identical in general characters, each presenting on a varying scale the same species of mural precipices, level meadows, and lofty waterfalls. The laws which preside over their distribution are as constant and apparent as those governing the distribution of forest trees. They occur only in the middle region of the chain, where the declivity is considerable and where the granite is similar in its internal structure. The position of each valley upon the yosemite zone indicates a marked and inseparable relation to the ancient glaciers, which, when fully deciphered, amounts to cause and effect. So constant and obvious is this connection between the various yosemites and the *névé* amphitheaters which fountained the ancient ice rivers, that an observer, inexperienced in these phenomena, might easily anticipate the position and size of any yosemite by a study of the glacial fountains above it, or the position and size of the fountains by a study of their complementary yosemite. *All yosemites occur at the junction of two or more glacial canyons.* Thus the greater and lesser yosemites of the Merced, Hetch Hetchy, and those of the upper Tuolumne, those of Kings River, and the San Joaquin, all occur immediately below the confluences of their ancient glaciers. If, in following down the canyon channel of the Merced Glacier, from its origin in the *névé* amphitheaters of the Lyell group, we should find that its sudden expansion and deepening at Yosemite occurs without a corresponding union of glacial tributary canyons, and without any similar expansion elsewhere, then we might well be driven to the doctrine of special marvels. But this emphatic deepening and widening becomes harmonious when we observe smaller yosemites occurring at intervals all the way down, across the yosemite zone, *wherever a tributary canyon unites with the trunk,* until, on reaching Yosemite; where the enlargement is greatest, we find the number of confluent glacier canyons is also greatest, as may be observed by references to Figure 1. Still further, the aggregate areas of their cross sections is approximately equal to the area of the cross sections of the several resulting yosemites, just as the cross section of a tree trunk is about equal to the sum of the sections of its branches. *Furthermore, the trend of yosemite valleys is always a direct resultant of the sizes, directions, and declivities of their confluent canyons,* modified by peculiarities of structure in their rocks. Now, all the canyons mentioned above are the abandoned channels of glaciers; therefore, these yosemites and their glaciers are inseparably related. Instead of being local in character, or formed by obscure and lawless forces, *these valleys are the only great sculpture phenomena whose existence and exact positions we may confidently anticipate.*

Much stress has been laid on the mere uncompared arithmetical depth of Yosemite, but this is a character of no consequence to the consideration of its origin. The greatest Merced yosemite is 3000 feet deep; the Tuolumne, 2000; another, 1000; but what geologist would be so unphilosophical as to decide against the identity of their origin from difference in depth only. One pine tree is 100 feet high, lean and crooked, from repressing winds and the poverty of the soil which nourished it; while another, more fortunate in the conditions of its life, is 200 feet high, erect and vigorous. So, also, one yosemite is 3000 feet deep, because of the favorable structure of its rocks and the depth and number of the ice rivers that excavated it; another is half as deep, because of the strength of its rocks, or the scantiness of the glacial force exerted upon it. What would be thought of a botanist who should announce that our gigantic sequoia was not a tree at all, offering as a reason that it was too large for a tree, and, in describing it, should confine himself to some particularly knotty portion of the trunk? In Yosemite there is an evergreen oak double the size of ordinary oaks of the region, whose trunk is craggy and angular as the valley itself, and colored like the granite boulders on which it is growing. At a little distance this trunk would scarcely be recognized as part of a tree, until viewed in relation to its branches, leaves, and fruit. It is an admirable type of the craggy Merced canyon tree, whose angular yosemite does not appear as a natural portion thereof until viewed in its relation to its wide-spreading branches, with their fruit and foliage of meadow and lake.

We present a ground plan of three yosemite valleys, showing the positions of their principal glaciers, and the relation of their trends and areas to them. The large arrows in Figures 1, 2, 3, show the positions and directions of movement of the main confluent glaciers concerned in the erosion of three yosemites. With regard to the number of their main glaciers, the Tuolumne yosemite may be called a yosemite of the *third* power; the Kings River yosemite, of the fourth power; and the Merced yosemite, of the fifth power. The granite in which each of these three yosemites is excavated is of the same general quality; therefore, the differences of width, depth, and trend observed, are due almost entirely to the number, magnitude, declivity and mode of combination of the glacial system of each. The similarity of their ground plans is obvious

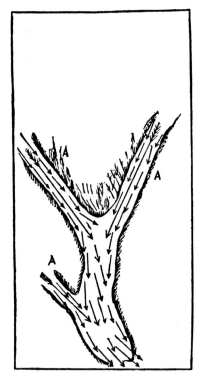

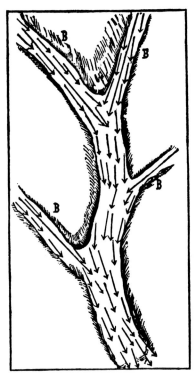

FIG. 1 *Tuolumne Yosemite.*   Fig. 2 *Kings River Yosemite.*
      (*AAA, Glaciers*)   (*B B B B, Glaciers*)

from a single glance at the figures; their cross sections are no less similar. One of the most characteristic from each of the valleys under consideration is shown in Figures 4, 5, and 6, drawn on the same scale.

The perpendicularity of yosemite walls is apt to be greatly overestimated. If the slopes of the Merced yosemite walls were to be carefully measured with a clinometer at intervals of say 100 yards, it would be found that the average angle they make with the horizon is less than 50 degrees, as shown in Figure 7. It is not possible that the bottom could drop out of a valley thus shaped, no matter how great the upheaval or down-heaval, or side-heaval.

Having shown that Yosemite, so-called, is not unique in its ground plan or cross sections, we will now consider some of the most remarkable of its rock forms. The beautiful San Joaquin Dome in the canyon of the San

FIG. 3 *Merced Yosemite glaciers.*
(A, Yosemite Creek;
B, Hoffmann; C, Tenaya;
D, South Lyell; E. Illilouette;
F, Pohono)

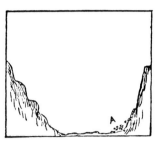

FIG. 4 *Section across the*
Hetch Hetchy Valley,
or lower Tuolumne Yosemite

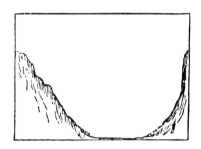

FIG. 5 *Section across the*
Kings River Yosemite

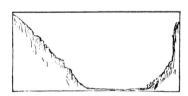

FIG. 6 *Section across*
Merced Yosemite

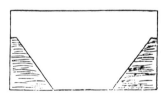

FIG. 7 *Idealized section across*
Merced Yosemite

Joaquin, near the confluence of the South Fork, looking south (Figure 9), shows remarkable resemblance to the Yosemite Half Dome, as seen from Tenaya Canyon (Figure 8). They are similarly situated with reference to the glaciers that denuded them, Half Dome having been assailed by the combined Tenaya and Hoffman glaciers, on the one side, and by the South Lyell or Merced Glacier on the other; the San Joaquin Dome, by the combined glaciers of the Middle and North forks, on one side, and by the glaciers of the South Fork on the other. The split dome of Kings River yosemite is a worthy counterpart of the great Half Dome of the Merced yosemite. They occur at about the same elevation, and are similarly situated with reference to the ancient glacial currents, which first overswept them and then guided heavily by on either side, breaking them up in chips and slabs, until fashioned and sculptured to their present condition. The Half Dome is usually regarded as being the most mysterious and unique rock form in the valley, or, indeed, in the world, yet when closely approached and studied, its history becomes plain.

FIG. 8   FIG. 9

From A to B, Figure 10, the height is about 1800 feet; from A to the base, 3000. The upper portion is almost absolutely plain and vertical, the lower is inclined at an angle with the horizon of about 37 degrees. The observer may ascend from the south side to the shoulder of the dome at D, and descend along the face toward A H. In the notch at F a section of the dome may be seen, showing that it is there made up of immense slabs set on edge. These evidently have been produced by the development of cleavage planes, which, cutting the dome perpendicularly, have determined the plane of its face, which is the most striking characteristic of the rock. Along the front toward A H may be seen the stumps of slabs which have been successively split off the face. At H may be seen the edges of residual fragments of the same slabs. At the summit, we perceive the cut edges of the concentric layers which have given the curved dome outline, B B. At D, a small gable appears, which has been produced by the development of diagonal cleavage planes which have been cut in front by vertical planes. After the passage of the main Tenaya Glacier in the direction of the arrows, small glacierets seem to have flowed down in front, eroding shallow groove channels in the direction of greatest declivity; and even before the total recession of the main glacier a wing-shaped ice slope probably leaned back in the shadow, and with slow action eroded the upper portion of the dome. All the rocks forming the south walls of deep yosemite canyons exhibit more or less of this light after-sculpture, effected in the shade after the north sun-beaten rocks were finished.

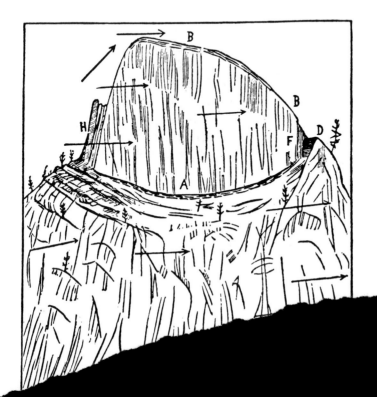

The south side of the dome has been heavily moutonéed by the Lyell Glacier, but is, nevertheless, nearly as vertical as the north split side. The main body of the rock corresponds in form and attitude with every other rock similarly situated with reference to ice rivers, and to elevation above sea level, the special split dome-top being, as we have seen, a result of special structure in the granite out of which it was formed. Numerous examples of this interesting species of rock may be culled from the various yosemites, illustrating every essential character on a gradually changing scale.

ace of Half Dome of Kings River Yosemite Valley

Half Dome, Yosemite,
El Capitan of
Capitan

FIG. 12

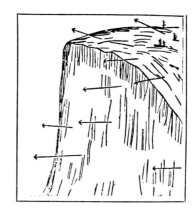

FIG. 13

FIG. 14

FIG. 15

The far-famed El Capitan rock presents a sheer cleaved front, over three thousand feet high, and is scarcely less impressive than the great dome. We have collected fine specimens of this clearly defined rock form from all the principal yosemites of the region. Nevertheless, it also has been considered exceptional. Their origin is easily explained. They are simply *split ends of ridges which have been broken through by glaciers.*

For their perfect development the granite must be strong, and have some of its vertical cleavage planes well developed, nearly to the exclusion of all the others, especially of those belonging to the diagonal and horizontal series. A powerful trunk glacier must sweep past in front nearly in the direction of its cutting planes, with small glaciers, tributary to the first, one on each side of the ridge out of which the Capitan is to be made.

This arrangement is illustrated in Figure 16, where A represents a horizontal section of a Capitan rock, exposing the edges of the cleavage planes which determined the characters of its face; B, the main glacier sweeping down the valley in front; and C C, the tributaries isolating it from the adjacent softer granite. The three Capitans figured stand thus related to the glaciers of the region where they are found. I have met with many others, all of which are thus situated, though in some instances one or both of the side glaciers had been wanting, leaving the resulting Capitan less perfect, considering the bold advancing Yosemite Capitan as a typical form.

When the principal surface features of the Sierra were being blocked out, the main ice sheet was continuous and moved in a southerly direction, therefore the most perfect Capitans are invariably found on the north sides of valleys trending east and west.

To illustrate still further how fully the split fronts of rocks facing deep canyons have the angles at which they stand measured by their cleavage planes, we give two examples (Figures 17 and 18) of leaning fronts from the canyon of the North Fork of the San Joaquin River. Sentinel and Cathedral rocks also are found in other glacial canyons, and in every instance their forms, magnitudes, and positions are obviously the necessary results of the internal structure and general mechanical characters of the rocks out of which they were made, and of the glacial energy that has been brought to bear on them. The abundance, therefore, of lofty angular rocks, instead of rendering Yosemite unique, is the characteristic which unites it most intimately with all the other similarly situated valleys in the range.

"Studies in the Sierra, No. II,"
The Overland Monthly, June 1874

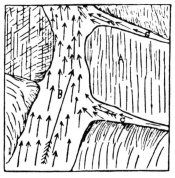

Fig. 16

Fig. 17

Fig. 18

5. ORIGIN OF THE PEAKS

"Patient observation and constant brooding above the rocks, lying upon them for years as the ice did, is the way to arrive at the truths which are graven so lavishly upon them," Muir said in one of his letters to Mrs. Carr. When he wrote the seven articles for The Overland Monthly *which comprised his "Studies in the Sierra," he had brooded for five years and arrived at the truths which were to upset Whitney's stubbornly held theories of cataclysm and subsidence. The amateur geologist, lacking even a bachelor's degree, had applied his powers of imagination, observation, and logic to better effect than the professional.*

Years later other investigations, including the definitive work of François E. Matthes, both in Yosemite and Sequoia national parks, sharpened and clarified knowledge of the role of glaciers and other forces in shaping the mountains we call the Sierra Nevada. Nevertheless, Muir's contribution was most significant. Fritiof Fryxell has written that he was "more intimately familiar with the facts and more nearly right in their interpretation than any professional geologist of his time."

This final paper in the Overland *series, in abstract form, was read by Professor Asa Gray at the August 1874 meeting of the American Association for the Advancement of Science under the title "Studies in the Formation of Mountains in the Sierra Nevada. California."*

Glaciated rock detail,
Horseshoe Lakes Basin,
Kings Canyon National Park

Middle Fork of the Kings Canyon from Windy Ridge, Kings Canyon National Park

This study of mountain building refers particularly to that portion of the range embraced between latitudes 36° 30′ and 39°. It is about 200 miles long, sixty wide, and attains an elevation along its axis of from 8000 to nearly 15,000 feet above the level of the sea. The individual mountains that are distributed over this vast area, whether the lofty and precipitous alps of the summit, the more beautiful and highly specialized domes and mounts dotted over the undulating flanks, or the huge bosses and angles projecting horizontally from the sides of canyons and valleys, have all been sculptured and brought into relief during the glacial epoch by the direct mechanical action of the ice sheet, with the individual glaciers into which it afterward separated. Our way to a general understanding of all this has been made clear by previous studies of valley formations— studies of the physical characters of the rocks out of which the mountains under consideration have been made, and of the widely contrasted methods and quantities of glacial and post-glacial denudation.

Notwithstanding the accessibility and imposing grandeur of the summit alps, they remain almost wholly unexplored. A few nervous raids have been made among them from random points adjacent to trails, and some of the more easily accessible, such as mounts Dana, Lyell, Tyndall, and Whitney, have been ascended, while the vast wilderness of mountains in whose fastnesses the chief tributaries of the San Joaquin and Kings rivers take their rise, have been beheld and mapped from a distance, without any attempt at detail. Their echoes are never stirred even by the hunter's rifle, for there is no game to tempt either Indian or white man as far as the frosty lakes and meadows that lie at their bases, while their avalanche-swept and crevassed glaciers, their labyrinths of yawning gulfs and crumbling precipices, offer dangers that only powerful motives will induce anyone to face.

The view southward from the colossal summit of Mount Humphreys[1] is indescribably sublime. Innumerable gray peaks crowd loftily into the keen azure, infinitely adorned with light and shade; lakes glow in lavish abundance around their bases; torrents whiten their denuded gorges; while many a glacier and bank of fountain *névé* leans back in their dark recesses. Awe-inspiring, however, as these vast mountain assemblies are, and incomprehensible as they may at first seem, their origin and the principal facts of their individual histories are problems easily solved by the patient student.

[1] The peak Muir had climbed the previous year was probably in the Evolution group south of Humphreys.

Beginning with pinnacles, which are the smallest of the summit mountainets: no geologist will claim that these were formed by special upheavals, nor that the little chasms which separated them were formed by special subsidences or rivings asunder of the rock; because many of these chasms are as wide at the bottom as at the top, and scarcely exceed a foot in depth; and many may be formed artificially by simply removing a few blocks that have been loosened.

The Sierra pinnacles are from less than a foot to nearly a thousand feet in height, and in all the cases that have come under my observation their forms and dimensions have been determined, not by cataclysmic fissures, but by the gradual development of orderly joints and cleavage planes, which gave rise to leaning forms where the divisional planes are inclined, as in Figure 19, or to vertical where the planes are vertical, as in Figure 20. Magnificent crests tipped with leaning pinnacles adorn the jagged flanks of Mount Ritter, and majestic examples of vertical pinnacle architecture abound among the lofty mountain cathedrals on the heads of Kings and Kern rivers. The Minarets to the south of Mount Ritter are an imposing series of partially separate pinnacles about 700 feet in height, set upon the main axis of the range. Glaciers are still grinding their eastern bases, illustrating in the plainest manner the blocking out of these imposing features from the solid. The formation of small peaklets that roughen the flanks of large peaks may in like manner be shown to depend, not upon any up-thrusting or down-thrusting forces, but upon the orderly erosion and transportation of the material that occupied the intervening notches and gorges.

FIG. 19

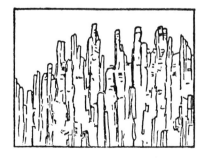

FIG. 20

The same arguments we have been applying to peaklets and pinnacles are found to be entirely applicable to the main mountain peaks; for careful detailed studies demonstrate that as pinnacles are separated by eroded chasms, and peaklets by notches and gorges, so the main peaks are separated by larger chasms, notches, gorges, valleys, and wide ice-womb amphitheaters. When across hollows we examine contiguous sides of mountains, we perceive that the same mechanical structure is continued across intervening spaces of every kind, showing that there has been a removal of the material that once filled them—the occurrence of large veins oftentimes rendering this portion of the argument exceedingly conclusive, as in two peaks of the Lyell group (Figure 21), where the wide veins, N N, are continued across the valley from peak to peak. We frequently find rows of pinnacles set upon a base, the cleavage of which does not admit of pinnacle formation, and in an analogous way we find immense slate mountains, like Dana and Gibbs, resting upon a plain granite pavement, as if they had been formed elsewhere, transported and set down in their present positions, like huge erratic boulders. It appears, therefore, that the loftiest mountains as well as peaklets and pinnacles of the summit region are residual masses of the once solid wave of the whole range, and that all that would be required to unbuild and obliterate these imposing structures would simply be the filling up of the labyrinth of intervening chasms, gorges, canyons, etc., which divide them, by the restoration of rocks that have disappeared. Here the important question comes up, What has become of the missing material, not the millionth part of which is now to be seen? It has not been engulfed, because the bottoms of all the dividing valleys and basins are unmistakably solid. It must, therefore, have been carried away; and because we find portions of it scattered far and near

Fig. 21

in moraines, easily recognized by peculiarities of mineralogical composition, we infer that glaciers were the transporting agents. That glaciers have brought out the summit peaks from the solid with all their imposing architecture, simply by the formation of the valleys and basins in which they flowed, is a very important proposition, and well deserves careful attention.

We have already shown that all the valleys of the region under consideration, from the minute striae and scratches of the polished surfaces less than the hundredth part of an inch in depth, to the yosemite gorges half a mile or more in depth, were all eroded by glaciers, and that post-glacial streams, whether small glancing brooklets or impetuous torrents, had not yet lived long enough to fairly make their mark, no matter how unbounded their eroding powers may be. Still, it may be conjectured that pre-glacial rivers furrowed the range long ere a glacier was born, and that when at length the ice winter came on with its great skyfuls of snow, the young glaciers crept into these river channels, overflowing their banks, and deepening, widening, grooving, and polishing them without destroying their identity. For the destruction of this conjecture it is only necessary to observe that the trends of the present valleys are strictly glacial, and glacial trends are extremely different from water trends; pre-glacial rivers could not, therefore, have exercised any appreciable influence upon their formation.

Neither can we suppose fissures to have wielded any determining influence, there being no conceivable coincidence between the zigzag and apparently accidental trends of fissures and the exceedingly specific trends of ice currents. The same argument holds good against primary foldings of the crust, dislocations, etc. Finally, if these valleys had been hewn or dug out by any pre-glacial agent whatever, traces of such agent would be visible on mountain masses which glaciers have not yet segregated; but no such traces of valley beginnings are anywhere manifest. The heads of valleys extend back into mountain masses just as far as glaciers have gone and no farther.

Granting, then, that the greater part of the erosion and transportation of the material missing from between the mountains of the summit was effected by glaciers, it yet remains to be considered what agent or agents shaped the upper portions of these mountains, which bear no traces of glacial action, and which probably were always, as they now are, above the reach of glaciers. Even here we find the glacier to be indirectly the most influential agent, constantly eroding backward, thus undermining their bases, and enabling gravity to drag down large masses, and giving greater effectiveness to the winter avalanches that sweep and furrow their sides.

All the summit peaks present a crumbling, ruinous, unfinished aspect. Yet they have suffered very little change since the close of the glacial period, for if denudation had been extensively carried on, their separating pits and gorges would be choked with debris; but, on the contrary, we find only a mere sprinkling of post-glacial detritus, and that the streams could not have carried much of this away is conclusively shown by the fact that the small lake bowls through which they flow have not been filled up . . .

Mount Ritter lies a few miles to the south of Lyell and is readily accessible to good mountaineers by way of the Mono plains. The student of mountain-building will find it a kind of textbook, abounding in wonderfully clear and beautiful illustrations of the principles of Sierra architecture we have been studying. Upon the north flank a small active glacier may still be seen at work blocking out and separating a peak from the main mass, and its whole surface is covered with clearly cut inscriptions of the frost, the storm wind, and the avalanche. Though not the very loftiest, Ritter is to me far the noblest mountain of the chain. All its neighbors stand well back, enabling it to give full expression to its commanding individuality; while living glaciers, rushing torrents, bright-eyed lakes, gentian meadows; flecks of lily and anemone, shaggy thickets and groves, and polleny zones of sun-filled *compositae,* combine to irradiate its massive features, and make it as beautiful as noble . . .

The truly magnificent group of nameless granite mountains stretching in a broad swath from the base of Mount Humphreys forty miles southward, is far the largest and loftiest of the range. But when we leisurely penetrate its wild recesses, we speedily perceive that, although abounding in peaks 14,000 feet high, these, individually considered, are mere pyramids, 1000 or 2000 feet in height, crowded together upon a common base, and united by jagged columns that swoop in irregular curves from shoulder to shoulder. That all this imposing multitude of mountains was chiseled from one grand pre-glacial mass is everywhere proclaimed in terms understandable by mere children.

Mount Whitney lies a few miles to the south of this group, and is undoubtedly the highest peak of the chain, but, geologically or even scenically considered, it possesses no special importance. When beheld either from the north or south, it presents the form of a helmet, or, more exactly, that of the Scotch cap called the "Glengarry." The flattish summit curves gently toward the valley of the Kern on the west, but falls abruptly toward Owens River Valley on the east, in a sheer precipice near 2000 feet deep. Its north and southeast sides are scarcely less precipitous, but these gradually yield to accessible slopes, round from southwest to northwest. Although highest of all the peaks, Mount Whitney is far surpassed in colossal grandeur and general impressiveness of physiognomy, not only by Mount Ritter, but by mounts Dana, Humphreys, Emerson, and many others that are nameless. A few meadowless lakes shine around its base, but it possesses no glaciers, and, toward the end of summer, very little snow on its north side, and none at all on the south. Viewed from Owens Valley, in the vicinity of Lone Pine, it appears as one of many minute peaklets that adorn the massive uplift of the range like a cornice. Toward the close of the glacial epoch, the gray porphyritic summit of what is now Mount Whitney peered a few feet above a zone of *névé* that fed glaciers which descended into the valleys of the Owens and Kern rivers. These, eroding gradually deeper, brought all that specially belongs to Mount Whitney into relief. Instead of a vast upheaval, it is merely a remnant of the common mass of the range, which, from relative conditions of structure and position, has suffered a little less degradation than the portions circumjacent to it.

Regarded as measures of mountain-building forces, the results of erosion are negative rather than positive, expressing more directly what has *not* been done than what *has* been done. The difference between the peaks and the passes is not that the former are elevations, the latter depressions; both are depressions, differing only in degree. The abasement of the peaks having been effected at a slower rate, they were, of course, left behind as elevations.

The transition from the spiky, angular summit mountains to those of the flanks with their smoothly undulated outlines is exceedingly well marked; weak towers, pinnacles, and crumbling, jagged crests at once disappear, leaving only hard, knotty domes and ridge waves as geological illustrations, on the grandest scale, of the survival of the strongest.

Figure 22 illustrates, by a section, the general cause of the angularity of summit mountains, and curvedness of those of the flanks; the former

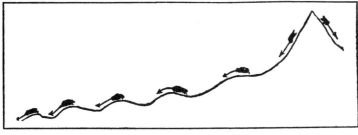

Fig. 22

having been *down*-flowed, the latter *over*-flowed. As we descend from the alpine summits on the smooth pathways of the ancient ice currents, noting where they have successively denuded the various rocks—first the slates, then the slaty-structured granites, then the curved granites—we detect a constant growth of specialization and ascent into higher forms. Angular masses, cut by cleavage planes, begin to be comprehended in flowing curves. These masses, in turn, become more highly organized, giving rise by the most gradual approaches to that magnificent dome scenery for which the Sierra is unrivaled. In the more strongly specialized granite regions, the features, and, indeed, the very existence, of the over-flowed mountains are in great part due neither to ice, water, nor any eroding agent whatsoever, but to building forces—crystalline, perhaps—which put them together and bestowed all that is more special in their architectural physiognomy, while they yet lay buried in the common fountain mass of the range.

The same silent and invisible mountain builders performed a considerable amount of work upon the down-flowed mountains of the summit, but these were so weakly put together that the heavy hand of the glacier shaped and molded, without yielding much compliance to their undeveloped forms. Had the unsculptured mass of the range been every way homogeneous, glacial denudation would still have produced summit mountains, differing not essentially from those we now find, but the rich profusion of flank mountains and mountainets, so marvelously individualized, would have had no existence, as the whole surface would evidently have been planed down into barren uniformity.

Thus the want of individuality which we have been observing among the summit mountains is obviously due to the comparatively uniform structure and erodibility of the rocks out of which they have been developed; their forms in consequence being greatly dependent upon the developing glaciers; whereas the strongly structured and specialized flank mountains, while accepting the ice currents as developers, still defended themselves from their destructive and form-bestowing effects.

The wonderful adaptability of ice to the development of buried mountains, possessing so wide a range of form and magnitude, seems as perfect as if the result of direct plan and forethought. Granite crystallizes into landscapes; snow crystallizes above them to bring their beauty to the light. The grain of no mountain oak is more gnarled and interfolded than that of Sierra granite, and the ice sheet of the glacial period is the only universal mountain eroder that works with reference to the grain. Here it smooths a pavement by slipping flatly over it, removing inequalities like a carpenter's plane; again it *makes* inequalities, gliding moldingly over and around knotty dome clusters, groping out every weak spot, sparing the strong, crushing the feeble, and following lines of predestined beauty obediently as the wind.

Rocks are brought into horizontal relief on the sides of valleys wherever superior strength of structure or advantageousness of position admits of such development, just as they are elsewhere in a vertical direction. Some of these projections are of a magnitude that well deserves the name of *horizontal mountain*. That the variability of resistance of the rocks themselves accounts for the variety of these horizontal features is shown by the prevalence of this law. *Where the uniformity of glacial pressure has not been disturbed by the entrance of tributaries, we find that where valleys are narrowest their walls are strongest; where widest, weakest.*

In the case of valleys with sloping walls, their salient features will be mostly developed in an oblique direction; but neither horizontal nor oblique mountainets or mountains can ever reach as great dimensions as the vertical, because the retreating curves formed in weaker portions of valley walls are less eroded the deeper they become, on account of receiving less and less pressure, while the alternating salient curves are more heavily pressed and eroded the farther they project into the past-squeezing glacier; thus tending to check irregularity of surface beyond a certain limit, which limit is measured by the resistance offered by the rocks to the glacial energy brought to bear upon them. So intense is this energy in the case of large steeply inclined glaciers, that many salient bosses are broken off on the lower or downstream side with a fracture like that produced by blasting. These fractures occur in all deep yosemite canyons, forming the highest expressions of the intensity of glacial force I have observed.

The same tendency toward maintaining evenness of surface obtains to some extent in vertical erosion also; as when hard masses rise abruptly from a comparatively level area exposed to the full sweep of the over-passing current. If vertical cleavage be developed in such rocks, mouton-néed forms will be produced with a split face turned away from the direction of the flow. These forms, measuring from a few inches to a thousand feet or more in height, abound in hard granitic regions. If no cleavage be developed, then long ovals will be formed, with their greater diameters extended in the direction of the current. The general tendency, however, in vertical erosion is to make the valleys deeper and ridges relatively higher, the ice currents being constantly attracted to the valleys, causing erosion to go on at an accelerated rate, and drawn away from the resisting ridges until they emerge from the ice sheet and cease to be eroded; the law here applicable being, "to him that hath shall be given."

Thus it appears that, no matter how the pre-glacial mass of the range came into existence, all the separate mountains distributed over its surface between latitude 36° 30′ and 39°, whether the lofty alps of the summit, or richly sculptured dome clusters of the flank, or the burnished bosses and mountainets projecting from the sides of valleys—all owe their development to the ice sheet of the great winter and the separate glaciers into which it afterward separated. In all this sublime fulfillment there was no upbuilding, but a universal razing and dismantling, and of this every mountain and valley is the record and monument.

"Studies in the Sierra, No. VII,"
The Overland Monthly, January 1875

BIRDS, GARDENS, AND ANIMAL MOUNTAINEERS

. . . when the divine balanced beauty of the trees and flowers seemed to be reflected and doubled by all the onlooking rocks and streams as though they were mirrors, while they in turn were mirrored in every garden and grove.

1. FOREST DEPTHS

Years of "sauntering" in the Mariposa and other groves, and travels to the south including his long tour as far as Tule River in 1875, enabled Muir to create a rich texture of fact and feeling in his writings about the Big Trees. In this portion of the Sequoia chapter in Our National Parks *he recollects the flora and fauna and the march of the seasons under the forest roof.*

Little is to be learned in confused, hurried tourist trips, spending only a poor noisy hour in a branded grove with a guide. You should go looking and listening alone on long walks through the wild forests and groves in all the seasons of the year. In the spring the winds are balmy and sweet, blowing up and down over great beds of chaparral and through the woods now rich in softening balsam and rosin and the scent of steaming earth. The sky is mostly sunshine, oftentimes tempered by magnificent clouds, the breath of the sea built up into new mountain ranges, warm during the day, cool at night, good flower-opening weather. The young cones of the Big Trees are showing in clusters, their flower time already

Forest pond near San Joaquin River,
Minarets Wilderness Area

past, and here and there you may see the sprouting of their tiny seeds of the previous autumn, taking their first feeble hold of the ground and unpacking their tender whorls of cotyledon leaves. Then you will naturally be led on to consider their wonderful growth up and up through the mountain weather, now buried in snow bent and crinkled, now straightening in summer sunshine like uncoiling ferns, shooting eagerly aloft in youth's joyful prime, and towering serene and satisfied through countless years of calm and storm, the greatest of plants and all but immortal.

Under the huge trees up come the small plant people, putting forth fresh leaves and blossoming in such profusion that the hills and valleys would still seem gloriously rich and glad were all the grand trees away. By the side of melting snowbanks rise the crimson sarcodes, round-topped and massive as the sequoias themselves, and beds of blue violets and larger yellow ones with leaves curiously lobed; azalea and saxifrage, daisies and lilies on the mossy banks of the streams; and a little way back of them, beneath the trees and on sunny spots on the hills around the groves, wild rose and rubus, spiraea and ribes, mitella, tiarella, campanula, monardella, forget-me-not, etc., many of them as worthy of lore immortality as the famous Scotch daisy, wanting only a Burns to sing them home to all hearts.

In the midst of this glad plant work the birds are busy nesting, some singing at their work, some silent, others, especially the big pileated woodpeckers, about as noisy as backwoodsmen building their cabins. Then every bower in the groves is a bridal bower, the winds murmur softly overhead, the streams sing with the birds, while from far-off waterfalls and thunderclouds come deep rolling organ notes.

In summer the days go by in almost constant brightness, cloudless sunshine pouring over the forest roof, while in the shady depths there is the subdued light of perpetual morning. The new leaves and cones are growing fast and make a grand show, seeds are ripening, young birds learning to fly, and with myriads of insects glad as birds keep the air whirling, joy in every wingbeat, their humming and singing blending with the gentle ah-ing of the winds; while at evening every thicket and grove is enchanted by the tranquil chirping of the blessed hylas, the sweetest and most peaceful of sounds, telling the very heart-joy of earth as it rolls through the heavens.

In the autumn the sighing of the winds is softer than ever, the gentle ah-ah-ing filling the sky with a fine universal mist of music, the birds have little to say, and there is no appreciable stir or rustling among the trees save that caused by the harvesting squirrels. Most of the seeds are ripe and away, those of the trees mottling the sunny air, glinting, glancing through the midst of the merry insect people, rocks and trees, everything alike drenched in gold light, heaven's colors coming down to the meadows and groves, making every leaf a romance, air, earth, and water in peace beyond thought, the great brooding days opening and closing in divine psalms of color.

Winter comes suddenly, arrayed in storms, though to mountaineers silky streamers on the peaks and the tones of the wind give sufficient warning. You hear strange whisperings among the treetops, as if the giants were taking counsel together. One after another, nodding and swaying, calling and replying, spreads the news, until all with one accord break forth into glorious song, welcoming the first grand snowstorm of the year, and looming up in the dim clouds and snowdrifts like lighthouse towers in flying scud and spray. Studying the behavior of the giants from some friendly shelter, you will see that even in the glow of their wildest enthusiasm, when the storm roars loudest, they never lose their god-like composure, never toss their arms or bow or wave like the pines, but only slowly, solemnly nod and sway, standing erect, making no sign of strife, none of rest, neither in alliance nor at war with the winds, too calmly, unconsciously noble and strong to strive with or bid defiance to anything. Owing to the density of the leafy branchlets and great breadth of head the Big Tree carries a much heavier load of snow than any of its neighbors, and after a storm, when the sky clears, the laden trees are a glorious spectacle, worth any amount of cold camping to see. Every bossy limb and crown is solid white, and the immense height of the giants becomes visible as the eye travels the white steps of the colossal tower, each relieved by a mass of blue shadow.

In midwinter the forest depths are as fresh and pure as the crevasses and caves of glaciers. Grouse, nuthatches, a few woodpeckers, and other hardy birds dwell in the groves all winter, and the squirrels may be seen every clear day frisking about, lively as ever, tunneling to their stores, never coming up empty-mouthed, diving in the loose snow about as quickly as ducks in water, while storms and sunshine sing to each other.

One of the noblest and most beautiful of the late winter sights is the blossoming of the Big Tree like gigantic goldenrods and the sowing of their pollen over all the forest and the snow-covered ground—a most glorious view of Nature's immortal virility and flower love.

Our National Parks, 1901

2. A MEADOW GARDEN

As a naturalist Muir observed and wrote of a broad range of phenomena, but his first love was botany. The travels of his youth were in pursuit of flowers, ferns, and grasses, and his loathing for the domestic sheep was strongly motivated by the disastrous effects of their grazing on the wild flora of the Sierra. Some of his most lyric writing was devoted to glacier meadows and the flowering of herbs, heaths, and forest trees, which he never failed to note in his journals and letters.

This characteristic meadow scene is from one of his early newspaper reports.

South Fork of Kings River

We camped on the riverbank a mile or two up the valley near a small circular meadow, that is one of the most perfect and downright flower gardens I have ever discovered in the mountains. The trampling mules, whom I would fain have kept out, fairly disappeared beneath the broad, overarching ferns that encircled the garden proper. It was filled with lilies and violets, and orchids, and sun-loving goldenrods and asters, and oenothera, and purple geraniums, and epilobium, with a hundred others all in bloom, but whose names no one would read, though all the world would love to revel in their beauty as they grow. One of the tiger lilies that I measured was six feet long, and had eleven open flowers, five of them in prime beauty. The wind rocked this splendid orange panicle above the heads of the geraniums and brier roses, forming a spectacle of pure beauty exquisitely poised and harmonized in all its parts. It was as if nature had fingered every leaf and petal that very day, readjusting every curve, and touching the colors of every corolla . . . Many other wild gardens occur along the riverbank, and in cool side dells where a stream comes out of a canyon, but neither at this time nor during my former visit to the valley were any discovered so perfect as this one. The lower half of the valley consists of sugar-pine groves divided by sunny park-like openings on which manzanita and several species of ceanothus form a scanty covering. Some of these openings are dry and gravelly and grow fine crops of monardella for the bees, together with eriogonae and the most sun-loving compositae for butterfly and hummingbird pastures. Toward the upper end of the valley there is quite an extensive meadow that reaches from wall to wall. The riverbank, groves and borders are made up chiefly of alder, poplar and willow, and a rich measure of azalea, brier rose and wild honeysuckle, all combined with reference to the best beauty, and to the special wants of the wide crystal river.

San Francisco *Daily Evening Bulletin,*
August 13, 1875

3. TROUT

"If I were limited to just one more fishing trip," wrote Charles McDermand, "I would want it to be there"—on the South Fork of the Kings River. But Muir, who could be infinitely patient in his transactions with deer, wild sheep, squirrels, and birds, seems never to have been tempted to stand by a stream and cast a lure for fish. Nor did he carry a gun, although he accepted meat from hunters and was not above eating bear muffins and bear flapjacks when there was bear oil. As he predicted so tolerantly, all the streams of the Sierra and most of the lakes have been stocked with trout. They catch thousands of us every year.

None of the high-lying mountain lakes or branches of the rivers above sheer falls had fish of any sort until stocked by the agency of man. In the high Sierra, the only river in which trout exist naturally is the Middle Fork of Kings River. There are no sheer falls on this stream; some of the rapids, however, are so swift and rough, even at the lowest stage of water, that it is surprising any fish can climb them. I found trout in abundance in this fork up to seventy-five hundred feet. They also run quite high on the Kern. On the Merced they get no higher than Yosemite Valley, four thousand feet, all the forks of the river being barred there by sheer falls, and on the main Tuolumne they are stopped by a fall below Hetch Hetchy, still lower than Yosemite. Though these upper waters are inaccessible to the fish, one would suppose their eggs might have been planted there by some means. Nature has so many ways of doing such things. In this case she waited for the agency of man, and now many of these hitherto fishless lakes and streams are full of fine trout, stocked by individual enterprise, Walton clubs, etc., in great part under the auspices of the United States Fish Commission. A few trout carried into Hetch Hetchy in a common water bucket have multiplied wonderfully fast. Lake Tenaya, at an elevation of over eight thousand feet, was stocked eight years ago by Mr. Murphy, who carried a few trout from Yosemite. Many of the small streams of the eastern slope have also been stocked with trout transported over the passes in tin cans on the backs of mules. Soon, it would seem, all the streams of the range will be enriched by these lively fish, and will become the means of drawing thousands of visitors into the mountains. Catching trout with a bit of bent wire is a rather trivial business, but fortunately people fish better than they know. In most cases it is the man who is caught. Trout fishing regarded as bait for catching men, for the saving of both body and soul, is important, and deserves all the expense and care bestowed on it.

Our National Parks, 1901

4. BEAR AND DEER

The black bear (Ursus americanus) *which forages in our parks and forests, all too often among the debris left by campers, was well known to Muir. In his day so were bear hunters, and he sometimes shared their kill. Occasionally he saw one of the grizzlies, that more fearsome species which is honored in the state flag but has since become extinct in California.*

The mule deer (Odocoileus hemionus californicus) *is still common and attracts both hunters and tourists. Few of the latter, however, unless they camp in wilderness and practice the art of quiet observation, ever enjoy such an experience of communion with this ruminative animal as Muir describes here.*

Just before sundown I reached a charming campground, with new sequoias to study and sleep beneath. It was evidently a well-known and

favorite resort of bears, which are always wise enough to choose homes
in charming woods where they are secure, and have the luxury of cool
meadow patches to wallow in, and clover to eat, and plenty of acid ants,
wasps, and pine nuts in their season. The bark of many of the trees was
furrowed picturesquely by their matchless paws, where they had stood
up stretching their limbs like cats. Their tracks were fresh along the
streamside, and I half expected to see them resting beneath the brown
trunks, or standing on some prostrate log snuffing and listening to learn
the nature of the disturbance. Brownie listened and looked cautiously
around, as if doubting whether the place were safe. All mules have the
fear of bears before their eyes, and are marvelously acute in detecting
them, either by night or day. No dog can scent a bear farther, and as long,
therefore, as your mule rests quietly in a bear region, you need have no
fears of their approach. But when bears *do* come into camp, mules
tethered by a rope too strong to break are not infrequently killed in trying
to run away. Guarding against this danger, I usually tie to an elastic
sapling, so as to diminish the shock in case of a stampede, and perhaps
thus prevent either neck or rope from breaking.

The starry night circled away in profound calm, and I lay steeped in
its weird beauty, notwithstanding the growing danger of being snowbound,
and feeling more than commonly happy, for while climbing the river
canyon I had made a fine geological discovery concerning the formation
and origin of the quartz sands of the great "dead river" deposits of the
northern Sierra.

Two days beyond this bear dell I enjoyed a very charming meeting
with a group of deer in one of nature's most sequestered gardens—a spot
never, perhaps, neared by human foot.

The garden lies high on the northern cliffs of the South Fork. The
Kaweah goes foaming past 2000 feet below, while the sequoia forest
rises shadowy along the ridge on the north. It is only about half an acre
in size, full of goldenrods and eriogonae and tall vase-like tufts of waving
grasses with silky panicles, not crowded like a field of grain, but planted
wide apart among the flowers, each tuft with plenty of space to manifest
its own loveliness both in form and color and wind-waving, while the
plantless spots between are covered with dry leaves and burrs, making
a fine brown ground for both grasses and flowers. The whole is fenced
in by a close hedge-like growth of wild cherry, mingled with California
lilac and glossy evergreen manzanita, not drawn around in strict lines,
but waving in and out in a succession of bays and swelling bosses exquisitely painted with the best Indian summer light, and making a perfect

Sixty Lakes Basin, Kings Canyon National Park

paradise of color. I found a small silver fir nearby, from which I cut plushy boughs for a bed, and spent a delightful night sleeping away all canyon-climbing weariness.

Next morning shortly after sunrise, just as the light was beginning to come streaming through the trees, while I lay leaning on my elbow taking my bread and tea, and looking down across the canyon, tracing the dip of the granite headlands, and trying to plan a way to the river at a point likely to be fordable, suddenly I caught the big bright eyes of a deer gazing at me through the garden hedge. The expressive eyes, the slim black-tipped muzzle, and the large ears were as perfectly visible as if placed there at just the right distance to be seen, like a picture on a wall. She continued to gaze, while I gazed back with equal steadiness, motionless as a rock. In a few minutes she ventured forward a step, exposing her fine arching neck and forelegs, then snorted and withdrew.

This alone was a fine picture—the beautiful eyes framed in colored cherry leaves, the topmost sprays lightly atremble, and just glanced by the level sunrays, all the rest in shadow.

But more anon. Gaining confidence, and evidently piqued by curiosity, the trembling sprays indicated her return, and her head came into view; then another and another step, and she stood wholly exposed inside the garden hedge, gazed eagerly around, and again withdrew, but returned a moment afterward, this time advancing into the middle of the garden; and behind her I noticed a second pair of eyes, not fixed on me, but on her companion in front, as if eagerly questioning, "What in the world do you see?" Then more rustling in the hedge, and another head came slipping past the second, the two heads touching; while the first came within a few steps of me, walking with inimitable grace, expressed in every limb. My picture was being enriched and enlivened every minute; but even this was not all. After another timid little snort, as if testing my good intentions, all three disappeared; but I was true, and my wild beauties emerged once more, one, two, three, four, slipping through the dense hedge without snapping a twig, and all four came forward into the garden, grouping themselves most picturesquely, moving, changing, lifting their smooth polished limbs with charming grace—the perfect embodiment of poetic form and motion. I have oftentimes remarked in meeting with deer under various circumstances that curiosity was sufficiently strong to carry them dangerously near hunters; but in this instance they seemed to have satisfied curiosity, and began to feel so much at ease in my company that they all commenced feeding in the garden—eating breakfast with me, like gentle sheep around a shepherd—while I observed keenly, to learn their gestures and what plants they fed on. They are

First State Lake, Kings Canyon National Park

very brink of a precipice, and, examining it, I found a deer bed beneath it, completely protected and concealed by drooping branches—a fine refuge and lookout as well as resting place. About an hour before dark I heard the clear, sharp snorting of a deer, and looking down on the brushy, rocky canyon bottom, discovered an anxious doe that no doubt had her fawns concealed nearby. She bounded over the chaparral and up the farther slope of the wall, often stopping to look back and listen— a fine picture of vivid, eager alertness. I sat perfectly still, and as my shirt was colored like the juniper bark I was not easily seen. After a little she came cautiously toward me, sniffing the air and grazing, and her movements, as she descended the canyon side over boulder piles and brush and fallen timber, were admirably strong and beautiful; she never strained or made apparent efforts, although jumping high here and there. As she drew nigh she sniffed anxiously, trying the air in different directions until she caught my scent; then bounded off, and vanished behind a small grove of firs. Soon she came back with the same caution and insatiable curiosity—coming and going five or six times. While I sat admiring her, a Douglas squirrel, evidently excited by her noisy alarms, climbed a boulder beneath me, and witnessed her performances as attentively as I did, while a frisky chipmunk, too restless or hungry for such shows, busied himself about his supper in a thicket of shad-bushes, the fruit of which was then ripe, glancing about on the slender twigs lightly as a sparrow.

Our National Parks, 1901

5. WILD SHEEP

John Muir earned his bread and mutton herding sheep in the San Joaquin Valley and the Sierra before he was able to support himself in Yosemite in other ways. His experience and observations led him to condemn the devastation wrought by the grazing of "hoofed locusts" and created a lifelong prejudice against the domestic sheep. When he encountered its wild cousin he was quick to contrast their qualities, both physical and spiritual, and to praise the proud bearing of the bighorn with which he identified so much of the mountaineer in himself.

The essay on the wild sheep, a portion of which follows, is one of the earliest he published. Although a bit textbookish, it contains an exciting account of Muir's adventure with a high-ranging band during the previous summer. An authoritative study of the survivors of this princely race, in 1948, showed only five remaining bands in the Sierra Nevada and none in the San Joaquin yosemite where Muir and Ovis canadensis *observed each other in 1873. The species can be found in other mountains and there are more exact descriptions, but Muir's intensely felt, first-person narrative tells us something not to be discovered in purely scientific writings. An essay on "Wild Wool," collected in* Steep Trails, *elaborates the transcendental theme of perfection in untamed nature.*

In California, the wild sheep ranks among the noblest of animal mountaineers. Possessed of keen sight, immovable nerve, and strong limbs, he dwells secure amid the loftiest summits of the Sierra, leaping unscathed from crag to crag, crossing foamy torrents and slopes of frozen snow, exposed to the wildest storms, yet maintaining a brave life, and developing from generation to generation in perfect strength and beauty. Compared with the Asian argali, which, considering its size and the vast extent of its range, is perhaps the most important of all the wild sheep, the horns of our species are more regularly curved and less divergent at the base and near the tips; moreover, the argali may not be quite so large, but their more important characters are essentially the same, some of the best naturalists maintaining that they are only varied forms of one species . . .

Compared with the best known domestic breeds, we find that our wild species is two or three times as large, full-grown specimens weighing from 200 to 350 pounds. Instead of wool, they are covered with a thick mattress of coarse hair, like that of the deer, with only a very little fine wool at the bottom; but, though coarse, this hair is soft and spongy, and lies smoothly, as if carefully tended with comb and brush. I have frequently observed some of the same kind of coarse hair mixed with the wool of Mexican sheep. The predominant color is brownish gray, varying somewhat with the seasons; the belly and a large conspicuous patch on the buttocks are white, and the tail, which is very short, is black, with a yellowish border. The horns of the male are of immense size, measuring in their greater diameter from five to six inches, and in length around the curve from two to three feet. They are yellowish white in color, and ridged transversely, like those of the domestic ram. Their cross section

*Cow parsnip, Giant Forest,
Sequoia National Park*

near the base is somewhat triangular in outline. In rising from the head
they curve gently backward and outward, then forward and outward,
until about three-fourths of a circle has been described, and until the
tips, which are flattened and blunt, are about two feet apart. Two specimens found last summer on the headwaters of the San Joaquin measured
as follows: Circumference at the base, 13½ and 16¼ inches; distance
across from tip to tip, 22 and 24 inches. Those of the female are more
flattened, less curved, and much smaller, measuring only six or seven
inches in length along the curve . . . Besides these differences in size,
color, and clothing, we might note that in form the domestic sheep is
expressionless, like a round bundle of something only half alive; the wild
is elegant as a deer, and every muscle glows with life. The tame is timid;
the wild is bold. The tame is always ruffled and soiled; the wild is trim
and clean as the flowers of its pasture . . .

A few of the more energetic of the Mono Indians hunt the sheep every
season among the slate summits between Castle Peak and Mount Lyell,
this section of the Sierra being comparatively easy of access, and here,
from having been pursued, they are now extremely wary; but farther
to the south, in the wilderness of snowy peaks where the many rugged
branches of the San Joaquin and Kings rivers take their rise, they fear
no hunter save the wolf, and are more guileless and approachable than
any of their tame kindred.

I have been greatly interested in studying their habits during the last
four years, while engaged in the work of exploring these high regions.
In spring and summer the males form separate bands. They are usually
met in small flocks, numbering from three to twenty, feeding along the
edges of glacier meadows, or resting among the castle-like crags of lofty
summits; and, whether feeding or resting, or scaling wild cliffs for pleasure, their noble forms, the very embodiment of muscular beauty, never
fail to strike the beholder with liveliest admiration. Their resting places
seem to be chosen with reference to sunshine and a wide outlook, and,
most of all, to safety from the attacks of wolves. Their feeding grounds
are among the most beautiful of the wild Sierra gardens, bright with
daisies and gentians, and mats of blooming shrubs. These are hidden
away high on the sides of rough canyons, where light is abundant, or
down in the valleys, along lake borders, and streambanks, where the
plushy turf is greenest, and the purple heather grows. Sweet grasses also
grow in these happy alpine gardens, but the wild sheep eats little besides
the spicy leaves and shoots of the various shrubs and bushes, perhaps

relishing both their taste and beauty, although tame men are slow to suspect wild sheep of seeing more than grass. When winter storms fall, decking their summer pastures in the lavish bloom of snow, then, like the bluebirds, and robins, our brave sheep gather and go to warmer climates, usually descending the eastern flank of the range to the narrow, birch-filled gorges that open into the sage plains, where snow never falls to any great depth, the elevation above the sea being about from 5000 to 7000 feet. Here they sojourn until spring sunshine unlocks the canyons and warms the pastures of their glorious Alps.

In the months of June and July[1] they bring forth their young, in the most solitary and inaccessible crags, far above the nest of the eagle. I have frequently come upon the beds of the ewes and lambs at an elevation of from 12,000 to 13,000 feet above sea level. These beds consist simply of an oval-shaped hollow, pawed out among loose disintegrating rock chips and sand, upon some sunny spot commanding a good outlook, and partially sheltered from the winds that sweep passionately across those lofty crags almost without intermission. Such is the cradle of the little mountaineer, aloft in the sky, rocked in storms, curtained in clouds, sleeping in thin, icy air; but wrapped in his hairy coat, nourished by a warm, strong mother, defended from the talons of the eagle and teeth of the sly coyote, the bonnie lamb grows apace. He learns to nibble the purple daisy and leaves of the white spiraea; his horns begin to shoot, and, ere summer is done, he is strong and agile, and goes forth with the flock, shepherded by the same Divine love that tends the more helpless human lamb in its warm cradle by the fireside.

Like the Alp-climbing ibex of Europe, our mountaineer is said to plunge fearlessly down the faces of sheer precipices, and alight on his huge elastic horns. I know only two hunters who claim to have witnessed this feat; I never was so fortunate. They describe the act as a diving head-foremost. Some of the horns that I have examined with reference to this question are certainly much battered in front, and are so large at the base that they cover all the upper portion of the head down nearly to a level with the eye; moreover, the skull of a wild sheep is stronger than a bull's. I struck an old bleached specimen on Mount Ritter a dozen blows with my ice ax without breaking it. Such skulls would not fracture very readily by the wildest rock-diving; but other bones might, and the numerous mechanical difficulties in the way of controlling the movements of their bodies after striking upon an irregular rock surface would seem

[1] Changed to "May and June" in the version which was published in *Scribner's Monthly* in 1881.

to make such a boulder-like method of progression improbable, even for the big-horned rams, much more for the ewes. Perhaps when a great leap is made they may endeavor to lighten the shock upon their legs, and assist in arresting farther progress, by striking their horns against any rock that may chance to be favorably situated for the purpose, just as men mountaineers do with their hands.

Nothing is more commonly remarked by travelers in the high Sierra than the absence of animal life; but if such would go singly, without haste or noise, away from the region of trails and pack trains, they would speedily learn that these mountain mansions are not without inhabitants, many of whom, confiding and gentle, would be glad to make their acquaintance. Last September, I was following the South Fork of the San Joaquin up its wild canyon to its farthest icy fountains. It was the season of mountain Indian summer. The sun beamed lovingly, squirrels were nutting amid the pine cones, butterflies hovered about the last of the goldenrods, willow and maple groves were yellow, the meadows were brown, and the whole mellow landscape glowed like a countenance with the deepest and sweetest repose. On my way along the rocky riverside, I came to a fine meadowy expansion of the canyon, about two miles long and half a mile wide, inclosed with picturesque granite walls like those of Yosemite, and with the river sweeping through its groves and meadows in magnificent curves. This little yosemite was full of wild life. Deer with their fawns constantly bounded from thicket to thicket as I advanced. Grouse kept rising from the brown grass with a great whirring of wings, and, alighting on low branches of the poplar or pine, allowed a near approach, as if pleased to be observed. A broad-shouldered wildcat showed himself, coming out of a grove and crossing the river upon a flood jam of logs. The bird-like tamias frisked about among pine needles and seedy grass tufts. Cranes waded the shallows of the river bends, the king-fisher rattled from perch to perch, and the blessed ouzel sung with the leaping spray of every cascade. Purple evening came as I lingered in the company of these mountain dwellers, and, as darkness fell, I awoke from their enchantment and sought a camping spot near the river. I slept among the yellow leaves of an aspen grove, and, pushing forward next morning, discovered yet grander landscapes and grander life. The scenery became more alpine. The lofty sugar pine and silver fir gave place to the hardier cedar and dwarf pine, the canyon walls became more jagged and bare, and gentians became more abundant in the gardens of the riverbank. In the afternoon, I came to a valley strikingly wild in all its features. As regards area of bottom, it is one of the very smallest of

San Joaquin yosemites; but its walls are sublime, rising from 2000 to 4000 feet above the river. At the head of the valley, the river forks, as is found to be the case in all yosemites. Its formation was accomplished by the action of two vast ice rivers, whose fountains were on the flanks of mounts Humphreys and Emerson, and mountains farther south.[2] On their recession at the close of the great winter, this valley basin became first a lake; then a sedgy meadow; then, filled with flood boulders and logs, and planted with bushes and grass, it became the yosemite of today—a range for wild sheep, whose tracks I saw printed everywhere along its briery lanes and gulches.

The chafed river sings loud on its way down the valley, but above its deafening songs I could hear the heavier booming of a waterfall, which caused me to push eagerly forward. Emerging from the tangled groves at the head of the valley, I beheld the young San Joaquin coming from its fountains in a glorious cascade. Scanning the steep incline down which the white waters thundered, I discovered a crooked seam, by which I climbed to the edge of a narrow terrace, which, crossing the canyon, divides the cascades nearly in the middle. Here I sat down to take breath and to make some entries in my notebook, taking advantage of my elevated position to gaze back down over the valley into the heart of the glorious landscape, little knowing the while what neighbors were near. Chancing to look across the cascade, there stood three wild sheep within a few yards, calmly observing me. Never did the sudden appearance of human friend, or mountain, or waterfall, so forcibly seize and rivet my attention. Anxiety to observe accurately on so rare an opportunity checked enthusiasm. Eagerly I marked the flowing undulations of their firm-braided limbs; their strong, straight legs, size, color, ears, eyes, heads; their graceful rounded necks, the upsweeping cycloidal curve of their noble horns. When they moved, I devoured every gesture; while they, in nowise disconcerted either by my attention or by the loud roar of the waters, advanced slowly up the rapids, often turning to look at me. Presently, they made a dash at a steep ice-polished incline, and reached the top without a struggle, by a succession of short, stiff leaps, bringing their hoofs down sharply with a patting sound. This was the most astounding feat of mountaineering I had ever witnessed. Just a few days previous, my cautious, iron-shod mules fell, on good rough ground, descending the canyonside in lawless avalanche; and many a time I have been compelled to tie my shoes and stockings to my belt, and creep up far easier slopes with the utmost caution. No wonder, then, I watched

[2] Not the present Humphreys and Emerson. Was this Evolution Valley?

the progress of these animal mountaineers with intensest sympathy, and exulted in the boundless sufficiency of wild nature displayed in their invention, construction, and keeping. But judge the measure of my over-joy when, a few moments later, I caught sight of a dozen more in one flock near the base of the upper cascade. They were on the same side of the river with me, distant only twenty-five or thirty yards, and looking as unworn, calm, and bright, as if created on the spot. It appears that when I came up the canyon, they were all feeding together in the valley, and in their haste to reach high ground, where they could look about them to ascertain the nature of the disturbance, they were divided, three having ascended on one side of the cascade, the rest on the other. The main flock, headed by an experienced chief, began to cross the rapids soon after I first observed them. The crossing of swift torrents on chance boulders is nerve-trying work even for men mountaineers, yet these shepherdless sheep leaped from boulder to boulder, and held themselves in perfect poise above the whirling current, as if doing nothing extraor-dinary. The immediate foreground of the rare picture before me was glossy ice-planed granite, traversed by seams in which grew rock ferns and tufts of heathy bryanthus, the gray canyon walls on both sides splendidly sculptured, and adorned with brown cedars and pines; in the distance, lofty mountains rising far into the thin blue sky; in the center, the snowy cascade, the voice and the soul of all, fringing shrubs waving time to its thunder tones; and in front, the brave sheep, their gray forms slightly obscured in the spray, yet firmly defined on the close, dense white of the cataract, their huge rough horns rising in the midst like upturned roots of dead pine trees—the setting sun lighting the canyon, purpling and glorifying all.

Fallen log by Glacier Lake,
Kings Canyon National Park

After crossing the river, the dauntless climbers, led by their chief, at once began to scale the canyon wall; now right, now left, in long single file, leaping in succession from cliff to cliff; now ascending slippery dome curves; now walking the edges of precipices, stopping at times to gaze down at me from some flat-topped rock, with heads held aslant, as if curious to find out whether I was about to follow. When they had reached the top of the wall, 1500 to 2000 feet high, I could still see their noble forms outlined on the sky as they lingered, looking down in groups of two or three, giving rare animation to the sublime cliffs. Throughout the whole ascent, I did not observe a single awkward step or unsuccessful effort. I have often seen tame sheep in the mountains jump upon a sloping rock surface, hold on tremulously a few seconds, and fall back baffled and irresolute; but in the most trying dangers, where the slightest inaccuracy would have resulted in destruction, these moved with magnificent reliance on their strength and skill, the limits of which they never seemed to know.

Moreover, each one of the flock, though acknowledging the right of leadership to the most experienced, climbed with intelligent independence—a perfect individual, capable of separate existence whenever it should choose to secede from the little clan. But the domestic sheep is only a fraction of an animal, a whole flock being required to form an individual, just as numerous florets are required for the making of one complete sunflower. Shepherds acquainted with mountain dangers, who in watching by night and day have beheld their feeble flocks broken by bears, crushed and disintegrated by storms, and scattered diverse in the rocks like wind-driven chaff, will in some measure appreciate the strong self-reliance and noble individuality of nature's sheep . . .

"The Wild Sheep of California,"
The Overland Monthly, April 1874

6. RODENTS AND ROCK RABBITS

A wilderness bachelor like Muir grows to depend on small, warm-blooded creatures for company. He particularly loved that "fiery, sputtering little bolt of life," the tamias or chickaree, which he said always cheered his lonely wanderings. There were other mammals, as well, not those he admired or respected for size, strength, or agility which rivaled his own, but lesser ones with which it was easier to feel a certain intimacy.

Every climber of the talus slopes comes to know the yellow-bellied marmot, the shaggy, slow-moving proprietor of the routes to the peaks. His tribe aroused Muir's fertile curiosity, as did those of the mountain beaver, pocket gopher, pika (or rock rabbit) and acquisitive wood rat. Muir's indulgent reception of the bushy-tailed, thieving neotoma, which threatened to carry away even his ice ax, shows how ready he was to find companionship in the most improbable corners of wild nature.

The woodchuck (*Arctomys monax*)[1] dwells on high bleak ridges and boulder piles; and a very different sort of mountaineer is he—bulky, fat, aldermanic, and fairly bloated at times by hearty indulgence in the lush pastures of his airy home. And yet he is by no means a dull animal. In the midst of what we regard as storm-beaten desolation, high in the frosty air, beside the glaciers he pipes and whistles right cheerily and lives to a good old age. If you are as early a riser as he is, you may oftentimes see him come blinking out of his burrow to meet the first beams of the morning and take a sunbath on some favorite flat-topped boulder. Afterward, well warmed, he goes to breakfast in one of his garden hollows, eats heartily like a cow in clover until comfortably swollen, then goes a-visiting, and plays and loves and fights . . .

In the spring of 1875, when I was exploring the peaks and glaciers about the head of the Middle Fork of the San Joaquin, I had crossed the range from the head of Owens River, and one morning, passing around a frozen lake where the snow was perhaps ten feet deep, I was surprised to find the fresh track of a woodchuck plainly marked, the sun having softened the surface. What could the animal be thinking of, coming out so early while all the ground was snow-buried? The steady trend of his track showed he had a definite aim, and fortunately it was toward a mountain thirteen thousand feet high that I meant to climb. So I followed to see if I could find out what he was up to. From the base of the mountain the track pointed straight up, and I knew by the melting snow that I was not far behind him. I lost the track on a crumbling ridge, partly projecting through the snow, but soon discovered it again. Well toward the summit of the mountain, in an open spot on the south side, nearly inclosed by disintegrating pinnacles among which the sun heat reverberated, making an isolated patch of warm climate, I found a nice garden, full of rock cress, phlox, silene, draba, etc., and a few grasses; and in this garden I overtook the wanderer, enjoying a fine fresh meal,

[1] Yellow-bellied marmot (*Marmota flaviventris*).

perhaps the first of the season. How did he know the way to this one
garden spot, so high and far off, and what told him that it was in bloom
while yet the snow was ten feet deep over his den? For this it would
seem he would need more botanical, topographical, and climatological
knowledge than most mountaineers are possessed of.

The shy, curious mountain beaver, haplodon,[2] lives on the heights,
not far from the woodchuck. He digs canals and controls the flow of small
streams under the sod. And it is startling when one is camped on the
edge of a sloping meadow near the homes of these industrious mountaineers, to be awakened in the still night by the sound of water rushing
and gurgling under one's head in a newly formed canal. Pouched gophers[3]
also have a way of awakening nervous campers that is quite as exciting
as the haplodon's plan; that is, by a series of firm upward pushes when
they are driving tunnels and shoving up the dirt. One naturally cries
out, "Who's there?" and then discovering the cause, "All right. Go on.
Good night," and goes to sleep again.

The haymaking pika,[4] bob-tailed spermophile, and wood rat are also
among the most interesting of the Sierra animals. The last, neotoma,[5]
is scarcely at all like the common rat, is nearly twice as large, has a
delicate, soft, brownish fur, white on the belly, large ears thin and trans-
lucent, eyes full and liquid and mild in expression, nose blunt and
squirrelish, slender claws sharp as needles, and as his limbs are strong
he can climb about as well as a squirrel; while no rat or squirrel has so
innocent a look, is so easily approached, or in general expresses so much
confidence in one's good intentions. He seems too fine for the thorny
thickets he inhabits, and his big, rough hut is as unlike himself as possible.
No other animal in these mountains makes nests so large and striking
in appearance as his. They are built of all kinds of sticks (broken
branches, and old rotten moss-grown chunks and green twigs, smooth or
thorny, cut from the nearest bushes), mixed with miscellaneous rubbish
and curious odds and ends—bits of cloddy earth, stones, bones, bits
of deerhorn, etc.: the whole simply piled in conical masses on the ground
in chaparral thickets. Some of these cabins are five or six feet high, and
occasionally a dozen or more are grouped together; less, perhaps, for
society's sake than for advantages of food and shelter.

[2] *Aplodontia rufa.*
[3] Pocket gopher, genus *Thomomys.*
[4] Cony (*Ochotona princeps*).
[5] Bushy-tailed wood rat (*Neotoma cinerea*), larger than the dusky-footed wood
rat of the foothills.

Coming through deep, stiff chaparral in the heart of the wilderness, heated and weary in forcing a way, the solitary explorer, happening into one of these curious neotoma villages, is startled at the strange sight, and may imagine he is in an Indian village, and feel anxious as to the reception he will get in a place so wild. At first, perhaps, not a single inhabitant will be seen, or at most only two or three seated on the tops of their huts as at the doors, observing the stranger with the mildest of mild eyes. The nest in the center of the cabin is made of grass and films of bark chewed to tow, and lined with feathers and the down of various seeds. The thick, rough walls seem to be built for defense against ene-mies—fox, coyote, etc.—as well as for shelter, and the delicate creatures in their big, rude homes suggest tender flowers, like those of *Salvia carduacea,* defended by thorny involucres.

Sometimes the home is built in the forks of an oak, twenty or thirty feet from the ground, and even in garrets. Among housekeepers who have these bushmen as neighbors or guests they are regarded as thieves, because they carry away and pile together everything transportable (knives, forks, tin cups, spoons, spectacles, combs, nails, kindling wood, etc., as well as eatables of all sorts), to strengthen their fortifications or to shine among rivals. Once, far back in the high Sierra, they stole my snow goggles, the lid of my teapot, and my aneroid barometer; and one stormy night, when encamped under a prostrate cedar, I was awakened by a gritting sound on the granite, and by the light of my fire I discovered a handsome neotoma beside me, dragging away my ice hatchet, pulling with might and main by a buckskin string on the handle. I threw bits of bark at him and made a noise to frighten him, but he stood scolding and chattering back at me, his fine eyes shining with an air of injured innocence.

Our National Parks, 1901

7. GROUSE

Even today the trail or cross-country traveler in the Sierra often is startled by a dusky grouse booming out of its pine or fir shelter, perhaps a hen whose young ones also are stirred by his approach to fly "up and away in a blurry birr and whir." This and the sage grouse of the eastern slopes and plains are the two species of these

large, chicken-like birds which inhabit our mountains. Muir ob-
served them attentively, in Yosemite and to the south, and found
a new object of envy in their grand independence.

The sage cock (*Centrocercus urophasianus*) is the largest of the Sierra
game birds and the king of American grouse. It is an admirably strong,
hardy, handsome, independent bird, able with comfort to bid defiance
to heat, cold, drought, hunger, and all sorts of storms, living on whatever
seeds or insects chance to come in its way, or simply on the leaves of
sagebrush, everywhere abundant on its desert range. In winter, when the
temperature is oftentimes below zero, and heavy snowstorms are blowing,
he sits beneath a sage bush and allows himself to be covered, poking his
head now and then through the snow to feed on the leaves of his shelter.
Not even the Arctic ptarmigan is hardier in braving frost and snow and
wintry darkness. When in full plumage he is a beautiful bird, with a long,
firm, sharp-pointed tail, which in walking is slightly raised and swings
sidewise back and forth with each step. The male is handsomely marked
with black and white on the neck, back, and wings, weighs five or six
pounds, and measures about thirty inches in length. The female is clad
mostly in plain brown, and is not so large. They occasionally wander from
the sage plains into the open nut-pine and juniper woods, but never enter
the main coniferous forest. It is only in the broad, dry, half-desert sage
plains that they are quite at home, where the weather is blazing hot in
summer, cold in winter. If anyone passes through a flock, all squat on
the gray ground and hold their heads low, hoping to escape observation;
but when approached within a rod or so, they rise with a magnificent burst
of wingbeats, looking about as big as turkeys and making a noise like
a whirlwind.

On the 28th of June, at the head of Owens Valley, I caught one of
the young that was then just able to fly. It was seven inches long, of a
uniform gray color, blunt-billed, and when captured cried lustily in a shrill
piping voice, clear in tone as a boy's small willow whistle. I have seen
flocks of from ten to thirty or forty on the east margin of Yosemite Park,
where the Mono Desert meets the gray foothills of the Sierra; but since
cattle have been pastured there they are becoming rarer every year.

Another magnificent bird, the blue or dusky grouse,[1] next in size to
the sage cock, is found all through the main forest belt, though not in
great numbers. They like best the heaviest silver-fir woods near garden

[1] *Dendragapus obscurus.*

and meadow openings, where there is but little underbrush to cover the approach of enemies. When a flock of these brave birds, sauntering and feeding on the sunny, flowery levels of some hidden meadow or yosemite valley far back in the heart of the mountains, see a man for the first time in their lives, they rise with hurried notes of surprise and excitement and alight on the lowest branches of the trees, wondering what the wanderer may be, and showing great eagerness to get a good view of the strange vertical animal. Knowing nothing of guns, they allow you to approach within a half dozen paces, then quietly hop a few branches higher or fly to the next tree without a thought of concealment, so that you may observe them as long as you like, near enough to see the fine shading of their plumage, the feathers on their toes, and the innocent wonderment in their beautiful wild eyes. But in the neighborhood of roads and trails they soon become shy, and when disturbed fly into the highest, leafiest trees, and suddenly become invisible, so well do they know how to hide and keep still and make use of their protective coloring. Nor can they be easily dislodged ere they are ready to go. In vain the hunter goes round and round some tall pine or fir into which he has perhaps seen a dozen enter, gazing up through the branches, straining his eyes while his gun is held ready; not a feather can he see unless his eyes have been sharpened by long experience and knowledge of the blue grouse's habits. Then, perhaps, when he is thinking that the tree must be hollow and that the birds have all gone inside, they burst forth with a startling whir of wingbeats, and after gaining full speed go skating swiftly away through the forest arches in a long, silent, wavering slide, with wings held steadily.

During the summer they are most of the time on the ground, feeding on insects, seeds, berries, etc., around the margins of open spots and rocky moraines, playing and sauntering, taking sun baths and sand baths, and drinking at little pools and rills during the heat of the day. In winter they live mostly in the trees, depending on buds for food, sheltering beneath dense overlapping branches at night and during storms on the lee-side of the trunk, sunning themselves on the southside limbs in fine weather, and sometimes diving into the mealy snow to flutter and wallow, apparently for exercise and fun.

I have seen young broods running beneath the firs in June at a height of eight thousand feet above the sea. On the approach of danger, the mother with a peculiar cry warns the helpless midgets to scatter and hide beneath leaves and twigs, and even in plain open spaces it is almost impossible to discover them. In the meantime the mother feigns lameness, throws herself at your feet, kicks and gasps and flutters, to draw your

Glacier Lake with view north to Evolution Country, Kings Canyon National Park

attention from the chicks. The young are generally able to fly about the middle of July; but even after they can fly well they are usually advised to run and hide and lie still, no matter how closely approached, while the mother goes on with her loving, lying acting, apparently as desperately concerned for their safety as when they were featherless infants. Sometimes, however, after carefully studying their circumstances, she tells them to take wing; and up and away in a blurry birr and whir they scatter to all points of the compass, as if blown up with gunpowder, dropping cunningly out of sight three or four hundred yards off, and keeping quiet until called, after the danger is supposed to be past. If you walk on a little way without manifesting any inclination to hunt them, you may sit down at the foot of a tree near enough to see and hear the happy reunion. One touch of nature makes the whole world kin; and it is truly wonderful how love-telling the small voices of these birds are, and how far they reach through the woods into one another's hearts and into ours. The tones are so perfectly human and so full of anxious affection, few mountaineers can fail to be touched by them.

They are cared for until full grown. On the 20th of August, as I was passing along the margin of a garden spot on the headwaters of the San Joaquin, a grouse rose from the ruins of an old juniper that had been uprooted and brought down by an avalanche from a cliff overhead. She threw herself at my feet, limped and fluttered and gasped, showing, as I thought, that she had a nest and was raising a second brood. Looking for the eggs, I was surprised to see a strong-winged flock nearly as large as the mother fly up around me.

Instead of seeking a warmer climate when the winter storms set in, these hardy birds stay all the year in the high Sierra forests, and I have never known them to suffer in any sort of weather. Able to live on the buds of pine, spruce, and fir, they are forever independent in the matter of food supply, which gives so many of us trouble, dragging us here and there away from our best work. How gladly I would live on pine buds, however pitchy, for the sake of this grand independence! With all his superior resources, man makes more distracting difficulty concerning food than any other of the family.

Our National Parks, 1901

8. WATER OUZEL

"The best biography yet given of any bird," wrote David Starr Jordan of this loving evocation of the modest, hardy little dipper, the "hummingbird of the California waterfalls." Jordan camped in "the Alps of the Kings-Kern Divide" in 1899 and mapped the glaciated north slope of Mount Brewer which he then named the Ouzel Basin. He said this was where Muir had studied the bird and sketched his essay. It is true that Muir was in the area in 1873 and 1875, but he must have found the ouzel often in Yosemite and throughout the mountains, as we still do.

The waterfalls of the Sierra Nevada are frequented by only one bird, the ouzel or water thrush (*Cinclus mexicanus,* Sw.). He is a singularly joyous and lovable little fellow, about the size of a robin, clad in a plain waterproof suit of a blackish, bluish gray, with a tinge of chocolate on the head and shoulders. In form he is about as smoothly plump and compact as a pothole pebble; the flowing contour of his body being interrupted only by his strong feet and bill, and the crisp wingtips, and upslanted wrenish tail.

Among all the countless waterfalls I have met in the course of eight years' explorations in the Sierra, whether in the icy Alps, or warm foothills, or in the profound yosemite canyons of the middle region, not one was found without its ouzel. No canyon is too cold for him, none too lonely, provided it be rich in white falling water. Find a fall, or cascade, or rushing rapid, anywhere upon a clear crystalline stream, and there you will surely find its complementary ouzel, flitting about in the spray, diving in foaming eddies, whirling like a leaf among beaten foam bells; ever vigorous and enthusiastic, yet self-contained, and neither seeking nor shunning your company.

If disturbed while dipping about in the margin shallows, he either sets off with a rapid whir to some other feeding ground up or down the stream, or alights on some half-submerged rock or snag out in the foaming current, and immediately begins to nod and curtsy like a wren, turning his head from side to side and performing many other odd dainty manners as if he had been trained at some bird dancing-school.

He is the mountain streams' own darling—the hummingbird of blooming waters, loving rocky ripple-slopes and sheets of foam, as a bee loves flowers—as a lark loves sunshine and meadows. Among all the mountain birds, none has cheered me so much in my lonely wanderings—none so unfailingly. For winter and summer he sings, independent alike of sunshine and love; requiring no other inspiration than the stream on which he dwells. While water sings, so must he; in heat or cold, calm or storm, ever attuning his voice in sure accord; low in the drouth of summer and drouth of winter, but never silent.

During the golden days of Indian summer the mountain streams are feeble—a succession of silent pools, linked together with strips of silvery lacework; then the song of the ouzel is at its lowest ebb. But as soon as the winter clouds have bloomed, and the mountain treasuries are once more replenished with snow, the voices of the streams and ouzels begin to increase in strength and richness until the flood season of early summer. Then the glad torrents chant their noblest anthems, and then too is the floodtime of our songster's melody. But as to the influence of the weather, dark days and sun days are the same to him. The voices of most song-birds, however joyous, suffer a long winter eclipse; but the ouzel sings on around all the seasons, and through every kind of storm. Indeed no storm can be more violent than those of the waterfalls in the midst of which he delights to dwell. At least, from whatever cause, while the weather is darkest and most boisterous, snowing, blowing, cloudy or clear, all the same he sings, and never a note of sadness. No need of spring sunshine to thaw *his* song, for it never freezes. Never shall you hear anything wintry from *his* warm breast; no pinched cheeping, no wavering notes between sadness and joy; his mellow, fluty voice is ever tuned to down-right gladness, as free from every trace of dejection as cockcrowing.

What may be regarded as the separate songs of the ouzel are exceed-ingly difficult of description, because they are so variable and at the same time so confluent. I have been acquainted with my favorite for eight years, and though, during most of this time, I have heard him sing nearly every day, I still detect notes and strains that are quite new to me. Nearly all of his music is very sweet and tender, lapsing from his round breast like water over the smooth lip of a pool, then breaking farther on into a rich sparkling foam of melodious notes, which glow with subdued enthusiasm, yet without expressing much of the strong, gushing ecstasy of the bobolink or skylark.

The more striking strains are perfect arabesques of melody, composed of a few full, round, mellow notes, embroidered with a great variety of delicate trills which fade in long, slender cadences like the silken fringes of summer clouds melting in the azure. But as a whole, his music is that of the stream itself, infinitely—organized, spiritualized. The deep booming notes of the falls are in it, the trills of rapids, the swirling and gurgling of potholes, low hushes of levels, the rapturous bounce and dance of rocky cascades, and the sweet tinkle of separate drops oozing from the ends of mosses and falling into tranquil pools.

The ouzel never sings in chorus with other birds, nor with his kind, but only with the streams. And like flowers that bloom beneath the surface of the ground, some of our favorite's best song blossoms never rise above the surface of the heavier music of the water. I have oftentimes observed him singing in the midst of beaten spray, his music completely buried beneath the water's roar; yet I knew he was surely singing by the movements of his bill.

His food consists of all kinds of water insects, which in summer are chiefly procured along shallow margins. Here he wades about ducking his head under water, and deftly turning over pebbles and fallen leaves with his bill, seldom choosing to go into deep water where he has to use his wings in diving.

He seems to be especially fond of the larvae of mosquitoes, found in great quantities attached to the bottom of smooth rock channels where the current is swift and shallow. When feeding in such places he wades upstream, and oftentimes while his head is under water the swift current is deflected upward along the glossy curves of his neck and shoulders, in the form of a clear, crystalline shell, which fairly incloses him like a bell glass, the shell being constantly broken and re-formed as he lifts and dips his head; while ever and anon he sidles out to where the too powerful current carries him off his feet, and sweeps him rapidly downstream; then he dexterously rises on the wing and goes gleaning again in shallower places.

But during the winter, when the stream banks are all deeply embossed in snow, and the streams themselves are chilled nearly to the freezing point, so that the snow falling into them in stormy weather is not wholly dissolved, but forms a thin blue sludge, thus rendering the current opaque—then he seeks the deeper portions of the main rivers, where he may dive to clear portions of the channel beneath the sludge. Or he repairs to some open lake or millpond, at the bottom of which he feeds in perfect safety.

When thus compelled to betake himself to a lake, he does not plunge into it at once like a duck, but always alights in the first place upon some rock or fallen pine along the shore, then flying out thirty or forty yards, more or less, according to the character of the bottom, he alights with a dainty glint on the surface, swims about, looks down, finally makes up his mind and disappears with a sharp stroke of his wings. After feeding for two or three minutes he suddenly reappears, showers the water from his wings with one vigorous shake, and rises abruptly into the air as if pushed up from beneath, comes back to his perch, sings a few minutes and goes out to dive again; thus coming and going, singing and diving at the same places for hours.

The ouzel alone of all birds dares to enter a white torrent. And though strictly terrestrial in structure, no other is so inseparably related to water, not even the duck, or bold ocean albatross, or storm petrel. Ducks go ashore when they have done feeding in undisturbed places, and frequently make long overland flights from lake to lake or from field to field. The same is true of most other aquatic birds. But our ouzel, born on the very brink of a stream, seldom leaves it for a single moment. For, notwithstanding he is often on the wing, he never flies overland, but whirs with rapid, quail-like beat above the stream, tracing all its winding modulations with great minuteness. Even when the stream is quite small, say from five to ten feet wide, he will not try to shorten his flight by crossing a bend, however abrupt it may be; and even when disturbed by meeting someone on the bank, he prefers to fly over one's head, to dodging out over the ground. When therefore his flight along a crooked stream is viewed endwise, it appears most strikingly wavered—an interpretation of every curve inscribed with lightning-like rapidity on the air.

Mist Falls, Paradise Valley,
Kings Canyon National Park

The vertical curves and angles of the most precipitous alpine torrents he traces with the same rigid fidelity. Swooping down the inclines of cascades, dropping sheer over dizzy falls amid the spray, and ascending with the same fearlessness and ease, seldom seeking to lessen the steepness of the acclivity by beginning to ascend before reaching the base of the fall. No matter how high it may be, he holds straight on as if about to dash headlong into the throng of booming rockets, then darts abruptly upward, and, after alighting at the top of the precipice to rest a moment, proceeds to feed and sing. His flight is solid and impetuous without any intermission of wingbeats—one homogeneous buzz like that of a laden bee on its way home. And while thus buzzing freely from fall to fall, he is frequently heard giving utterance to a long outdrawn train of unmodulated notes, in no way connected with his song, but corresponding closely with his flight, both in sustained vigor, and homogeneity of substance.

Were the flights of every individual ouzel in the Sierra traced on a chart, they would indicate the direction of the flow of the entire system of ancient glaciers, from about the period of the breaking up of the ice sheet until near the close of the glacial winter; because the streams which the ouzels so rigidly follow, are, with the unimportant exceptions of a few side tributaries, all flowing in channels eroded for them out of the solid flank of the range by the vanished glaciers—the streams tracing the glaciers, the ouzels tracing the streams. Nor do we find so complete compliance to glacial conditions in the life of any other mountain bird, or animal of any kind. Bears frequently accept the pathways laid down by the glaciers as the easiest to travel; but then, they often leave them and cross over from canyon to canyon. So also, most birds found in rocky canyons at all usually fly across at right angles to the courses of the vanished glaciers, because the main forests of these regions to which they come and go are growing upon the lateral moraines which always stretch along the tops of the canyon walls.

The ouzel's nest is one of the most extraordinary pieces of bird architecture I ever beheld; so odd and novel in design, and so perfectly fresh and beautiful, and in every way so fully worthy of the genius of the little builder. It is about a foot in diameter, round and bossy in outline, with a neatly arched opening near the bottom, somewhat like an old-fashioned brick oven, or Hottentot's hut. It is built almost exclusively of green and yellow mosses, chiefly the beautiful fronded hypnum that covers the rocks and old drift logs in the vicinity of waterfalls. These are deftly interwoven, and felted together into a charming little hut; and so situated that many of the outer mosses continue to flourish as if they had not been plucked. A few fine silky-stemmed grasses are occasionally found interwoven with the mosses, but, with the exception of a thin layer lining the floor, their presence seems accidental, as they are of a species found growing with the mosses and are probably plucked with them. The site chosen for this curious mansion is usually some little rock shelf within reach of the spray of a waterfall, so that its walls are kept green and growing, at least during the time of high water.

No harsh lines are presented by any portion of the nest as seen *in situ,* but when removed from its shelf, the back and bottom, and sometimes a portion of the top, is found quite sharply angular because it is made to conform to the surface of the rock, upon which and against which it is built; the little architect always taking advantage of slight crevices and protuberances that may chance to offer, to render his structure stable, by means of a kind of gripping and dovetailing.

In choosing a building spot, concealment does not seem to be taken into consideration at all; yet notwithstanding the nest is so large, and so guilelessly exposed to view, it is far from being easily detected, chiefly because it swells forward like any other bulging moss cushion growing naturally in such situations. This is more especially the case where the nest is kept fresh by being well sprinkled. Sometimes these romantic little huts have their beauty enhanced by tasteful decorations or rock ferns and grasses, that spring up around the walls or in front of the doorsill, all dripping with crystal beads.

Furthermore, at certain hours of the days when the sunshine is poured down at the required angle, the whole mass of the spray enveloping the fairy establishment is brilliantly irised; and it is through so glorious a rainbow atmosphere as this that some of our blessed ouzels obtain their first peep at the world.

In these moss huts are laid, three or four eggs—white, like foam bubbles; and well may the little ouzels hatched from them sing water songs, for they hear them all their lives, and even before they are born.

I have oftentimes observed the young just out of the nest making their odd gestures, and seeming in every way as much at home as their experienced parents—like young bees in their first excursions to the flower fields. No amount of familiarity with people and their ways seems to change them in the least. To all appearance their behavior is just the same on seeing a man for the first time, as when seeing him every day.

On the lower reaches of the rivers where mills are built, they sing on through the din of the machinery, and all the concomitant confusion of dogs, cattle, and workmen. On one occasion, while a woodchopper was at work on the river bank, I observed one cheerily singing within reach of the flying chips. Nor does any kind of unwonted disturbance put him in bad humor, or frighten him out of a calm self-possession. In passing through a narrow gorge, I drove one ahead of me from rapid to rapid, disturbing him four times in quick succession, where he could not very well fly past me on account of the narrowness of the channel. Most birds under similar circumstances fancy themselves pursued, and become suspiciously uneasy; but, instead of growing nervous about it, he made his usual dippings, and sang one of his most tranquil strains. When observed within a few yards their eyes are seen to express remarkable gentleness and intelligence; but they seldom allow a sufficiently near approach. On one occasion, while rambling along the shore of a mountain lake, where the birds, at least those born that season, had never seen a man, I sat down to rest upon a large stone close to the water's edge, upon which it seemed the ouzels and sandpipers were in the habit of alighting when they came to feed on that part of the shore, and some of the other birds also, when they came down to wash or drink. After I had sat a few minutes, along came a whirring ouzel and alighted on the stone beside me, within reach of my hand. Then observing me, all at once he stooped nervously as if about to fly on the instant, but as I remained motionless as the stone, he gained confidence, and looked me steadily in the face for about a minute, then flew quietly to the outlet and began to sing. A sandpiper came next and gazed at me with much the same guileless expression of eye as the ouzel. Lastly, down with a swoop came a Steller's jay out of a fir tree, probably with the intention of moistening his noisy throat. But instead of sitting confidingly as my other visitors had done, he rushed off at once, nearly tumbling heels over head into the lake in his suspicious confusion, and with loud screams roused the neighborhood.

Grass on pond near Bullfrog Lake,
Kings Canyon National Park

The species is distributed all along the mountain ranges of the Pacific coast from Alaska to Mexico, and east to the Rocky Mountains. Nevertheless, it is as yet but little known, even among naturalists. Audubon and Wilson did not meet it at all. Swainson was, I believe, the first to describe a specimen from Mexico. Specimens were shortly afterward procured by Drummond near the sources of the Athabasca River, between the fifty-fourth and fifty-sixth parallels; and it has been collected by nearly all of the numerous exploring expeditions undertaken of late through our western states and territories; for it never fails to engage the attention of naturalists in a very particular manner.

Such, then, is the life of our little cinclus, beloved of everyone who is so happy as to know him. Tracing on strong wing every curve of the most precipitous torrent, from one extremity of the Californian Alps to the other; not fearing to follow them through their darkest gorges, and coldest snow tunnels; acquainted with every waterfall, echoing their divine music; and throughout the whole of their beautiful lives interpreting all that we in our unbelief call terrible in the utterances of torrents, as only varied expressions of God's eternal love.

"The Humming-Bird of the California Water-Falls,"
Scribner's Monthly, February 1878

9. DOUGLAS SQUIRREL

The little red tree squirrel or Sierra chickaree (Tamiasciurus douglasii) *was another of Muir's favorites. He apologizes for writing so much about his Douglas neighbors, but explains how much he values both their instinctive forestry and their "unmistakable humanity." Sally Carrighar, in telling the story of the chickaree in her book,* One Day on Beetle Rock (*1944*), *conveys similar insight into the mammalian soul of Muir's "bright chip of nature."*

The Douglas squirrel is by far the most interesting and influential of all the California *sciuridae,* surpassing every other species in force of character, numbers, extent of range, and in the amount of influence he brings to bear upon the health and distribution of the vast forests he inhabits.

Go where you will throughout the noble woods of the Sierra Nevada—among the giant pines and spruces of the lower zones, up through the towering silver firs to the storm-bent thickets of the Alps, you everywhere find this little squirrel the master existence. Though only a few inches long, so intense is his fiery vigor and restlessness, he stirs every grove with wild life, and makes himself more important than even the huge bears that shuffle through the tangled underbrush beneath him. Every wind is fretted by his voice, almost every bole and branch feels the sting of his sharp feet. How much the growth of the trees is stimulated by this means it is not easy to learn, but his action in manipulating their seeds is more appreciable. Nature has made him master forester and committed almost the whole of her coniferous crops to his paws. Probably over fifty per cent of all the cones ripened on the Sierra are cut off and handled by the Douglas alone, and of those of the Big Trees (*Sequoia gigantea*), forming an interrupted belt nearly two hundred miles long, perhaps ninety per cent pass through his hands. The greater portion is of course stored away for food during the winter and spring, but some of them are tucked separately into holes, and loosely covered, where they germinate and become trees.

The only one of the family to which the Douglas is very closely allied is the red squirrel or chickaree of the eastern woods. Ours may be a lineal descendant of this species, probably distributed westward to the Pacific by way of the great lakes, and thence southward along our forested ranges. This view is suggested by the fact that our species becomes redder and more chickaree-like in general, the farther it is traced back along the course indicated above. But whatever their relationship, and the evolutionary forces that have acted upon them, the Douglas is now the larger and more beautiful animal.

From the nose to the root of the tail, he measures about eight inches; and his tail, which he so effectively uses in interpreting his feelings, is about six inches in length. He wears dark bluish gray over the back and halfway down the sides, bright buff on the belly, with a stripe of dark gray, nearly black, separating the upper and under colors. This dividing stripe, however, is not very sharply defined. He has long black whiskers, which gives him a rather fierce look when observed closely, strong claws, sharp as fishhooks, and the brightest of bright eyes, full of telling speculation.

A Kings River Indian told me that they call him "pillillooeet," which, rapidly pronounced with the first syllable heavily accented, is not unlike the lusty exclamation he utters on his way up a tree when excited. Most mountaineers in California call him the pine squirrel, and when I asked an old trapper the other day whether he knew our little forester, he replied with brightening countenance:

"Oh yes, of course I know him; everybody knows him. When I'm hunting in the woods, I often find out where the deer are by his barking at them. I call 'em lightnin' squirrels, because they're so mighty quick and peert."

All the true squirrels are more or less bird-like in speech and movements; but the Douglas is pre-eminently so, possessing, as he does, every attribute peculiarly squirrelish enthusiastically concentrated. He is the squirrel of squirrels, flashing from branch to branch of his favorite evergreens, crisp and glossy, and undiseased as a sunbeam. Give him wings, and he would outfly any bird in the woods. His big, gray cousin[1] is a looser animal, seemingly light enough to float on the wind. Yet when leaping from limb to limb, or out of one treetop to another, he sometimes halts to gather strength, as if making efforts concerning the upshot of which he could not always feel exactly confident. But the Douglas, with his denser body, leaps and glides in hidden strength, seemingly as independent of common muscles as a mountain stream. He threads the tasseled branches of the pines, stirring their needles like a rustling breeze; now shooting across openings in arrowy lines; now launching in curves, glinting deftly from side to side in sudden zigzags, and swirling in giddy loops and spirals around the knotty trunks; getting into what seem to be the most impossible situations, without sense of danger; now on his haunches, now on his head; yet ever graceful, and punctuating his most irrepressible outbursts of energy with little dots and dashes of perfect repose. He is, without exception, the wildest animal I ever saw—a fiery, sputtering little bolt of life, luxuriating in quick oxygen and the woods' best juices. One can hardly think of such a creature being dependent, like the rest of us, on climate and food. But, after all, it requires no long acquaintance to learn he is human, for he works for a living. His busiest time is in the Indian summer. Then he gathers burrs and hazelnuts like a plodding farmer, working continuously every day for hours; saying not a word; cutting off the ripe cones at the top of his speed, as if employed by the job, and examining every branch in regular order, as if careful that not one should escape him; then, descending, he stores them away beneath logs and stumps, in anticipation of the pinching hunger days of winter. He seems himself a kind of coniferous fruit, both fruit and flower. The rosiny essences of the pines pervade every pore of his body, and eating his flesh is like chewing gum.

[1] California gray squirrel (*Sciurus griseus*).

One never tires of this bright chip of nature—this brave little voice crying in the wilderness—observing his many works and ways, and listening to his curious language. His musical, piney gossip is savory to the ear as balsam to the palate; and, though he has not exactly the gift of song, some of his notes are sweet as those of a linnet—almost flute-like in softness; while others prick and tingle like thistles. He is the mocking-bird of squirrels, pouring forth mixed chatter and song like a perennial fountain. Barking like a dog, screaming like a hawk, whistling like blackbirds and sparrows; while in bluff, audacious noisiness he is a jay.

No other of the Sierra animals of my acquaintance is better fed, not even the deer, amid abundance of sweet herbs and shrubs, or the mountain sheep, or omnivorous bears. His food consists of hazelnuts, chinquapins, and the nuts and seeds of all the coniferous trees without exception—pine, fir, spruce, libocedrus, torreya, juniper and sequoia—he is fond of them all, and they all agree with him, green or ripe. No cone is too large for him to manage, none so small as to be beneath his notice. The smaller ones, such as those of the Williamson and Douglas spruce and the two-leafed pine, he cuts off and eats on a branch of the tree, without allowing them to fall; beginning at the bottom of the cone and cutting away the scales to expose the seeds; not gnawing by guess like a bear, but turning them round and round in regular order, in compliance with their spiral arrangement.

When thus employed, his location in the tree is betrayed by a dribble of scales, shells, and seed wings, and, every few minutes, by the stripped axis of the cone. Then of course he is ready for another, and if you are watching you may catch a glimpse of him as he glides silently out to the end of a branch and see him examining the cone clusters until he finds one to his mind, then, leaning over, pull back the springy needles out of his way, grasp the cone with his paws to prevent its falling, snip it off in an incredibly short time, seize it with jaws grotesquely stretched, and return to his chosen seat near the trunk. But the immense size of the cones of the sugar pine—from sixteen to twenty inches in length—and those of the yellow pine, compels him to adopt a quite different method. He cuts them off without attempting to hold them, then goes down and drags them from where they have chanced to fall up to the bare, swelling ground around the instep of the tree, where he demolishes them in the same methodical way, beginning at the bottom and following the scale spirals to the top.

From a single sugar-pine cone he gets from two to four hundred seeds about half the size of a hazelnut, so that in a few minutes he can procure

enough to last a week. He seems, however, to prefer those of the two
silver firs above all others; perhaps because they are most easily obtained,
as the scales drop off when ripe without needing to be cut. Both species
are filled with an exceedingly pungent, aromatic oil, which spices all
his flesh, and is of itself sufficient to account for his lightning energy.

You may easily know this little workman by his chips. On sunny hillsides around the principal trees they lie in big piles—bushels and
basketfuls of them, all fresh and clean, making the most beautiful
kitchen-middens imaginable. The brown and yellow scales and nutshells
are as abundant and as delicately penciled and tinted as the shells along
the seashore; while the red and purple seed wings mingled with them
would lead one to fancy that innumerable butterflies had met their fate
there.

He feasts on all the species long before they are ripe, but is wise
enough to wait until they are fully matured before he gathers them into
his barns. This is in October and November, which with him are the two
busiest months of the year. All kinds of burrs, big and little, are now cut
off and showered down alike, and the ground is speedily covered with
them. A constant thudding and bumping is kept up; some of the larger
cones chancing to fall on old logs make the forest re-echo with the sound.
Other nut-eaters less industrious know well what is going on, and
hasten to carry away the cones as they fall. But however busy the har-
vester may be, he is not slow to descry the pilferers below, and instantly
leaves his work to drive them away. The little striped tamias[2] is a thorn
in his flesh, stealing persistently, punish him as he may. The large gray
squirrel gives trouble also, although the Douglas has been accused of
stealing from him. Generally, however, just the opposite is the case.

The excellence of the Sierra evergreens is beginning to be well known;
consequently there is considerable demand for their seeds. The greater
portion of the supply is procured by chopping down the trees in the more
accessible sections of the forests alongside of bridle paths that cross the
range. Sequoia seeds bring about eight or ten dollars per pound, and
therefore are eagerly sought after. Some of the smaller fruitful trees are
cut down in the groves not protected by government, especially those of
Fresno and Kings River. Most of them, however, are of so gigantic a size
that the seedsmen have to look for the greater portion of their supplies
to the Douglas, who soon learns that he is no match for these freebooters.
He is wise enough, however, to cease working the instant he perceives
them, and never fails to embrace every opportunity to recover his burrs
whenever they happen to be stored in any place accessible to him, and

[2] Lodgepole chipmunk (*Eutamias speciosus*).

the busy seedsmen often find on returning to camp that the little Douglas
has very exhaustively spoiled the spoiler. I know one seed-gatherer who,
whenever he robs the squirrels, scatters wheat or barley beneath the
trees for conscience money.

The want of appreciable life remarked by so many travelers in the
Sierra forests is never felt at this time of year. Banish all the humming
insects and the birds and quadrupeds, leaving only Sir Douglas, and the
most solitary of our so-called solitudes would still throb with ardent
life. But if you should go impatiently even into the most populous of the
groves on purpose to meet him, and walk about looking up among the
branches, you will see very little of him. You should lie down at the foot
of one of the trees and he will come. For, in the midst of the ordinary
forest sounds, the falling of burrs, piping of quails, the screams of the
Clark crow, and the rustling of deer and bears among the chaparral,
he is quick to detect your strange footsteps, and will hasten to make a
good, close inspection of you as soon as you are still. First, you may hear
him sounding a few notes of curious inquiry, but more likely the first
intimation of his approach will be the prickly sounds of his feet as he descends the tree overhead, just before he makes his savage onrush to
frighten you and proclaim your presence to every other squirrel and
bird in the neighborhood. If you are now capable of remaining perfectly
motionless, he will make a nearer and nearer approach, and probably
set your flesh a-tingle by frisking across your body. Once, while seated
at the foot of a Williamson spruce in one of the most inaccessible of the
San Joaquin yosemites engaged in sketching, a reckless fellow came up
behind me, passed under my bended arm, and jumped on my paper. And
while an old friend of mine was reading one warm afternoon out in the
shade of his cabin, one of his Douglas neighbors jumped from the gable
upon his head, then with admirable assurance ran down over his shoulder
and onto the book he held in his hand.

Though I cannot of course expect all my readers to sympathize fully
in my admiration of this little animal, few I hope will think this sketch
of his life too long. I cannot begin to tell here how much he has cheered
my lonely wanderings during all the years I have been pursuing my
studies in these glorious wilds; or how much unmistakable humanity I
have found in him. Take this for example: One calm, creamy, Indian
summer morning, when the nuts were ripe, I was camped in the upper
pinewoods of the South Fork of the San Joaquin, where the squirrels
seemed to be about as plentiful as the ripe burrs. They were taking an
early breakfast before going to their regular harvest work. While I was
busy with my own breakfast I heard the thudding fall of two or three

heavy cones from a yellow pine near me, and stole noiselessly forward within about twenty feet of the base of it to observe. In a few moments down came the Douglas. The breakfast burrs he had cut off had rolled on the gently sloping ground into a clump of ceanothus bushes, but he seemed to know exactly where they were, for he found them at once, apparently without searching for them. They were more than twice as heavy as himself, but after turning them into the right position for getting a good hold with his long sickle teeth he managed to drag them up to the foot of the tree he had cut them from, moving backward. Then seating himself comfortably, he held them on end, bottom up, and demolished them with easy rapidity. A good deal of nibbling had to be done before he got anything to eat, because the lower scales are barren, but when he had patiently worked his way up to the fertile ones he found two sweet nuts at the base of each, shaped like trimmed hams, and purple-spotted like birds' eggs. And notwithstanding these cones were dripping with soft balsam, and covered with prickles, and so strongly put together that a boy would be puzzled to cut them open with a jackknife, he accomplished his meal with easy dignity and cleanliness, making less effort apparently than a man would in eating soft cookery from a plate.

Breakfast done, I thought I would whistle a tune for him before he went to work, curious to see how he would be affected by it. He had not seen me all this while; but the instant I began he darted up the tree nearest to him, and came out on a small dead limb opposite me, and composed himself to listen. I sang and whistled more than a dozen tunes, and as the music changed his eyes sparkled, and he turned his head quickly from side to side, but made no other response. Other squirrels, hearing the strange sounds, came around on all sides, chipmunks also, and birds. One of the birds, a handsome, speckle-breasted thrush, seemed even more interested than the squirrels. After listening for a while on one of the lower dead sprays of a pine, he came swooping forward within a few feet of my face, where he remained fluttering in the air for half a minute or so, sustaining himself with whirring wingbeats, like a hummingbird in front of a flower, while I could look into his eyes and see his innocent wonder.

By this time my performance must have lasted nearly half an hour. I sang or whistled "Bonnie Doon," "Lass o' Gowrie," "O'er the Water to Charlie," "Bonnie Woods o' Cragie Lee," etc., all of which seemed to be listened to with bright interest, my first Douglas sitting patiently through it all, with his telling eyes fixed upon me until I ventured to give the "Old Hundredth," when he screamed his Indian name, Pillill-ooeet, turned tail, and darted with ludicrous haste up the tree out of sight, his voice and actions in the case leaving a somewhat profane impression, as if he had said, "I'll be hanged if you get me to hear anything so solemn and unpiney." This acted as a signal for the general dispersal of the whole hairy tribe, though the birds seemed willing to wait further developments, music being naturally more in their line.

No one who makes the acquaintance of our forester will fail to admire him; but he is far too self-reliant and war-like ever to be taken for a darling.

I have no idea how long he lives. The young seem to sprout from knotholes—perfect from the first, and as enduring as their own trees. It is difficult, indeed, to realize that so condensed a piece of sun-fire should ever become dim or die at all. He is seldom killed by hunters, for he is too small to encourage much of their attention, and when pursued in settled regions becomes excessively shy, and keeps close in the furrows of the highest trunks, many of which are of the same color as himself. Indian boys, however, lie in wait with unbounded patience to shoot them with arrows. A few fall prey to rattlesnakes in the lower and middle zones. Occasionally he is pursued by hawks and wildcats, etc. But, upon the whole, he dwells safely in the deep bosom of the woods, the most highly favored of all his happy tribe. May his tribe increase!

"The Douglass Squirrel of California,"
Scribner's Monthly, December 1878

THE BIG TREES

. . . where the sequoia becomes more exuber-
ant and numerous, the rival trees become less
so; and where they mix with sequoia, they
mostly grow up beneath them like slender
grasses among stalks of Indian corn.

1. POST-GLACIAL HISTORY

One of Muir's main purposes in traveling southward from Yo-
semite was to study the extent and ecology of Sequoia gigantea,
which he called "the king of all the conifers in the world." He first
saw the forests that became part of Sequoia National Park in the
autumn of 1873, and returned for two months of intensive ex-
ploration and observation in 1875, at which time, he later said, he
originated the name "Giant Forest." (There is evidence of an earlier
use of the name.) The Big Trees held his interest throughout his
life; in 1902 he hurried from Fresno to Converse Basin with a
steel tape to verify the report of a "largest tree," and he rode an
automobile to Giant Forest in 1912.

Of all the phenomena in the mountains, it was the great sequoias
Muir reverenced most. Nearing threescore and ten, himself, he wrote
to a friend, "That I may see you again ere long and that you may
have a full century at least, bearing the big years like a noble
Sequoia, I devoutly hope and pray." His empathy for all life led to
his wonder and delight in the serene longevity of this "greatest of
living things," and to some of his finest descriptive prose when he
wrote about the Big Trees. It also inspired the indignation at the
man-made scourges of overgrazing, destructive cutting, and fires,
which launched Muir as a leader in the conservation movement.

The American Association for the Advancement of Science, with
the good offices of Professor Asa Gray whom Muir had met and
guided in Yosemite, published the following paper in its Proceedings
of 1876. Through the careful reasoning shines the radiance and
passion of the already devoted conservationist. It was entitled
"On the Post-Glacial History of Sequoia Gigantea. By John Muir,
of San Francisco, Cal."

Giant Forest, Sequoia National Park

During the past summer I explored the sequoia belt of the Sierra Nevada, tracing its boundaries and learning what I could of the post-glacial history of the species, and of its future prospects. Perhaps the most important of the questions put to the forests are as follows:

What area does Sequoia now occupy as the principal tree? Was the species ever more extensively distributed on the Sierra during post-glacial times? Is the species verging to extinction? And if so, then, to what causes will its extinction be due? What have been its relations to climate, to soil, and to other coniferous trees with which it is associated? What are those relations now? What are they likely to be in the future?

Some of the answers obtained to these questions, seem plain and full of significance, and cannot, I think, fail to interest every student of natural history. I shall endeavor, therefore, to present them in as clear and com-pact a shape as possible.

The sequoia belt extends from the well-known Calaveras groves on the north, to the head of Deer Creek, on the south, a distance of about 200 miles. The northern limit being a little above the 38th parallel, the southern a little below the 36th, and the elevation above sea level varies from about 5000, to 8000 feet.[1]

From the Calaveras to the South Fork of Kings River, the species occurs only in small isolated groves and patches, so sparsely distributed along the belt, that two gaps occur nearly forty miles in width, one between the Calaveras and Tuolumne groves, the other between those of the Fresno and Kings River. Hence southward the trees are nowhere gathered in small sequestered groups, but stretch majestically across the broad and rugged basins of the Kaweah and Tule in noble forests, a distance of nearly seventy miles, and with a width of from three to ten miles; the continuity of the belt being broken here only by deep sheer-walled canyons.

The Fresno group, the largest sequoia congregation of the north, occu-pies an area of three or four square miles. From the so-called Kings River Grove[2] in the neighborhood of Thomas Mill, I pushed off in a north-easterly direction, along the bevelled rim of the canyon of the South Fork of Kings River. Here I discovered a majestic forest of sequoia, nearly six miles long, by two wide; not hemmed in by pines and firs, but growing as the predominant species, in brave and comfortable inde-

[1] It has since been found that the northernmost grove of sequoia is in Placer County, about the 39th parallel. The southernmost is in Tulare County, about 250 miles away. Elevation of Big Trees is as low as 4500 feet.
[2] General Grant Grove.

pendence, over hill, and dale, and rocky ridgetop. This is the north-ernmost assemblage of sequoias that may fairly be called a forest.

Descending the precipitous divide between Kings River and the Kaweah, we enter the colossal forests of the main continuous portion of the sequoia belt. As we advance southward, the trees become more and more irrepressibly exuberant, tossing their massive crowns against the sky from every ridgetop, and waving onward in graceful compliance to the complicated topography of the basins of the Kaweah and Tule.

The finest of the Kaweah portion of the belt is located on the broad, lofty ridge separating the waters of Marble Creek from the Middle Fork, and extends from the granite headlands overlooking the hot plains, back within a few miles of the cool glacial fountains.[3]

The extreme upper limit of the belt is reached between the Middle and South forks at an elevation of 8400 feet above the sea.

The most compact and majestic portion of the Tule forests, lies on the North Fork, forming, I think, the finest block of sequoia in the entire belt.

Southward from here I thought I could detect a slight decrease in the general thrift of the forests; this being the only indication of approach to the southern limit. But shortly after crossing the divide between the basins of the Tule and Deer Creek, the belt is abruptly contracted, and terminated. I made a careful survey of the southern boundary, and of the woods beyond, without discovering a single sequoia, or any trace of their former existence.

I was greatly interested, however, to find that the species had crossed over from the head of Deer Creek into the valley of the Upper Kern, and planted colonies northward along the eastern slopes of the western summit or Greenhorn Range.[4] The western summit puts out from the main backbone of the range at the head of Kings River, trending southward, and enclosing the Upper Kern valley on the west, and it is just where this lofty spur begins to break down, on its approach to its southern termination, that the sequoia has been able to cross it.

Though the area occupied by the species increases from north to south, there is no corresponding increase in the size of the trees; a diameter of twenty feet, and height of 275, is, perhaps, about the average for full-grown trees; specimens twenty-five feet in diameter are not rare, and a good many approach 300 feet in height. Occasionally one meets a specimen thirty feet in diameter, and rarely one that is larger. The largest I have yet seen and measured is a majestic stump on the south

[3] Giant Forest. Marble Creek is now called the Marble Fork of the Kaweah.
[4] Great Western Divide.

side of Kings River. It measures thirty-five feet eight inches in diameter inside the bark four feet from the ground, and a plank thus wide of solid wood could be obtained from it without a decaying fiber.

The main continuous portion of the sequoia belt, stretching across the basins of the Kaweah and Tule, forms by far the greater portion of the entire coniferous belt, and is plainly visible from the San Joaquin Valley, the light fringe of pines in front not being dense enough to hide it, while it extends so far up the range, there is but little space left for pines or firs above it.

It appears then from this general survey of the sequoia forests, that notwithstanding the colossal dimensions of the trees, and their peculiarly interesting character, more than ninety per cent of the whole number of individuals have hitherto remained unknown.

Was the species ever more extensively distributed on the Sierra in post-glacial times?

I have been led to the conclusion that it never was. Because careful search along the margins of the groves, and in the gaps between, fails to discover a single trace of its previous existence beyond its present bounds.

Notwithstanding I feel confident, that if every sequoia in the range were to die today, numerous monuments of their existence would remain, of so imperishable a nature as to be available for the student more than ten thousand years hence.

In the first place we might notice that no species of coniferous tree in the range keeps its individuals so well together as sequoia; a mile is perhaps the greatest distance of any straggler from the main body, and all of those stragglers that have come under my observation are *young,* instead of old monumental trees, relics of a more extended growth.

Again, we might notice in this connection, the well-known longevity of sequoia. A tree was felled last summer in the old Kings River Grove, whose annual rings, counted by three different persons, numbered from 2125, to 2137; and this specimen was by no means a very aged-looking tree, and measured only twenty-three feet in diameter inside the bark, while the giant of the New Kings River forest, to which I have already called attention, is nearly twice as large, and probably about twice as old; for it is standing on dry gravelly ground where the growth has been slow, the annual rings measuring only about the one-thirtieth of an inch throughout a considerable portion of the diameter.

Again, sequoia trunks frequently endure for centuries after they fall. I have a specimen block, cut from a fallen trunk, which is hardly distinguishable from specimens cut from living trees, although the old trunk fragment from which it was derived has lain exposed in the damp forest more than 380 years, probably thrice as long. The time measure, in the case, is simply this. When the ponderous trunk, to which the old vestige belonged, fell, it sunk itself into the ground, thus making a long straight ditch, and in the middle of this ditch, a silver fir is growing, that is now four feet in diameter, and 380 years old, as determined by cutting it half through and counting the rings, thus demonstrating that the remnant of the trunk that made the ditch, has lain on the ground *more* than 380 years. For it is evident that to find the whole time, we must add to the 380 years, the time that the vanished portion of the trunk lay in the ditch before being burned out of the way, plus the time that passed ere the seed from which the monumental fir sprang fell into the prepared soil and took root. Now, because sequoia trunks are never wholly consumed in one forest fire, and those fires recur only at considerable intervals, and because sequoia ditches after being cleared are often left unplanted for centuries, it becomes evident that the trunk remnant in question may probably have lain a thousand years or more. And this instance is by no means a rare one.

But admitting that upon those areas supposed to have been once covered with sequoia every tree may have fallen, and every trunk burned or buried, leaving not a remnant, many of the ditches made by the fall of the ponderous trunks, and the bowls made by their upturning roots, would remain patent for thousands of years after the last vestige of the trunks that made them had vanished. Much of this ditch-writing would no doubt be quickly effaced by the flood action of overflowing streams, and rain-washing; but no inconsiderable portion would remain enduringly engraved on ridgetops beyond all such destructive action; for, where all the conditions are favorable, it is almost absolutely imperishable. *Now these historic ditches and root bowls occur in all the present sequoia groves and forests, but not the faintest vestige of one presents itself outside of them.*

We therefore conclude that the area covered by sequoia has not been diminished during the last eight or ten thousand years, and probably not at all in post-glacial times.

Is the species verging to extinction? What are its relations to climate, soil, and associated trees?

All the phenomena bearing on these questions, also throw light, as we shall endeavor to show, upon the peculiar distribution of the species, and sustain the conclusion already arrived at on the question of extension.

In the northern groups there are few young trees or saplings growing up around the failing old ones to perpetuate the race, and inasmuch as

those aged sequoias, so nearly childless, are the only ones commonly
known, the species seems doomed to speedy extinction, as being nothing
more than an expiring remnant, vanquished in the so-called struggle for
life, by pines and firs, that have driven it into its last strongholds, in
moist glens where climate is exceptionally favorable. But the language of
the majestic continuous forests of the south, creates a very different impression. No tree of all the forest is more enduringly established in concordance with climate and soil. It grows heartily everywhere, on moraines,
rocky ledges, along watercourses, and in the deep moist alluvium of
meadows; with a multitude of seedlings, and saplings crowding up around
the aged, seemingly abundantly able to maintain the forest in prime
vigor. For every old storm-stricken tree, there is one or more in all the
glory of prime; and for each of these, many young trees, and crowds of
exuberant saplings. So that if all the trees of any section of the main
sequoia forest were ranged together according to age, a very promising
curve would be presented, all the way up from last year's seedlings to
giants, and with the young and middle-aged portion of the curve, many
times longer than the old portion. Even as far north as the Fresno, I
counted 536 saplings and seedlings growing promisingly upon a piece of
rough avalanche soil not exceeding two acres in area. This soil bed is
about seven years old, and had been seeded almost simultaneously by
pines, firs, libocedrus, and sequoia; presenting a remarkably simple and
instructive illustration of the struggle for life among the rival species;
and it was interesting to note that the conditions thus far affecting
them have enabled the young sequoias to gain a marked advantage
over all the others.

In every instance like the above, I have observed that the seedling
sequoia is capable of growing on both drier and wetter soil than its rivals,
but requires more sunshine than they; the latter fact being clearly shown
wherever a sugar pine or fir is growing in close contact with a sequoia of
about equal age and size, and equally exposed to the sun, the branches
of the latter are always less leafy. Toward the south, however, where
the sequoia becomes *more* exuberant and numerous, the rival trees become
less so; and where they mix with sequoias, they mostly grow up beneath
them like slender grasses among stalks of Indian corn. Upon a bed of
sandy flood soil I counted ninety-four sequoias, from one to twelve feet
high, on a patch of ground once occupied by four large sugar pines which
lay crumbling beneath them; an instance of conditions which have enabled sequoia to crowd out the pines.

I also noted eighty-six vigorous saplings upon a piece of fresh ground
prepared for their reception by fire. Thus fire, the great destroyer of

sequoia, also furnishes bare virgin ground, one of the conditions essential for its growth from the seed. Fresh ground is thus upturned and mellowed, and many trees are also planted for every one that falls. Landslips and floods also give rise to bare virgin ground; and a tree now and then owes its existence to a burrowing wolf or squirrel, but the main supply of fresh soil is furnished by the fall of aged trees.

The climatic changes in progress in the Sierra, bearing on the tenure of tree life, are entirely misapprehended, especially as to the *time,* and the means, employed by nature in effecting them. It is constantly asserted in a vague way, that the Sierra was vastly wetter than now, and that the increasing drouth will of itself extinguish sequoia, leaving its ground to other trees supposed capable of flourishing in a drier climate. But that Sequoia can and does grow on as dry ground as any of its present rivals, is manifest in a thousand places. "Why then," it will be asked, "are sequoias always found in *greatest abundance* in well watered places where streams are exceptionally abundant?" Simply because a growth of sequoias always *creates* those streams. The thirsty mountaineer knows well that in every sequoia grove he will find running water, but it is a very complete mistake to suppose that the water is the *cause* of the grove being there; for on the contrary, the grove is the entire cause of the *water* being there; drain off the water if possible, and the trees will remain, but cut off the trees, and the streams will vanish. Never was cause more completely mistaken for effect than in the case of these related phenomena of sequoia woods and perennial streams, and I confess that at first I shared in the blunder.

When attention is called to the method of sequoia stream-making, it will be apprehended at once. The roots of this immense tree cover the ground, forming a thick continuous, capacious sponge, that absorbs, and holds back the rains and melting snows, only allowing them to ooze and flow gently. Indeed every fallen leaf, and rootlet, as well as long clasping root, and prostrate trunk, may be regarded as dams, hoarding the bounty of storm clouds, and dispensing it as blessings all through the summer, instead of allowing it to go headlong in short-lived floods. Evaporation is also checked by the dense sequoia foliage to a greater extent than by any other Sierra tree and the air is entangled in masses and broad sheets, that are quickly saturated; while thirsty winds are not allowed to go sponging and licking along the ground.

So great is the retention of water in many places in the main belt that bogs and meadows are created by the killing of the trees; a single trunk falling across a stream in the woods often forms a dam 200 feet long, and from ten to thirty feet high, giving rise to a pond, which kills the trees within its reach. These dead trees fall in turn, thus making a clearing, while sediments gradually accumulate changing the pond into a bog, or meadow, for a growth of carices and sphagnum. In some instances a chain of small bogs or meadows rise above one another on a hillside, which are gradually merged into one another, forming sloping bogs or meadows which form very striking features of sequoia woods, and since all the trees that have fallen into them have been preserved, they contain records of the generations that have passed since they began to form.

Since then it is a fact that thousands of sequoias are growing thriftily on what is termed dry ground, and even clinging like mountain pines to rifts in granite precipices; and since it has also been shown that the extra moisture found in connection with the denser growths is an *effect* of their presence, instead of a *cause* of their presence; then the notions as to the former extension of the species, and its near approach to extinction, based upon its supposed dependence on greater moisture are seen to be erroneous.

The decrease in the rain and snowfall since the close of the glacial epoch in the Sierra is much less than is commonly guessed. The highest post-glacial watermarks are well preserved in all the upper river channels, and they are not greatly higher than the spring floodmarks of the present; showing conclusively that no extraordinary decrease has taken place in the volume of post-glacial Sierra streams since they came into existence. But in the meantime eliminating all this complicated question of climatic change, the plain fact remains; that *the present rain and snowfall is abundantly sufficient for the luxuriant growth of sequoia forests.* Indeed all my observations tend to show that in case of prolonged drouth, the sugar pines and firs would die before sequoia, not alone because of the greater longevity of individual trees, but because the species can endure more actual drouth, and make the most of whatever moisture falls. Only a few of the very densest fir and pine woods felt and weave a root sponge sufficiently thick and extensive for the maintenance of perennial springs, while *every* sequoia grove does.

Again, if the restriction and irregular distribution of the species be interpreted as a result of the desiccation of the range, then instead of increasing as it does in individuals toward the south where the rainfall is less, it should diminish.

If then the peculiar distribution of sequoia *has not* been governed by superior conditions of soil as to fertility or moisture, by what *has* it been governed?

Several years ago I observed that the northern groves, the only ones I was then acquainted with, were located on just those portions of the general forest soil belt that were first laid bare toward the close of the glacial period when the ice sheet began to break up into individual glaciers. And last summer while searching the wide basin of the San Joaquin, and trying to account for the absence of sequoia where every condition seemed favorable for its growth, it occurred to me that this remarkable gap in the sequoia belt is located exactly in the pathway of the vast *mer de glace* of the San Joaquin and Kings River basins, which poured its frozen floods to the plain, fed by the snows that fell on more than fifty miles of the summit. I then perceived that the other great gap in the belt, forty miles wide, extending between the Calaveras and Tuolumne groves, occurs exactly in the pathway of the great *mer de glace* of the Tuolumne and Stanislaus basins, and that the smaller gap between the Merced and Mariposa groves, occurs in the pathway of the smallest glacier of the Merced. *The wider the ancient glacier, the wider the corresponding gap in the sequoia belt.*

Finally, pursuing my investigations across the basins of the Kaweah and Tule, I discovered that the sequoia belt attained its greatest development, just where, owing to the topographical peculiarities of the region, the ground had been most perfectly protected from the main ice rivers, that continued to pour past from the summit fountains, long after the smaller local glaciers had been melted.

Beginning at the south, the majestic, ancient glaciers are seen to have been shed off right and left down the valleys of Kern and Kings rivers, by the lofty protective spurs outspread embracingly above the warm sequoia-filled basins of the Kaweah and Tule. Then next northward comes the wide sequoia-less channel of the ancient San Joaquin and Kings River *mer de glace*. Then the warm, protected spots of Fresno and Mariposa groves. Then the sequoia-less channel of the ancient Merced glacier. Next the warm, sheltered ground of the Merced and Tuolumne groves. Then the sequoia-less channel of the grand ancient *mer de glace* of the Tuolumne and Stanislaus; and lastly the warm, old ground of the Calaveras groves.

What the other conditions may have been that enabled sequoia to establish itself upon these oldest and warmest portions of the main glacial soil belt, I cannot say. I might venture to state, however, in this connection, that since the sequoia forests present a more and more ancient aspect as they extend southward, I am inclined to think that the species was distributed from the south. While the sugar pine, its great rival in the northern groves, seems to have come around the head of the Sacramento valley and down the Sierra from the north. Consequently when the Sierra soil beds were first thrown open to pre-emption on the melting of the ice

Crescent Meadow, Giant Forest,
Sequoia National Park

sheet, Sequoia may have established itself along the available portions of the south half of the range, prior to the arrival of the sugar pine; while the sugar pine took possession of the north half, prior to the arrival of Sequoia.

But, however much uncertainty may attach to this branch of the question, there are no obscuring shadows upon the grand general relationship we have pointed out between the present distribution of sequoia and the ancient glaciers of the Sierra. And when we distinctly bear in mind the great radical fact, that *all* the present forests of the Sierra are young, growing on moraine soil recently deposited, and that the flank of the range itself, with all its landscapes is newborn, recently sculptured and brought to the light of day from beneath the ice mantle of the glacial winter, then a thousand lawless mysteries disappear, and broad harmonies take their places.

But although all the observed phenomena bearing on the post-glacial history of this colossal tree point to the conclusion that it never was more widely distributed on the Sierra since the close of the glacial epoch—that its present forests are scarcely past prime, if indeed they have reached prime—that the post-glacial day of the species is not half done, yet, when from a wider outlook the vast antiquity of the genus is considered, and its ancient richness in species and individuals; comparing our Sierra Giant and *Sequoia sempervirens* of the coast, the only other living species, with the twelve fossil species already discovered, and described by Heer and Lesquereux, some of which seem to have flourished over vast areas around the polar zone, and in Europe, and our own territories, during tertiary and cretaceous times—then indeed it becomes plain that our two surviving species, restricted to narrow belts within the limits of California, are mere remnants of the genus, both as to species, and individuals; and that they probably are verging to extinction. But the verge of a period beginning in cretaceous times, may have a breadth of tens of thousands of years, not to mention the possible existence of conditions calculated to multiply and re-extend both species and individuals. This, however, is a branch of the question beyond the present discussion.[5]

In studying the fate of our forest king, we have thus far considered the action of purely natural causes only; but unfortunately *man* is in the woods, and waste and pure destruction are already making rapid headway. If the importance of forests were at all understood, even from an

[5] In 1944 living examples of a closely related genus, *Metasequoia,* the Dawn Redwood, were discovered in central China.

economic standpoint, their preservation would call forth the most watchful attention of government. In the meantime, however, scarce anything definite is known regarding them, and the simplest groundwork for available legislation is not yet laid, while every species of destruction is moving on with accelerated speed.

In the course of last year's explorations I have found no less than five mills located on, or near, the lower edge of the sequoia belt, all of which saw more or less of the Big Tree into lumber. One of these, located on the North Fork of the Kaweah, cut over two million feet of Big Tree lumber last season. Most of the Fresno group are doomed to feed the mills recently erected near them, and a company has been formed to cut the magnificent forest on Kings River. In these milling operations waste far exceeds use; for after the choice young manageable trees on any given spot have been felled, the woods are fired to clear the ground of limbs and refuse with reference to further operations, and of course most of the seedlings and saplings are destroyed.

These mill ravages however are small as compared with the comprehensive destruction caused by "Sheepmen." Incredible numbers of sheep are driven to the mountain pastures every summer, and their course is ever marked by desolation. Every wild botanic garden is trodden down, the shrubs are stripped of leaves as if devoured by locusts, and the woods are burned. Running fires are set everywhere, with a view to clearing the ground of prostrate trunks, to facilitate the movements of the flocks, and improve the pastures. The entire forest belt is thus swept and devastated from one extremity of the range to the other, and with the exception of the resinous *Pinus contorta,* sequoia suffers most of all. Indians burn off the underbrush in certain localities to facilitate deer-hunting. Mountaineers carelessly allow their campfires to run, so do lumbermen, but the fires of the sheepmen or *Muttoneers,* form more than ninety per cent of all destructive fires that range the Sierra forests.

Some years ago a law was enacted by the California legislature with special reference to the preservation of *Sequoia gigantea,* under which the cutting down of trees over sixteen feet in diameter became illegal, but on the whole, a more absurd and shortsighted piece of legislation could not be conceived; for all the young trees on which the permanence of the forest depend, may be either burned or cut with impunity, while the old trees may also be burned provided only they are not cut!

It appears, therefore, that notwithstanding our forest king might live on gloriously in nature's keeping, it is rapidly vanishing before the fire and steel of man; and unless protective measures be speedily invented and applied, in a few decades at the farthest, all that will be left of *Sequoia gigantea* will be a few hacked and scarred monuments.

Proceedings of the American Association
for the Advancement of Science, 25th Meeting,
August 1876

2. MORAINE SOIL

The very soil on which the giant trees flourished, Muir was delighted to report, was glacier ground. Like the cedars of Lebanon, about which the English botanist Sir Joseph Hooker had told him at one of their Shasta campfires, sequoias shared the earth and gravel of moraine deposits with certain other conifers. Thus the two chief preoccupations of Muir's southern travels, ancient glaciers and ancient trees, were fused in a single, insightful discovery.

The forests of the South Fork of the Kaweah extend up the range to a height of 8400 feet, which is the extreme upper limit of the entire sequoia belt, and here I was so fortunate as to settle definitely the question of the relationship of sequoia to the ancient glaciers, as to the soil they are growing upon. Hooker discovered that the cedars of Lebanon were growing upon an ancient moraine. So also are the giant trees of California. Several years ago, toward the commencement of my glacial studies, I clearly determined the fact that all the upper portion of the general forest belt was not growing upon soil slowly crumbled from the rock by rains and dews and the decomposing atmosphere, but upon *moraine* soil ground from the mountain flank by the ancient glaciers, and scarce at all modified by post-glacial agents. *Pinus contorta,*[1] *P. flexilis,*[2] *P. aristata,*[3] and *P. monticola*[4] are planted as regularly in moraine rows and curves as the corn of an Illinois farmer. So also is a considerable portion of the

[1] Lodgepole pine (*P. contorta* var. *latifolia*).
[2] Probably Whitebark pine (*P. albicaulis*).
[3] Bristlecone pine, actually not found in the Sierra.
[4] Western white pine.

Picea amabilis[5] which forms the upper portion of the main heavy coniferous belt of the Sierra. Next in descending order comes *Picea grandis,*[6] then *Pinus lambertiana,*[7] and *P. ponderosa,*[8] *Sequoia gigantea, Libocedrus decurrens,*[9] and *Abies douglasii,*[10] all growing upon moraine soil also, but so greatly modified and obscured by post-glacial weathering as to make its real origin dark or invisible to observers unskilled in glacial phenomena. Here, on the head of the South Fork of the Kaweah, the sequoias are established upon moraines of the ancient Kaweah glacier that flowed down the South Fork Canyon, and scarce more changed than those occupied by the summit pines.

"The New Sequoia Forests of California,"
Harper's Monthly, November 1878

3. NATURE'S FOREST MASTERPIECE

Twenty-five years of further experience and travel, in the Northwest and Alaska and across the continent, only deepened Muir's appreciation of the Big Trees he had tracked down the Sierra Nevada in the 1870s. Time also mellowed and intellectualized his prose style. When he wrote Our National Parks, *portions of which appeared as separate articles in the* Atlantic, *Muir was displaying to the world the treasures he had helped to discover and interpret, and arguing with all his might for their preservation. This was his tribute to the most perfect example of natural beauty, strength, and dignity he had ever found.*

[5] Silver fir (*Abies amabilis*).
[6] California red fir (*Abies magnifica*).
[7] Sugar pine.
[8] Western yellow pine.
[9] Incense cedar.
[10] Douglas fir (*Pseudotsuga taxifolia*).

No description can give any adequate idea of their singular majesty, much less of their beauty. Excepting the sugar pine, most of their neighbors with pointed tops seem to be forever shouting "Excelsior!" while the Big Tree, though soaring above them all, seems satisfied, its rounded head poised lightly as a cloud, giving no impression of trying to go higher. Only in youth does it show, like other conifers, a heavenward yearning, keenly aspiring with a long quick-growing top. Indeed the whole tree, for the first century or two, or until a hundred to a hundred and fifty feet high, is arrowhead in form, and, compared with the solemn rigidity of age, is as sensitive to the wind as a squirrel tail. The lower branches are gradually dropped as it grows older, and the upper ones thinned out, until comparatively few are left. These, however, are developed to great size, divide again and again, and terminate in bossy rounded masses of leafy branchlets, while the head becomes dome-shaped. Then poised in fullness of strength and beauty, stern and solemn in mien, it glows with eager, enthusiastic life, quivering to the tip of every leaf and branch and far-reaching root, calm as a granite dome—the first to feel the touch of the rosy beams of the morning, the last to bid the sun good night.

Perfect specimens, unhurt by running fires or lightning, are singularly regular and symmetrical in general form, though not at all conventional, showing infinite variety in sure unity and harmony of plan. The immensely strong, stately shafts, with rich purplish-brown bark, are free of limbs for a hundred and fifty feet or so, though dense tufts of sprays occur here and there, producing an ornamental effect, while long parallel furrows give a fluted, columnar appearance. The limbs shoot forth with equal boldness in every direction, showing no weather side. On the old trees the main branches are crooked and rugged, and strike rigidly outward, mostly at right angles from the trunk, but there is always a certain measured restraint in their reach which keeps them within bounds. No other Sierra tree has foliage so densely massed, or outlines so finely, firmly drawn, and so obediently subordinate to an ideal type. A particularly knotty, angular, ungovernable-looking branch, five to eight feet in diameter, and perhaps a thousand years old, may occasionally be seen pushing out from the trunk as if determined to break across the bounds of the regular curve; but, like all the others, as soon as the general outline is approached, the huge limb dissolves into massy bosses of branchlets and sprays, as if the tree were growing beneath an invisible bell glass, against the sides of which the branches were molded, while many small varied departures from the ideal form give the impression of freedom to grow as they like.

Except in picturesque old age, after being struck by lightning and broken by a thousand snowstorms, this regularity of form is one of the Big Tree's most distinguishing characteristics. Another is the simple sculptural beauty of the trunk, and its great thickness as compared with its height and the width of the branches; many of them being from eight to ten feet in diameter at a height of two hundred feet from the ground, and seeming more like finely modeled and sculptured architectural columns than the stems of trees, while the great strong limbs are like rafters supporting the magnificent dome head.

The root system corresponds in magnitude with the other dimensions of the tree, forming a flat, far-reaching, spongy network, two hundred feet or more in width without any taproot; and the instep is so grand and fine, so suggestive of endless strength, it is long ere the eye is released to look above it. The natural swell of the roots, though at first sight excessive, gives rise to buttresses no greater than are required for beauty as well as strength, as at once appears when you stand back far enough to see the whole tree in its true proportions. The fineness of the taper of the trunk is shown by its thickness at great heights—a diameter of ten feet at a height of two hundred being, as we have seen, not uncommon. Indeed the boles of but few trees hold their thickness so well as sequoia. Resolute, consummate, determined in form, always beheld with wondering admiration, the Big Tree always seems unfamiliar, standing alone, unrelated, with peculiar physiognomy, awfully solemn and earnest. Nevertheless, there is nothing alien in its looks. The madrone, clad in thin smooth red and yellow bark and big glossy leaves, seems, in the dark coniferous forests of Washington and Vancouver Island, like some lost wanderer from the magnolia groves of the South, while sequoia, with all its strangeness, seems more at home than any of its neighbors, holding the best right to the ground as the oldest, strongest inhabitant. One soon becomes acquainted with new species of pine and fir and spruce as with friendly people, shaking their outstretched branches like shaking hands, and fondling their beautiful little ones; while the venerable aboriginal sequoia, ancient of other days, keeps you at a distance, taking no notice of you, speaking only to the winds, thinking only of the sky, looking as strange in aspect and behavior among the neighboring trees as would the mastodon or hairy elephant among the homely bears and deer. Only the Sierra juniper is at all like it, standing rigid and unconquerable on glacial pavements or thousands of years, grim, rusty, silent, uncommunicative, with an air of antiquity about as pronounced as that so characteristic of sequoia.

The bark of full-grown trees is from one to two feet thick, rich cinnamon brown, purplish on young trees and shady parts of the old, forming magnificent masses of color with the underbrush and beds of flowers. Toward the end of winter the trees themselves bloom, while the snow is still eight or ten feet deep. The pistillate flowers are about three-eighths of an inch long, pale green, and grow in countless thousands on the ends of the sprays. The staminate are still more abundant, pale yellow, a fourth of an inch long, and when the golden pollen is ripe they color the whole tree, and dust the air and the ground far and near.

The cones are bright grass-green in color, about two and a half inches long, one and a half wide, and are made up of thirty or forty strong closely packed, rhomboidal scales, with four to eight seeds at the base of each. The seeds are extremely small and light, being only from an eighth to a fourth of an inch long and wide, including a filmy surrounding wing, which causes them to glint and waver in falling, and enables the wind to carry them considerable distances from the tree.

The faint lisp of snowflakes, as they alight, is one of the smallest sounds mortal can hear. The sound of falling sequoia seeds, even when they happen to strike on flat leaves or flakes of bark, is about as faint. Very different are the bumping and thudding of the falling cones. Most of them are cut off by the Douglas squirrel, and stored for the sake of the seeds, small as they are. In the calm Indian summer these busy harvesters with ivory sickles go to work early in the morning, as soon as breakfast is over, and nearly all day the ripe cones fall in a steady, pattering, bumping shower. Unless harvested in this way, they discharge their seeds, and remain on the tree for many years. In fruitful seasons the trees are fairly laden. On two small specimen branches, one and a half and two inches in diameter, I counted four hundred and eighty cones. No other California conifer produces nearly so many seeds, excepting perhaps its relative, the redwood of the Coast Mountains. Millions are ripened annually by a single tree, and the product of one of the main groves in a fruitful year would suffice to plant all the mountain ranges of the world.

The dense tufted sprays make snug nesting places for birds, and in some of the loftiest, leafiest towers of verdure thousands of generations have been reared, the great solemn trees shedding off flocks of merry singers every year from nests like the flocks of winged seeds from the cones.

The Big Tree keeps its youth far longer than any of its neighbors. Most silver firs are old in their second or third century, pines in their fourth or fifth, while the Big Tree, growing beside them, is still in the bloom of its youth, juvenile in every feature, at the age of old pines, and cannot be said to attain anything like prime size and beauty before its fifteen hundredth year, or, under favorable circumstances, become old before its three thousandth. Many, no doubt, are much older than this. On one of the Kings River giants, thirty-five feet and eight inches in diameter, exclusive of bark, I counted upwards of four thousand annual wood rings, in which there was no trace of decay after all these centuries of mountain weather.[2] There is no absolute limit to the existence of any tree. Their death is due to accidents, not, as of animals, to the wearing out of organs. Only the leaves die of old age—their fall is foretold in their structure; but the leaves are renewed every year, and so also are the other essential organs, wood, roots, bark, buds. Most of the Sierra trees die of disease. Thus the magnificent silver firs are devoured by fungi, and comparatively few of them live to see their three-hundredth birth year. But nothing hurts the Big Trees. I never saw one that was sick or showed the slightest sign of decay. It lives on through indefinite thousands of years, until burned, blown down, undermined, or shattered by some tremendous lightning stroke. No ordinary bolt every seriously hurts sequoia. In all my walks I have seen only one that was thus killed outright. Lightning, though rare in the California lowlands, is common on the Sierra. Almost every day in June and July small thunderstorms refresh the main forest belt. Clouds like snowy mountains of marvelous beauty grow rapidly in the calm sky about midday, and cast cooling shadows and showers that seldom last more than an hour. Nevertheless, these brief, kind storms wound or kill a good many trees. I have seen silver firs, two hundred feet high, split into long peeled rails and slivers down to the roots, leaving not even a stump; the rails radiating like the spokes of a wheel from a hole in the ground where the tree stood. But the sequoia, instead of being split and slivered, usually has forty or fifty feet of its brash knotty top smashed off in short chunks about the size of cordwood, the beautiful rosy-red ruins covering the ground in a circle a hundred feet wide or more. I never saw any that had been cut down to the ground, or even to below the branches, except one in the Stanislaus Grove,[3] about twelve feet in diameter, the greater part of which was smashed to fragments, leaving only a leafless stump about seventy-five feet high. It is a curious fact that all the very old sequoias have lost their heads by lightning. "All things come to him who waits"; but of all living things Sequoia is perhaps the only one able to wait long enough to make sure of being struck by lightning. Thousands of years it stands ready and waiting, offering its head to every passing cloud as if inviting its fate, praying for heaven's fire as a blessing; and when at last the old head is off, another of the same shape immediately begins to grow on. Every bud and branch seems excited, like bees that have lost their queen, and tries hard to repair the damage. Branches that for many centuries have been

---

[2] Scientists estimate the age of the oldest logged sequoia at no more than 3200 years.

[3] Calaveras Big Trees.

growing out horizontally at once turn upward, and all their branchlets arrange themselves with reference to a new top of the same peculiar curve as the old one. Even the small subordinate branches halfway down the trunk do their best to push up to the top and help in this curious head-making.

The great age of these noble trees is even more wonderful than their huge size, standing bravely up, millennium in, millennium out, to all that fortune may bring them; triumphant over tempest and fire and time, fruitful and beautiful, giving food and shelter to multitudes of small fleeting creatures dependent on their bounty. Other trees may claim to be about as large or as old: Australian gums, Senegal baobabs, Mexican taxodiums, English yews, and venerable Lebanon cedars, trees of renown, some of which are from ten to thirty feet in diameter. We read of oaks that are supposed to have existed ever since the creation, yet, strange to say, I can find no definite accounts of the age of any of these trees, but only estimates based on tradition and assumed average rates of growth. No other known tree approaches the sequoia in grandeur, height and thickness being considered, and none, as far as I know, has looked down on so many centuries or opens such impressive and suggestive views into history. The majestic monument of the Kings River Forest is, as we have seen, fully four thousand years old, and, measuring the rings of annual growth, we find it was no less than twenty-seven feet in diameter at the beginning of the Christian era, while many observations lead me to expect the discovery of others ten or twenty centuries older.[4]

"Hunting Big Redwoods," *The Atlantic Monthly,*
September 1901

[4] Bristlecone pines (*P. aristata*) in the White Mountains east of the Sierra Nevada include specimens older than the oldest known sequoias. Muir's estimate of 4000 years for a sequoia cannot be verified.

4. MEASURING A GIANT

Hunting big trees is a California tradition, and habit-forming. Muir, who did not intend to be taken in by tall stories, nevertheless was always open to the possibility of new data concerning the age or size of Sequoia gigantea. *When he was sixty-four years old, having just completed an exhausting mountain trip, he turned back to Converse Basin to check the report of a new record. The article he proposed to write, in this letter to Robert Underwood Johnson, was not published, but a manuscript found after his death may be related to it. (See "Save the Redwoods," page 250.)*

Martinez, September 15, 1902

Dear Mr. Johnson:

On my return from the Kern region I heard loud but vague rumors of the discovery of a giant sequoia in Converse Basin on Kings River, one hundred and fifty-three feet in circumference and fifty feet in diameter, to which I paid no attention, having heard hundreds of such "biggest-tree-in-the-world" rumors before. But at Fresno I met a surveyor who assured me that he had himself measured the tree and found it to be one hundred and fifty-three feet in circumference six feet above ground. So of course I went back up the mountains to see and measure for myself, carrying a steel tape-line.

At one foot above ground it is 108 feet in circumference
  ″ four feet   ″   ″   ″ ″ 97   ″   6 inches in ″
  ″ six   ″   ″   ″   ″ ″ 93   ″   ″ ″

One of the largest and finest every way of living sequoias that have been measured. But none can say it is certainly *the largest*. The immensely larger dead one that I discovered twenty-seven years ago stands within a few miles of this new wonder, and I think I have in my notebooks measurements of living specimens as large as the new tree, or larger. I have a photo of the tree and can get others, I think, from a photographer who has a studio in Converse Basin. I'll write a few pages on Big Trees in general if you like; also touching on the horrible destruction of the Kings River groves now going on fiercely about the mills . . .

The Life and Letters of John Muir

ONE GRAND
NATIONAL PARK

God's first temples—the noblest of a noble race.

1. GOD'S FIRST TEMPLES

From a solitary rambler seeking knowledge of the Yosemite wilderness to the "father of the forest reservation system of America" is a very long journey. It took John Muir more than twenty years. He made his biggest stride after he reached his farthest south, among the Tule River sequoias in October 1875, returning to Yosemite and then to civilization to brood over the question, "How shall we preserve our forests?"

Muir's answer, in phrases which echoed throughout his future writings, was a "letter" to the editors of the leading newspaper of California's state capital. Hopefully, it would influence legislators. Muir was to repeat the argument again and again, in lectures and private talks and newspaper and magazine articles which found a widening audience across the nation.

"God's First Temples," as the Sacramento Record-Union *headlined the piece, was a special plea for "the great master-existence of these noble woods,"* Sequoia gigantea. *Before the presidential proclamations of the 1890s which set aside the Sierra Forest and other Federal reserves, however, Muir extended his range and spoke for all the forests and potential parks.*

Senate Group, Giant Forest,
Sequoia National Park

"GOD'S FIRST TEMPLES."

The Question Considered by John Muir,
the California Geologist—The Views of a
Practical Man and a Scientific Observer
—A Profoundly Interesting Article.

——————

(Communicated to the *Record-Union*)

EDS. RECORD-UNION: The forests of coniferous trees growing on our mountain ranges are by far the most destructible of the natural resources of California. Our gold, and silver, and cinnabar are stored in the rocks, locked up in the safest of all banks, so that notwithstanding the world has been making a run upon them for the last twenty-five years, they still pay out steadily, and will probably continue to do so centuries hence, like rivers pouring from perennial mountain fountains. The riches of our magnificent soil beds are also comparatively safe, because even the most barbarous methods of wildcat farming cannot effect complete destruction, and however great the impoverishment produced, full restoration of fertility is always possible to the enlightened farmer. But our forest belts are being burned and cut down and wasted like a field of unprotected grain, and once destroyed can never be wholly restored even by centuries of persistent and painstaking cultivation.

THE PRACTICAL IMPORTANCE of the preservation of our forests is augmented by their relations to climate, soil and streams. Strip off the woods with their underbrush from the mountain flanks, and the whole state, the lowlands as well as the highlands, would gradually change into a desert. During rainfalls, and when the winter snow was melting, every stream would become a destructive torrent overflowing its banks, stripping off and carrying away the fertile soils, filling up the lower river channels, and overspreading the lowland fields with detritus to a vastly more destructive degree than all the washings from hydraulic mines concerning which we now hear so much. Dripping forests give rise to moist sheets and currents of air, and the sod of grasses and underbrush thus fostered, together with the roots of trees themselves, absorb and hold back rains and melting snow, yet allowing them to doze and percolate and flow gently in useful fertilizing streams. Indeed every pine needle and rootlet, as well as fallen trunks and large clasping roots, may be regarded as dams, hoarding the bounty of storm clouds, and dispensing it as blessings all through the summer, instead of allowing it to gather and rush headlong in short-lived devastating floods. Streams taking their rise in deep woods flow un-failingly as those derived from the eternal ice and snow of the Alps. So constant indeed and apparent is the relationship between forests and never-failing springs, that effect is frequently mistaken for cause, it being often asserted that fine forests will grow only along stream sides where their roots are well watered, when in fact the forests themselves produce many of the streams flowing through them.

THE MAIN FOREST BELT of the Sierra is restricted to the western flank, and extends unbrokenly from one end of the range to the other at an elevation of from three to eight thousand feet above sea level. The great master existence of these noble woods is *Sequoia gigantea,* or Big Tree. Only two species of sequoia are known to exist in the world. Both belong to California, one being found only in the Sierra, the other (*Sequoia sempervirens*) in the Coast Ranges, although no less than five distinct fossil species have been discovered in the tertiary and cretaceous rocks of Green-land. I would like to call attention to this noble tree, with special reference to its preservation. The species extends from the well-known Calaveras groves on the north, to the head of Deer Creek on the south, near the big bend of the Kern River, a distance of about two hundred miles, at an elevation above sea level of from about five to eight thousand feet. From the Calaveras to the South Fork of Kings River it occurs only in small isolated groves, and so sparsely and irregularly distributed that two gaps occur nearly forty miles in width, the one between the Calaveras and Tuolumne groves, the other between those of the Fresno and Kings rivers. From Kings River the belt extends across the broad, rugged basins of the Kaweah and Tule rivers to its southern boundary on Deer Creek, inter-rupted only by deep, rocky canyons, the width of this portion of the belt being from three to ten miles.

IN THE NORTHERN GROVES few young trees or saplings are found ready to take the places of the failing old ones, and because these ancient, childless sequoias are the only ones known to botanists, the species has been gen-erally regarded as doomed to speedy extinction, as being nothing more than an expiring remnant of an ancient flora, and that therefore there is no use trying to save it or to prolong its few dying days. This, however, is in the main a mistaken notion, for the Sierra as it now exists never had an ancient flora. All the species now growing on the range have been planted since the close of the glacial period, and the Big Tree has never formed a greater part of these post-glacial forests than it does today, however widely it may have been distributed throughout pre-glacial forests.

IN TRACING THE BELT southward, all the phenomena bearing upon its history goes to show that the dominion of *Sequoia gigantea,* as King of California trees, is not yet passing away. No tree in the woods seems more firmly established, or more safely settled in accordance with climate and soil. They fill the woods and form the principal tree, growing heartily on solid ledges, along water courses, in the deep, moist soil of meadows, and on avalanche and glacial debris, with a multitude of thrifty seedlings and saplings crowding around the aged, ready to take their places and rule the woods.

Nevertheless nature in her grandly deliberate way keeps up a rotation of forest crops. Species develop and die like individuals, animal as well as plant. Man himself will as surely become extinct as sequoia or mastodon, and be at length known only as a fossil. Changes of this kind are, however, exceedingly slow in their movements, and, as far as the lives of individuals are concerned, such changes have no appreciable effect. Sequoia seems scarcely further past prime as a species than its companion firs (*Picea amabilis* and *P. grandis*),[1] and judging from its present condition and its ancient history, as far as I have been able to decipher it, our sequoia will live and flourish gloriously until A.D. 15,000 at least—probably for longer—that is, if it be allowed to remain in the hands of nature.

WASTE AND DESTRUCTION. But waste and pure destruction are already taking place at a terrible rate, and unless protective measures be speedily invented and enforced, in a few years this noblest tree species in the world will present only a few hacked and scarred remnants. The great enemies of forests are fire and the ax. The destructive effects of these, as compared with those caused by the operations of nature, are instantaneous. Floods undermine and kill many a tree, storm winds bend and break, landslips and avalanches overwhelm whole groves, lightning shatters and burns, but the combined effects of all these amount only to a wholesome beauty-producing culture. Last summer I found some five sawmills located in or near the lower edge of the sequoia belt, all of which saw more or less of the Big Tree into lumber. One of these (Hyde's), situated on the North Fork of the Kaweah, cut no less than 2,000,000 feet of sequoia lumber last season. Most of the Fresno Big Trees are doomed to feed the mills recently erected near them, and a company has been formed by Chas. Converse to cut the noble forest on the South Fork of Kings River. In these milling operations waste far exceeds use. After the choice young manageable trees have been felled, the woods are cleared of limbs and refuse by burning,

[1] *Abies amabilis* and *A. magnifica.*

and in these clearing fires, made with reference to further operations, all the young seedlings and saplings are destroyed, together with many valuable fallen trees and old trees, too large to be cut, thus effectually cutting off all hopes of a renewal of the forest.

THESE RAVAGES, however, of mill fires and mill axes are small as compared with those of the "sheepmen's" fires. Incredible numbers of sheep are driven to the mountain pastures every summer, and in order to make easy paths and to improve the pastures, running fires are set everywhere to burn off the old logs and underbrush. These fires are far more universal and destructive than would be guessed. They sweep through nearly the entire forest belt of the range from one extremity to the other, and in the dry weather, before the coming on of winter storms, are very destructive to all kinds of young trees, and especially to sequoia, whose loose, fibrous bark catches and burns at once. Excepting the Calaveras, I, last summer, examined every sequoia grove in the range, together with the main belt extending across the basins of Kaweah and Tule, and found everywhere the most deplorable waste from this cause. Indians burn off underbrush to facilitate deer-hunting. Campers of all kinds often permit fires to run, so also do millmen, but the fires of "sheepmen" probably form more than ninety per cent of all destructive fires that sweep the woods.

FIRE, THEN, IS THE ARCH DESTROYER of our forests, and sequoia forests suffer most of all. The young trees are most easily fire-killed; the old are most easily burned, and the prostrate trunks, which *never rot* and would remain valuable until our tenth centennial, are reduced to ashes.

In European countries, especially in France, Germany, Italy, and Austria, the economics of forestry have been carefully studied under the auspices of Government, with the most beneficial results. Whether our loose-jointed Government is really able or willing to do anything in the matter remains to be seen. If our law makers were to discover and enforce any method tending to lessen even in a small degree the destruction going on, they would thus cover a multitude of legislative sins in the eyes of every tree lover. I am satisfied, however, that the question can be intelligently discussed only after a careful survey of our forests has been made, together with studies of the forces now acting upon them.

A law was constructed some years ago making the cutting down of sequoias over sixteen feet in diameter illegal. A more absurd and short-sighted piece of legislation could not be conceived. All the young trees might be cut and burned, and all the old ones might be burned but not cut.

JOHN MUIR

Sacramento *Record-Union,* February 5, 1876

2. NEED OF A PARK

The concluding paragraph of Muir's Century *article on Kings Canyon (1891) is printed here separately to underscore his advocacy of "one grand national park." Despite his efforts and those of others, the law-givers did not make haste. It was 1940 before Kings Canyon Wilderness National Park was established, and another twenty-five years before the two great yosemites of the South Fork and Middle Fork were included.*

So far, highway engineers have not been permitted to implement Muir's startling plan for a road from the South Fork, across the divide, down the Middle Fork, and up again to the Big Trees. We may hope that the Wilderness Act of 1964, together with other legal and physical deterrents, will continue to stand in their way.

I fancy the time is not distant when this wonderful region will be opened to the world—when a road will be built up the South Fork of Kings River through the sequoia groves, into the great canyon,[1] and thence across the divide and down the Middle Fork Canyon to Tehipite; thence through the valley and down the canyon to the confluence of the Middle and South forks, and up to the sequoia groves to the point of beginning. Some of the sequoia groves were last year included in the national reservations

[1] The road ends at Copper Creek, near Zumwalt Meadow on the South Fork.

Lower State Lake,
Kings Canyon National Park

of Sequoia and General Grant parks. But all of this wonderful Kings
River region, together with the Kaweah and Tule sequoias, should be comprehended in one grand national park. This region contains no mines of
consequence, it is too high and too rocky for agriculture, and even the
lumber industry need suffer no unreasonable restriction. Let our law-givers
then make haste before it is too late to set apart this surpassingly glorious
region for the recreation and well-being of humanity, and all the world
will rise up and call them blessed.

"A Rival of the Yosemite," *Century Magazine,*
November 1891

3. THE SIERRA RESERVE

*The Sierra Forest Reserve, proclaimed in 1893, was the first
result of Muir's vigorous reaction to the boundary limitations of
Sequoia and General Grant national parks. "It was Muir's idea
that the whole roof of the Sierra should be made a forest reservation," wrote Robert Underwood Johnson, who pursued the subject
with congressmen and with Secretary of Interior John W. Noble.
Special Agent B. F. Allen investigated, and with the aid of Muir
and directors of the new Sierra Club wrote a report advocating the
reservation. (Captain J. H. Dorst, in charge of the parks, estimated
a half million sheep were being grazed at the time in the Kings and
Kern canyons.)*

*Today's Sierra, Sequoia, and fifteen other national forests in Cali-
fornia include some 19 million acres nearly extending from Oregon
to Mexico. As for the four national parks of the 1890s, three of
them in California, they have grown, thanks to the movement Muir
inspired and fostered, to 225 parks, monuments and related areas
in the United States. In 1966, the fiftieth anniversary of the National Parks Act, 128 million visitors were expected and a program
for their safety was announced along with the slogan, "Discover
America."*

The wildest health and pleasure grounds accessible and available to tourists seeking escape from care and dust and early death are the parks and reservations of the West. There are four national parks—the Yellowstone, Yosemite, General Grant, and Sequoia—all within easy reach, and thirty forest reservations, a magnificent realm of woods, most of which, by railroads and trails and open ridges, is also fairly accessible, not only to the determined traveler rejoicing in difficulties, but to those (may their tribe increase) who, not tired, not sick, just naturally take wing every summer in search of wildness. The forty million acres of these reserves are in the main unspoiled as yet, though sadly wasted and threatened on their more open margins by the ax and fire of the lumberman and prospector, and by hoofed locusts, which, like the winged ones, devour every leaf within reach, while the shepherds and owners set fires with the intention of making a blade of grass grow in the place of every tree, but with the result of killing both the grass and the trees.

The Sierra of California is the most openly beautiful and useful of all the forest reserves, and the largest, excepting the Cascade Reserve of Oregon and the Bitter Root of Montana and Idaho. It embraces over four million acres of the grandest scenery and grandest trees on the continent, and its forests are planted just where they do the most good, not only for beauty, but for farming in the great San Joaquin Valley beneath them. It extends southward from the Yosemite National Park to the end of the range, a distance of nearly two hundred miles. No other coniferous forest in the world contains so many species or so many large and beautiful trees —*Sequoia gigantea,* king of conifers, "the noblest of a noble race," as Sir Joseph Hooker well says; the sugar pine, king of all the world's pines, living or extinct; the yellow pine, next in rank, which here reaches most perfect development, forming noble towers of verdure two hundred feet high; the mountain pine, which braves the coldest blasts far up the mountains on grim, rocky slopes; and five others, flourishing each in its place, making eight species of pine in one forest, which is still further enriched by the great Douglas spruce, libocedrus, two species of silver fir, large trees and exquisitely beautiful, the Paton hemlock, the most graceful of evergreens, the curious tumion, oaks of many species, maples, alders, poplars, and flowering dogwood, all fringed with flowery underbrush, manzanita, ceanothus, wild rose, cherry, chestnut, and rhododendron. Wandering at random through these friendly, approachable woods, one comes here and there to the loveliest lily gardens, some of the lilies ten feet high, and the smoothest gentian meadows, and yosemite valleys known only to mountaineers. Once I spent a night by a campfire on Mount Shasta with Asa Gray and Sir Joseph Hooker, and, knowing that they were acquainted with all the great forests of the world, I asked whether they knew any coniferous forest that rivaled that of the Sierra. They unhesitatingly said: "No. In the beauty and grandeur of individual trees, and in number and variety of species, the Sierra forests surpass all others."

This Sierra Reserve, proclaimed by the President of the United States in September, 1893, is worth the most thoughtful care of the government for its own sake, without considering its value as the fountain of the rivers on which the fertility of the great San Joaquin Valley depends. Yet it gets no care at all. In the fog of tariff, silver, and annexation politics it is left wholly unguarded, though the management of the adjacent national parks by a few soldiers shows how well and how easily it can be preserved. In the meantime, lumbermen are allowed to spoil it at their will, and sheep in uncountable ravenous hordes to trample it and devour every green leaf within reach; while the shepherds, like destroying angels, set innumerable fires, which burn not only the undergrowth of seedlings on which the permanence of the forest depends, but countless thousands of the venerable giants. If every citizen could take one walk through this reserve, there would be no more trouble about its care; for only in darkness does vandalism flourish.

"The Wild Parks and Forest Reservations of the West,"
Atlantic Monthly, January 1898

4. SAVE THE REDWOODS

As a partisan not only of the Big Trees of the Sierra but also of the Coast Redwoods, Sequoia sempervirens, *Muir visited and admired redwood groves from Santa Cruz north. During his lifetime he was honored by the establishment of Muir Woods National Monument, preserving such a grove in Marin County near the Golden Gate. When the Save-the-Redwoods League was beginning its campaign to establish a chain of California state parks in the redwood region, this undated manuscript, found among Muir's papers after his death, was published for the first time in the* Sierra Club Bulletin. *Congress has not yet acted on various proposals for a Redwood National Park.*

We are often told that the world is going from bad to worse, sacrificing everything to mammon. But this righteous uprising in defense of God's trees in the midst of exciting politics and wars is telling a different story, and every sequoia, I fancy, has heard the good news and is waving its branches for joy. The wrongs done to trees, wrongs of every sort, are done in the darkness of ignorance and unbelief, for when light comes the heart of the people is always right. Forty-seven years ago one of these Calaveras King Sequoias was laboriously cut down, that the stump might be had for a dancing floor. Another, one of the finest in the grove, more than three hundred feet high, was skinned alive to a height of one hundred and sixteen feet from the ground and the bark sent to London to show how fine and big that Calaveras tree was—as sensible a scheme as skinning our great men would be to prove their greatness. This grand tree is of course dead, a ghastly disfigured ruin, but it still stands erect and holds forth its majestic arms as if alive and saying, "Forgive them; they know not what they do." Now some millmen want to cut all the Calaveras trees into lumber and money. But we have found a better use for them. No doubt these trees would make good lumber after passing through a sawmill, as George Washington after passing through the hands of a French cook would have made good food. But both for Washington and the tree that bears his name[1] higher uses have been found.

Could one of these sequoia kings come to town in all its godlike majesty so as to be strikingly seen and allowed to plead its own cause, there would never again be any lack of defenders. And the same may be said of all the other sequoia groves and forests of the Sierra with their companions and the noble *Sequoia sempervirens,* or redwood, of the coast mountains.

In a general view we find that the *Sequoia gigantea,* or Big Tree, is distributed in a widely interrupted belt along the west flank of the Sierra, from a small grove on the Middle Fork of the American River to the head of Deer Creek, a distance of about two hundred and sixty miles, at an elevation of about five thousand to a little over eight thousand feet above the sea. From the American River grove to the forest on Kings River the species occurs only in comparatively small isolated patches or groves so sparsely distributed along the belt that three of the gaps in it are from forty to sixty miles wide. From Kings River southward the sequoia is not restricted to mere groves, but extends across the broad rugged basins of the Kaweah and Tule rivers in majestic forests a distance of nearly seventy miles, the continuity of this portion of the belt being but slightly broken save by the deep canyons.

[1] *Sequoia washingtonia* was one of the botanical names for the Big Tree which did not survive.

In these noble groves and forests to the southward of the Calaveras Grove the ax and saw have long been busy, and thousands of the finest sequoias have been felled, blasted into manageable dimensions, and sawed into lumber by methods destructive almost beyond belief, while fires have spread still wider and more lamentable ruin. In the course of my explorations twenty-five years ago, I found five sawmills located on or near the lower margin of the sequoia belt, all of which were cutting more or less Big Tree lumber, which looks like the redwood of the coast, and was sold as redwood. One of the smallest of these mills in the season of 1874 sawed two million feet of sequoia lumber. Since that time other mills have been built among the sequoias, notably the large ones on Kings River and the head of the Fresno. The destruction of these grand trees is still going on.

On the other hand, the Calaveras Grove for forty years has been faithfully protected by Mr. Sperry,[2] and with the exception of the two trees mentioned above is still in primeval beauty. The Tuolumne and Merced groves near Yosemite, the Dinkey Creek grove, those of the General Grant National Park, with several outstanding groves that are nameless on the Kings, Kaweah, and Tule river basins, and included in the Sierra forest reservation, have of late years been partially protected by the Federal Government; while the well-known Mariposa Grove has long been guarded by the State.

For the thousands of acres of sequoia forest outside of the reservation and national parks, and in the hands of lumbermen, no help is in sight. Probably more than three times as many sequoias as are contained in the whole Calaveras Grove have been cut into lumber every year for the last twenty-six years without let or hindrance, and with scarce a word of protest on the part of the public, while at the first whisper of the bonding of the Calaveras Grove to lumbermen most everybody rose in alarm. This righteous and lively indignation on the part of Californians after the long period of deathlike apathy, in which they have witnessed the destruction of other groves unmoved, seems strange until the rapid growth that right public opinion has made during the last few years is considered and the peculiar interest that attaches to the Calaveras giants. They were the first discovered and are best known. Thousands of travelers from every country have come to pay them tribute of admiration and praise, their reputation is world-wide, and the names of great men have long been associated with them—Washington, Humboldt, Torrey and Gray, Sir Joseph Hooker, and others. These kings of the forest, the noblest of a noble race, rightly

[2] James L. Sperry was proprietor of a hotel in Calaveras Big Trees for many years, before establishment of the state park there.

belong to the world, but as they are in California we cannot escape responsibility as their guardians. Fortunately the American people are equal to this trust, or any other that may arise, as soon as they see it and understand it.

Any fool can destroy trees. They cannot defend themselves or run away. And few destroyers of trees ever plant any; nor can planting avail much toward restoring our giant aboriginal giants. It took more than three thousand years to make some of the oldest of the sequoias, trees that are still standing in perfect strength and beauty, waving and singing in the mighty forests of the Sierra. Through all the eventful centuries since Christ's time, and long before that, God has cared for these trees, saved them from drought, disease, avalanches, and a thousand storms; but he cannot save them from sawmills and fools; this is left to the American people. The news from Washington is encouraging. On March third[3] the House passed a bill providing for the Government acquisition of the Calaveras giants. The danger these sequoias have been in will do good far beyond the boundaries of the Calaveras Grove, in saving other groves and forests, and quickening interest in forest affairs in general. While the iron of public sentiment is hot let us strike hard. In particular, a reservation or national park of the only other species of sequoia, the *sempervirens,* or redwood, hardly less wonderful than the *gigantea,* should be quickly secured. It will have to be acquired by gift or purchase, for the Government has sold every section of the entire redwood belt from the Oregon boundary to below Santa Cruz.

"Save the Redwoods," *Sierra Club Bulletin,*
January 1920

5. THE WORK OF PRESERVATION

Unlike the closely written, literary letters of his early years, Muir's correspondence in his last quarter-century was both business-like and breathless. His leadership among conservationists and his many friendships required constant letter-writing. He did not acquire a typewriter until very late, after his penmanship had become nearly a scrawl.

[3] The year was 1904. The legislation was never enacted.

These three examples indicate Muir's thoroughgoing activity for protection of the forests, for appreciation and growth of the parks, and for truth and accuracy in whatever was written. The reference in the 1907 letter is to a Sierra Club "Report on the Kings River Canyon and Vicinity" addressed to the President of the United States, the Secretary of Agriculture and the Forester, which Muir felt went too far in comparing the new region to Yosemite. The information requested in the letter of 1911 was provided by William Colby, Secretary of the Sierra Club, but was not used, after all, in the text of Muir's book, The Yosemite.

Martinez, January 10, 1899

[To Theodore P. Lukens]

. . . The sheep owners in particular are already giving trouble & promise more next season. I have just learned from Mr. Bartlett, Forest Supervisor of Sierra Reservation, that 200,000 sheep invaded & desolated the reservation last summer under a tempory concession made by the Secretary Bliss & now thus encouraged certain land & timber speculators combined with the sheep owners have sent on agents to Washington to obtain leases of the entire Reservation for sheep grazing during the coming season. We must at once get to work in quick hearty opposition to this, or soon there will be complete surrender at Washington & destruction of the forests & other interests depending on them . . .

Martinez, January 15, 1907

[To William Colby]

I herewith return the draft of a club report on Kings River region with my hearty approval excepting the first 2 pages of the MS in which the Yosemite & Kings River regions are compared. Every possible aid & encouragement should be given by the club for the preservation, road & trail building, etc. for the development of the magnificent Kings River region. But unjust one-sided comparisons seeking to build up & glorify one region at the expense of lowering the other is useless work & should be left to real estate agents, promoters, rival hotel & stage owners, etc. Certainly the Club has nothing to do with such stuff, "tremendous advantages" "wealth & variety of mountain sculpture" depending on greater "depths & heights" etc. suggest boys with eyes to depth & height of butter & honey seeing tremendous advantages in one slice of bread over another cut from the same loaf . . .

Los Angeles, January 16, 1911
325 West Adams Street

[To William Colby]

. . . I am now at work on the Kings River yosemites, and I would like to have the part of the Kings River region which ought to be added to the General Grant and Sequoia National Parks definitely described, because I wish to recommend the preservation of the region in the Yosemite Guidebook.

And please tell me how much of the new road to the Kings River canyon has been actually built, and describe its course, where it starts from, where it runs, and where it strikes the river below the mouth of the canyon.

Please tell me also what sort of a trail is the one which runs up Copper Creek and over the divide to Simpson Meadows and down to Tehipite, and also the trails out of the lower end of Tehipite on both sides.

I am afraid I am putting you to lots of trouble, but you are much more familiar with these roads and trails than I am, and I want to get them right. I find in this Yosemite book that it is taking in so much it is going to be difficult to keep it within bounds, and I want to make the description of roads and trails as short as possible . . .

6. NATURAL BOUNDARIES

The last of his books published in his lifetime, The Yosemite *was the one Muir had intended to describe "other yosemites" as well. But he was caught up in the heated controversy over damming the Tuolumne River at Hetch Hetchy Valley. He was seventy-four years old when the book was published, and sacrificed other things to make it a weapon in the last-ditch campaign to prevent the City of San Francisco from flooding a fine yosemite within the boundaries of a national park. Although Hetch Hetchy was lost, public concern over the issue helped, after Muir's death, to make possible the creation of the National Park System.*

This brief passage summed up the arguments, at the time, for enlarging the two small national parks, Sequoia and General Grant, to include most of the remaining Big Trees and the "sublime scenery" on the headwaters of the Kings and Kern. Repeated efforts in Congress finally brought about that result in the Greater Sequoia National Park (1926), Kings Canyon Wilderness National Park (1940), and extension of the latter to include Cedar Grove and Tehipite (1965).

So far as I am able to see at present only fire and the ax threaten the existence of these noblest of God's trees. In nature's keeping they are safe, but through the agency of man destruction is making rapid progress, while in the work of protection only a good beginning has been made. The Fresno Grove, the Tuolumne, Merced and Mariposa groves are under the protection of the Federal Government in the Yosemite National Park. So are the General Grant and Sequoia national parks; the latter, established twenty-one years ago, has an area of 240 square miles and is efficiently guarded by a troop of cavalry under the direction of the Secretary of the Interior; so also are the small General Grant National Park, established at the same time with an area of four square miles, and the Mariposa Grove, about the same size and the small Merced and Tuolumne group. Perhaps more than half of all the Big Trees have been thoughtlessly sold and are now in the hands of speculators and millmen. It appears, therefore, that far the largest and important section of protected Big Trees is in the great Sequoia National Park, now easily accessible by rail to Lemon Cove and thence by a good stage road into the giant forest of the Kaweah and thence by trail to other parts of the park; but large as it is it should be made much larger. Its natural eastern boundary is the high Sierra and the northern and southern boundaries are the Kings and Kern rivers. Thus could be included the sublime scenery on the headwaters of these rivers and perhaps nine-tenths of all the Big Trees in existence. All private claims within these bounds should be gradually extinguished by purchase by the Government. The Big Tree, leaving all its higher uses out of the count, is a tree of life to the dwellers of the plain dependent on irrigation, a never-failing spring, sending living waters to the lowland. For every grove cut down a stream is dried up. Therefore all California is crying, "Save the trees of the fountains." Nor, judging by the signs of the times, is it likely that the cry will cease until the salvation of all that is left of *Sequoia gigantea* is made sure.

The Yosemite, 1912

Let our law-givers then make haste before it is too late to set apart this surpassingly glorious region for the recreation and well-being of humanity, and all the world will rise up and call them blessed.

East Lake, Kings Canyon National Park

JOHN MUIR'S TRAVELS

SOUTH OF YOSEMITE

October 1872

With William Keith, Benoni Irwin, Thomas Ross, and Merrill Moores, from Yosemite Valley to Lyell Fork of the Tuolumne, thence alone to Mount Ritter; return via Lyell Fork.

August 11 to about September 1, 1873

Alone, from the Clark Range in Yosemite, via the Middle Fork of the San Joaquin to the Minarets and probably Rodgers Peak and Mount Davis; return via Mount Lyell to Yosemite Valley.

September 13 to late October, 1873

With Galen Clark, Dr. Albert Kellogg, and William Simms, from Clark's Station (Wawona) via Chiquito Creek and the Middle and South forks of the San Joaquin, and alone probably to the Evolution lakes and Mount Darwin. After Clark's departure, with the others via the divide between the North and Middle forks of the Kings to cross the main river below their confluence. Thence via Mill Creek to Thomas Mills, Grant Grove, and the divide between the Kings and Kaweah; to the South Fork canyon; alone, to peaks probably on the Kings-Kern Divide. Return to the South Fork canyon and back over Kearsarge Pass. Via Lone Pine and Hockett Trail to the valley of the Kern, alone, to climb Mount Langley and near summit of Mount Muir; return to Independence. Again alone, via eastern approach, to climb Mount Whitney; return to Independence, and with Kellogg and Simms to Lake Tahoe and Yosemite Valley.

June 15 to end of June or early July, 1875

With William Keith, John Swett, and J. B. McChesney, from Yosemite Valley, via Tuolumne Meadows and Mono Lake to the Owens Valley and the eastern slope of the Sierra at least beyond Red Slate Mountain; return to Yosemite Valley.

July 9 to July 30 or 31, 1875

With George Bayley, Charles Washburn, and "Buckskin Bill" and mules, from Yosemite Valley via Clark's Station and Mariposa Grove to the upper Fresno, Centerville crossing of Kings River, the Big Tree groves of the Kings, the South Fork canyon. Across the range to Independence and Lone Pine to climb Mount Whitney; return to Yosemite Valley.

August to October, 1875

Alone with mule, from Yosemite Valley via Mariposa Grove and Fresno Grove, to the sequoia forests of the Kings, Kaweah and Tule rivers; return to Yosemite Valley.

October 1877

Alone (or with John Rigby), from Visalia via Converse Basin to the South Fork canyon of the Kings, over the divide to the head of the main Middle Fork canyon, down the canyon to Tehipite Valley. Below the confluence of the Middle and South forks, to climb the canyon wall and return to Converse Basin, Hyde's Mill and Visalia.

May 30 to June 13, 1891

With Charles D. Robinson, John Fox, and a Mr. Lake, from Visalia via Mill Creek, Grant Grove, and Boulder Creek to Horse Corral, and thence to camp on the South Fork of the Kings; return via similar route.

July and August, 1902

With the annual Sierra Club outing for ten days in the South Fork canyon of the Kings. Thence with William Keith and others, on horseback, to Giant Forest and the valley of the Kern, to camp and climb Mount Whitney. Return via Giant Forest, Visalia, and Fresno. From Fresno, briefly, to Converse Basin and return.

July 1908

With the annual Sierra Club outing for a month in the Kern Canyon area. From Porterville, Springville, and Nelson's to the Kern lakes, thence to the main camp at the junction of the Kern and Big Arroyo. Return to Giant Forest via Mineral King and Redwood Meadow.

July 1912

By automobile from Santa Barbara and Paso Robles to Giant Forest and Yosemite, thence to Martinez.

SOURCES OF THE TEXT

BY JOHN MUIR

"A Rival of the Yosemite," *Century Magazine,* Nov. 1891

"God's First Temples," Sacramento *Daily Record and Union,* Feb. 5, 1876

"Hunting Big Redwoods," *The Atlantic Monthly,* Sept. 1901

"In the Heart of the California Alps," *Scribner's Monthly,* July 1880

John of the Mountains, edited by Linnie Marsh Wolfe (Boston: Houghton Mifflin Company, 1938)

"On the Post-Glacial History of Sequoia Gigantea," (Salem, Mass.: *Proceedings of the American Association for the Advancement of Science,* Vol. 25, 1877)

Our National Parks (Boston: Houghton Mifflin Company, 1901)

"Save the Redwoods," *Sierra Club Bulletin,* Jan. 1920

"Studies in the Sierra, No. II; Mountain Sculpture—Origin of Yosemite Valleys," *The Overland Monthly,* June 1874

"Studies in the Sierra, No. VII; Mountain-Building," *The Overland Monthly,* Jan. 1875

"Summering in the Sierra," *The Daily Evening Bulletin,* San Francisco, California, Aug. 13 and 24, Sept. 21, and Oct. 22, 1875

"The Douglass Squirrel of California," *Scribner's Monthly,* Dec. 1878

"The Humming-Bird of the California Water-Falls," *Scribner's Monthly,* Feb. 1878

The Life and Letters of John Muir, Vols. I and II, by W. F. Badé (Boston: Houghton Mifflin Company, 1924)

"The New Sequoia Forests of California," *Harper's Monthly,* Nov. 1878

"The Passes of the Sierra," *Scribner's Monthly,* March 1879

"The Wild Parks and Forest Reservations of the West," *The Atlantic Monthly,* Jan. 1898

"The Wild Sheep of California," *The Overland Monthly,* April 1874

The Yosemite (New York: The Century Company, 1912)

Interview with John Muir, *Tulare County Times,* Visalia, California, Aug. 28, 1902

Manuscript postcard to Mrs. John Bidwell, Oct. 21, 1877; and manuscript letters to William Colby, Jan. 15, 1907, and Jan. 16, 1911 (collection of Bancroft Library, University of California, Berkeley)

Manuscript letter to Theodore P. Lukens, Jan. 10, 1899 (collection of Huntington Library, San Marino, California)

INDEX